TRICK OR TREAT

TRICK OR TREAT

Rethinking Black
Economic Empowerment

Jenny Cargill

First published by Jacana Media (Pty) Ltd in 2010

10 Orange Street
Sunnyside
Auckland Park 2092
South Africa
+2711 628 3200
www.jacana.co.za

ISBN 978-1-77009-830-5

Set in Ehrhardt 11/15pt
Printed and bound by Ultra Litho (Pty) Limited, Johannesburg
Job No. 001204

See a complete list of Jacana titles at www.jacana.co.za

For my son Marc

Contents

Foreword

This book is the culmination of fifteen years of intensive work in the black economic empowerment space: researching, advising on, facilitating and constructing BEE deals. I first got to know Jenny during those early years of intensive debates about the future of the South African economy. Through the company she founded, BusinessMap, she facilitated many discussions between business and political leaders, and herself engaged continually with policy makers, business leaders, international investors, trade unionists and the beneficiaries of BEE to ensure that she understood the dynamics of South Africa's transition. BusinessMap produced what was arguably the most comprehensive database on BEE investments and companies. Together with her colleagues, she provided a unique account of the country's BEE journey over many years.

This book is the work of an insider who is taking stock of her own experiences, exploring the successes and challenges of BEE and looking at possible ways forward. I avoid the word 'failures'. It is clear that, to Jenny, what looks like failure today was often a groundbreaking idea yesterday that unlocked progress and created value. Her review of Malaysia's affirmative action experiences illustrates this – how the policy outlived its value, bringing unintended consequences that undermined the policy objectives.

She argues that the time has come to evaluate new ways of going forward. As she so aptly puts it, leadership is key to breaking the confines of the current BEE policy framework and looking at new ways to ensure that South Africa's black citizens share equitably in the productive wealth and activities of the economy. She puts cogent arguments forward for flexibility, innovation and pragmatism to manage the country's transformation in the midst of a complex and unpredictable global environment.

It is a courageous and balanced book about which one cannot maintain neutrality. It is courageous since it attempts to transparently and constructively analyse some of the complexities of BEE, not succumbing to the compulsion of orthodoxy. It is balanced not in the sense of looking at both sides, but of judging particular tactics and strategies against desired national outcomes. Its argument for nonracialism is compelling, though much work remains to be done to chart out the course and steps to be taken on this difficult journey. This book is an important addition to the number of voices that are articulating their concerns in one of the most important areas of our transformation.

Fred Phaswana
April 2010

Preface

I know from history that the world can perform acrobatically and turn expectations upside down. Yet, when this book was started, I would have been loath to pay the clairvoyant who told me the following: America would have a black president; the Royal Bank of Scotland would be owned by the British government; Lehman Brothers and General Motors would declare bankruptcy; little Iceland would send shivers through the global economy twice. These unprecedented events occurred in only two years – just when I was writing about a policy that aims to change business by applying a fixed system for a 10-year period.

For even longer – fifteen years – South Africa has been shaping its economy the way an emerging artist might start a painting, by laying down a background and defining the composition in bold lines to unite the disparate subject matter – people, landscape, water, buildings. Unfortunately the background is still wet and the drawing clumsy. The result is a disappointing blur.

What I am really describing is the realm and subject of this book, black economic empowerment (BEE). As I write, BEE is still very much a work in progress but that was not the original intention. The ANC government laid down a grand paint-by-numbers scheme dictating clear form and direction for racial transformation in the business environment – with little room for creative diversion. As anyone knows, numbers are to painting what statistics are to the real world – nowhere near the living reality. Everyday life calls for a truly creative, spontaneous approach accommodating chance and the recognition that people and the environment are not putty or paint. This is the core theme of my book.

In my view, the policy framework for BEE is a form of social engineering – particularly the Codes of Good Practice, through which black empowerment is expected to find expression. The Codes are essentially templates for business, based on race, containing scores of arithmetical formulas devised to calculate the achievement of black participation in the economy to fit predetermined targets. The ANC government has yet to devise another policy that so crucially intervenes and impacts on society. My concern is that it may actually undermine what it sets out to achieve – systemic economic change to enable black citizens all the freedoms, choices and opportunities of a well-functioning economy.

There are many powerful voices within black business to disagree with me, arguing for more and not less state intervention. Understandably distrustful of white business to do more than the minimum for black empowerment, they believe arm wrestling a necessity.

A conviction that any social policy should incorporate flexibility is based on my experience as an exile working for the ANC in Zimbabwe and many subsequent years of involvement as a researcher and consultant in empowerment. One of my tasks in exile was to draft strategies to advance underground operations and collect information for those involved. For several reasons the strategies were rarely adhered to or the intelligence acted upon. A major factor was uncertainty. Controlling the outcome of an operation was extremely difficult; a single arrest could unravel years of work or the loss of an entire network of operatives; information on border security, gathered painstakingly over a long period, might be rendered worthless when passed on to a double agent. As a matter of course I would annually shred former strategies and set about crafting afresh. This might have been frustrating if it were not for the eventual realisation that wise planning accommodates the permanence of uncertainty, the necessity for flexibility and the complexity of human interactions.

Working in BEE has only confirmed the wisdom of this approach. Black empowerment came together fast in the post-1994 era and unravelled at an even greater pace, with no one involved at fault. South Africa, like many other countries, failed to escape the impact of the Asian crisis of 1997/8. At that time, BEE was about the sale of corporate shareholding to newly formed black investor groups to ensure black ownership in the hitherto white-controlled private sector. No one had money to buy shares, and so they borrowed – there were willing lenders because this seemed the right thing to do in the political circumstances. Had uncertainty been properly factored into the financial arrangements, there might have been a different outcome – instead, the BEE deals were, on the whole, structured for the good times.

The many years spent advising on BEE transactions and in negotiations between BEE buyers and corporate sellers have given fly-on-the-wall insight into the enormous complexities of what we are aiming to achieve. Not only is South Africa trying to apply a national racial mix to ownership and employment, it is also facing the pressure of operating in an increasingly unpredictable and fluid global economy – a challenge escalating with climate change. With this in mind, 'nanny-knows-best' forms of state intervention to control our socio-economic environment are not only outdated but potentially harmful. Today's challenges can only be addressed out of the box with innovative thinking, flexible style, high levels of personal commitment and dynamic partnerships. The rigidly packed BEE Codes preempt such freedom.

I am aware I might be accused of focusing narrowly on only one aspect of BEE – ownership. Of course BEE encompasses much more: employment equity, training, enterprises development, preferential procurement and corporate social responsibility. In part, I am writing about ownership because that's what I know. However, policy affords much more importance to BEE ownership than meets the eye. Each element of the Codes has a composite of scores. Black ownership is a requirement in three elements – BEE ownership, as you would expect, and procurement and enterprise development. In aggregate, ownership accounts for almost 40% of the total BEE scorecard, and not the 20% usually cited.

Additionally, far more capital has been invested in the sale of shareholding to black groups than in other key areas of socio-economic transformation, such as low-income housing and land redistribution – at least R500 billion as against less than R150 billion on housing and land. There are also trade-offs between ownership and other transformational investments, since capital is a scarce resource.

BEE ownership therefore matters enormously. As a result, I pick at its consequences from a number of angles – its lack of productivity or contribution to new economic value; discouragement of real entrepreneurs; role in political patronage and corruption; and hidden costs. Yes, the Codes have been good for wealth redistribution, but it has been the kind achieved not by creating it but by attaching oneself to others who do.

Unexpected is the dominance of broad-based companies among productive BEE investors. They are the bright stars of empowerment. The phenomenon of broad-based ownership has grown substantially in recent years and I cover it extensively. While finding the best of BEE in this arena, I am wary of looking at it through rose-tinted spectacles as many are inclined to do. I question the current approach of distributing share ownership on the basis of debt-supported sales – is this really an appropriate way of redistributing wealth to South Africa's poorer black citizens?

I leave it up to the media to cover the titillating side of black empowerment – the WaBenzi – a hugely enriched and new black elite emerging from BEE, simultaneously a source of endless derision and fascination. However, excluding the colourful antics of the ANC Youth League leader Julius Malema proved impossible.

In researching this book I was drawn to writers and intellectuals who not only questioned what they saw as redundant social management systems and economic theories but offered insights into alternatives. I am indebted to them for their words, liberally quoted and adding flesh to many chapters, and for providing ways of re-viewing BEE and inspiring me to attempt something other than the traditional fare that dominates empowerment debates.

I am aware of the pitfalls involved in launching a book with hope but I can't avoid it. I unashamedly hope that among its readers are those sufficiently stimulated to think or act critically and creatively beyond BEE to other forms of socially relevant investment that may contribute to the success of South Africa's economic transformation.

Acknowledgements

Researching this book involved much interesting travel and meetings with wonderful people. Among the many Malaysians who offered help, Herbert Morais deserves special thanks. Although we never met, he opened doors that led to my meeting some of the early contributors to Malaysia's preferential policies almost forty years ago. The South African High Commission in Hanoi was equally helpful. On home ground in South Africa, I had the pleasure of visiting the extraordinary Richtersveld and its people, who unstintingly shared their firm opinions and sharp wit. I am grateful to their legal adviser, Henk Smith, for discussing their case at length. My heartfelt thanks to the Kalk Bay fishermen for their frank discussions and Horst Kleinschmidt for his salutary candour. Without the diligence of my research assistant Lyndsey Duff, I doubt that I would have succeeded in interviewing the many business and government leaders, policy makers and advisers whose contribution to this book has been invaluable. My former business partner, Renée Marais, contributed greatly to my understanding of financial risk and its implications on socio-political investment. My apologies to Gillian Cargill for refusing to allow her to turn this book into a novel, and to my able and long-suffering editor Priscilla Hall, who was forced to accept copy moments before delivery to the publisher.

Abbreviations

Basa	Banking Association of South Africa
BEE	Black economic empowerment
BEECom	Black Economic Empowerment Commission
CPA	Communal Property Association of the Richtersveld
CSI	corporate social investment
Ceppwawu	Chemical, Energy, Paper, Printing, Wood and Allied Workers Union
CI	Ceppwawu Investments
DMR	Department of Mineral Resources
DTI	Department of Trade and Industry
Esops	employee share ownership schemes
FSC	Financial Sector Charter
GLC	(Malaysian) government-linked company
GDP	gross domestic product
HCI	Hosken Consolidated Investments
HDSA	historically disadvantaged South African
Implats	Impala Platinum Holdings
ISS	Institute of Security Studies
JSE	Johannesburg Stock Exchange; JSE Securities Exchange
KTI	Kagiso Trust Investments
LRC	Legal Resources Centre
MCM	Department of Marine and Coastal Management
MIC	Mineworkers Investment Company

Abbreviations

MPRDA	Mineral and Petroleum Resources Development Act
Nafcoc	National African Federated Chamber of Commerce and Industry
NEC	National Empowerment Consortium
NEP	(Malaysian) New Economic Policy
NP	National Party
NPAT	net profit after tax
NUM	National Union of Mineworkers.
Numsa	National Union of Metalworkers of South Africa
PIC	Public Investment Corporation
RBH	Royal Bafokeng Holdings
RBN	Royal Bafokeng Nation
Remgro	Rembrant group
SIG	Sactwu Investment Group
SPV	special purpose vehicle
SRI	socially responsible investment
Wiphold	Women's Investment Portfolio Holdings

1

Introduction

BEE in the making

In September 2009 a prominent black–controlled company, the Mvelephanda Group, announced its withdrawal from future BEE investment. The landscape had changed. BEE investors, representing a broad base of black interests, had come to dominate transactional activity, squeezing out individually black-owned groups like Mvelephanda. Yet the statement attracted little public debate. A weariness had settled in the BEE arena as the global financial crisis reverberated in South Africa, decimating asset values and threatening to implode the debt–laden investments of black shareholders.

Nevertheless, Mvelephanda had drawn a line in the sand, leaving a clear message for the future of empowerment: it was time to cross the line and approach BEE differently. BEE had been brought to just such a line once before, after the Asian market collapse in the late Nineties. Back then I reported the challenge would be for a reconstructed second wave of empowerment to emerge. It had become clear then that demonstrable operational control and effective internal empowerment within organisations were needed. Control solely defined in terms of shareholder equity had realised its initial purpose and outlived its shelf life.[1]

The second wave rolled off the back of a new policy and regulatory framework that introduced high levels of state intervention. Clearly, neither government nor black business felt a need to review the value and character of BEE ownership. Instead, they significantly expanded the frame of black corporate shareholding that had existed before, but this time with an accoutrement of accessories designed to keep in check

1

the perverse side-effects that had become associated with BEE – most notably the unpalatable levels of enrichment and greed, opportunism and unproductive investments.

Regrettably, we are currently facing many of the same unwanted results we met in the first wave of empowerment – and in some cases, even worse. It is therefore important to question whether BEE ownership, as we know it, can offer much more for corporate transformation, and if so, consider where we should go from here.

After tripping over the same stones for fifteen years, it is crucial to start the questioning at the beginning, when corporate shareholding usurped other ideas and initiatives designed to redress the marginalisation of black South Africans from the mainstream economy.

ANC edges towards BEE

The ANC started off on an unsure footing. Business, black or white, had never been high on its agenda. Early engagements to win over the ANC to the cause of black business prompted one among them to accuse the ANC of being 'ignorant of black business. We feel rejected. We feel like lepers.'[2]

'There was caginess on both sides. BEE was one of our weakest areas and we had to absorb from other interest groups. Unashamed black capitalists wanted us to make them money and redistribute on their behalf,' said Joel Netshitenzhe, when head of policy in the Presidency.[3]

Glancing back even further, it is important to remember that for thirty years the ANC had lived a surreal existence in exile and underground. Few members had been touched by issues of economic power and pragmatism. Despite all the signs of major change ahead, the unbanning of the ANC in February 1990 was unexpected. I remember the early morning when I received a phone call from a journalist breaking the news. I rushed to tell Jacob Zuma, who as head of ANC intelligence at the time was preparing an exposé on the apartheid regime's death squads. Even he was surprised.

Only Thabo Mbeki might have had an inkling that the unbanning was imminent. In the mid-Eighties he began engaging with both white and black business establishments and created unease in underground ranks. Our myopic vision of a 'national democratic revolution' felt dislocated.

What was he thinking? Mbeki's journey towards BEE began back then, with the nurturing of what 'would become his prime constituency: the small but burgeoning black elite,' writes his biographer Mark Gevisser.[4] But at that time, scattered across the frontline states, we had no information to help us process what was going on. Inevitably, Mbeki's quiet diplomacy activated suspicion. His persuasiveness could not be acknowledged, as it was never seen and never put to any open forum for discussion.

Until then, the resources of the ANC were single-mindedly directed towards the overthrow of apartheid. Insurrection was the stated objective. Little thought had been devoted to the development of Africa's largest economy. 'We failed to understand that life continued [while the ANC functioned from exile] and that there was a stratum of black entrepreneurs with aspirations and with quite a significant influence on the black community. We had focused on nationalisation and not the rights of everyone to trade. Therefore the debate on black business got frozen until the mid-Eighties, when the ANC had to start engaging on the constitutional principles for a democratic South Africa. The debate then moved to a mixed economy,' says Netshitenzhe.[5]

The ANC might have been unclear about future economic policy but it was well aware of its inheritance of an economy long crumbling under apartheid. Damage aside, it was still well supported by a substantial industrial platform and sophisticated capital markets developed and maintained, on the whole, by a resident business community. Thus it may be said the ANC took over a reasonably sound foundation – albeit in need of structural renovations – that had no equal in post-Fifties independence and liberation movement experiences. South Africa therefore seemed well positioned to redesign the economy to include and empower black people. This motivated South Africans to think afresh about the future with virtually anyone free to state their views.

Missing the great BEE debate

The source of the ANC's vision, the Freedom Charter, inevitably receded as the new circumstances required attention to the detail necessary to create a new policy framework for the country. The ANC's economic policy unit stood at the centre of the debate, organising and participating in discussion designed to shape an exciting creation – the New South Africa. Policy making had never before – nor has it since – been so engaging. It was filled with a sense of anticipation and excitement not normally associated with such a dry, academic pursuit.

ANC figures leading the economic debate in the beginning went on to make an indelible impact on the structure and success of the post-apartheid South African economy. Trevor Manuel as minister of Finance, Tito Mboweni as governor of the Reserve Bank and Maria Ramos as National Treasury head were the most visible players in the early policy debates. They were the triumvirate that delivered a stable macro-economy – transformed from a virtually bankrupt government, with untenable foreign debt claims, budget deficits and high inflation. As I write, nearly sixteen years on, Mboweni has just left the Reserve Bank, Ramos has settled into the top seat at one of the country's largest banks, while her husband Trevor Manuel has crossed to the Presidency as government's chief planner (he was, incidentally, the only voice in the executive to place a question mark publicly behind BEE ownership).

The policy debates in the early Nineties barely touched on black corporate ownership; the dialogue on black redress tended to be contested within the economic paradigm of redistribution versus growth. Gevisser notes that Mbeki failed in an early attempt to place BEE on the ANC's economic agenda: 'In November 1990, Mbeki tried to sneak the beginnings of BEE policy into the ANC under the cover of a document on the phasing out of sanctions ... But so unpopular was his suggestion that sanctions be phased out that it [his proposal] was shouted down ... and the baby of BEE was chucked out with the bath water of sanctions policy reform.'[6] Instead, BEE, as a defined concept, emerged piecemeal in fits and starts while mainstream macro-economic policy evolved relatively consistently. As a result, BEE never quite became part of a coherent, integrated economic and investment policy. It is still something of a stepchild to economic policy in general, included on the basis of an assumption that it must be good for growth.

When the ANC dealt with racial exclusion in the economy, affirmative action, with the emphasis on employment-based discrimination, dominated, as did small business development. BEE barely featured in the ANC's early policy debates, but that is not to suggest that there was no engagement with the issue. In 1992 the businessman Don Mkwanazi, charged with heading the ANC's research into affirmative action, described BEE to me as 'ownership and control of the productive assets and resources of our country. If the economic power relations remain intact – that is, concentrated in a few hands – that will not be consistent with democracy.'[7]

Thebe, and the first lessons for BEE

Individuals within the ANC had aspirations and were already looking at business opportunities as the transition was taking place. Tokyo Sexwale features very early on. The first BEE-type enterprise, Thebe Investment Corporation, was launched way back in 1992 from within the ANC. Owned ostensibly by an investment trust (Batho Batho Trust), with the community earmarked as the beneficiary, a strong ANC coating stuck to Thebe. Sexwale and Vusi Khanyile (former ANC financial officer) were the main movers for Thebe, and the ANC stalwarts Nelson Mandela and Walter Sisulu were among the founding trustees.

Khanyile, an accountant and activist, stayed close to black business and discussions on the future of South African business while running the ANC's finances. 'Those discussions ended up saying that unless we have successful and viable black businesses, then the community cannot have its expression in the economy.'[8] With that vision in mind, Khanyile knew where his future lay; he turned down his nomination to parliament and carried his idealism into business.

Thebe's first activities produced many of the criticisms and contradictions that we still grapple with today. Less than a year after its establishment, Thebe began to be buffeted by disparaging media exposure. At the time, I was concerned about the absence of guidelines dealing with the economic interests of political party officials and felt the matter required attention before bad habits or inadequate practices began to coalesce.[9]

Khanyile insisted that Thebe would operate like any other business. I suspected the involvement of senior ANC leaders in Thebe would make the corporation appear like flypaper to a fly. Patently, any business wanting access to an appropriate politician would be attracted to a partnership with a company like Thebe. It was surprising how little debate there was into political–business linkages, considering the backdrop of four decades of collusion between the National Party and Afrikaner economic interests.[10]

To its credit Thebe managed to steer clear of much potentially murky water. I heard many a time, from ANC sources, that Khanyile did not play the game politically; through his quiet style, he asserted the company's independence. However, there were among the ANC leadership those who saw Thebe as accountable to the organisation. With Khanyile at the helm this concern may explain why the ANC later formed its own company, Chancellor House – raising even more relevant questions about merging political and business interests.

Thebe built up its investment portfolio with a high acquisition rate. Within less than four years, it had accumulated at least twenty investments covering financial services, aviation, media, entertainment, leisure and a range of industrial–type holdings.[11] It was certainly not alone. A handful of BEE companies laid claim to large numbers of transactions, although none quite surpassed the acquisitiveness of the trade union company Sahrwu Investments, who in one year concluded 14 transactions.[12]

But Thebe distinguished itself as well. This is where Khanyile's idealism mattered. The company built its own operational subsidiaries, based on his belief that they needed to play in the middle court. Here Khanyile expected to find both good opportunities for the company and a basis for transformation of the highly concentrated, white–controlled private sector. Essentially it targeted three sectors: airlines, liquid fuels and banking (the last in particular showed up the absence of an ANC strategy towards BEE). 'I used to say that the South African financial sector was efficient, with a few dominant institutions. Therefore anyone else who wanted to come in needed to be a niche player. I also remember as a child in a banking mall seeing how badly the bank treated an old woman who couldn't speak English. I saw a black–owned medium–sized bank being able to have an impact on the lives of people like this old woman,' says Khanyile.[13]

Thebe therefore started picking out middle-range banks to acquire, in equity partnership with FirstCorp. First, it created FBC Bank out of a merger of Future Bank, two building societies of the former black bantustans Ciskei and Bophuthatswana, and Citizen Bank. Later it tied up with Fidelity Bank, resulting in the financial group Fedsure becoming a shareholder in FBC Fidelity.

But Thebe's banking ambitions were quickly caught in the crosscurrents caused by the Asian crisis. Jitters first set in after the demise of the Malaysian-controlled New Republic Bank, headquartered in Durban. Khanyile remembers the day when the *Sunday Times* published a rumour of FBC being overly exposed. High drama followed. 'By 12 noon Monday, R400 million had been withdrawn, most by the corporations and state-owned enterprises. We tried to stem the tide with support from the Reserve Bank. We drafted a term sheet, but it required Treasury support. They told us that if banks aren't strong enough to survive on their own, they must go.'[14]

Bitter news indeed, particularly as, after FBC was placed in curatorship, the curator confirmed what Khanyile knew – that 'the bank is basically sound'.[15] It was too late and others went to the wall. Government ultimately stepped in when the largest of the smaller banks, BOE, wobbled. Had government thought about BEE and the creation of a black corporate presence within established business – as the Afrikaners had done for their own empowerment forty years earlier – there might well have been a very different outcome.

White corporates adjust

Those in big business were busy too, pondering how they should respond to their re-entry into global markets and a new political dispensation in which they would not be well placed to exert influence. They were fortunate that the ANC took a pragmatic and accommodative approach, derided by its critics for being neoliberal. With old communist supporters fading away and disintegration of the Cold War, the ANC quickly acknowledged that there was one large playing field – globalisation – and South Africa had to tread carefully as the new team in the league.

South Africa's conglomerates like Anglo American Corporation could look forward to significantly expanded markets, with access to foreign capital to enhance their presence on the global stage. First, however, they needed to change from being corporations with a mishmash of assets and businesses collected when locked into the South African economy by sanctions. The international preference for companies to focus on core business activities motivated South Africa's conglomerates to restructure and unload anything defined as non-core.

This dovetailed neatly with the political imperative to bring black South Africans into the inner circle of the business establishment. The former political activist and today a director of Anglo American, Mamphela Ramphele, writes, 'A post-apartheid South Africa in which only white people are wealthy is unsustainable.'[16] Few do or want to quibble with this as a general statement and BEE seemed a tantalisingly simple way to reconfigure the wealth distribution equation. Sell a slice of corporate South Africa, adorned with the right kind of icing (enough political clout mixed with mass appeal) and hey presto, a Rainbow Nation with BEE the New Economic Insurance.

So big business promptly got down to accommodating BEE. Anglo's Michael Spicer was charged with looking at the General Mining deal that the mining group had transacted some forty years earlier with Afrikaner business and which entrenched the presence of a large Afrikaner-owned and -controlled mining company. Could this provide a model? They felt it did, starting with the sale of African Life to the former Anglo manager Don Ncube, then on to a range of industrial assets packaged into Johnnic and including newspaper interests, and then the mining house, JCI – stripped of its platinum assets, which Anglo wanted to keep.

Spicer argues the case: 'You can't have political liberation without economic liberation. There had to be an artificial intervention to deal with there being no black capital. Moeletsi [Mbeki] fingers us for being the architects of a flawed system, but what else were we to do? It [BEE] required trial and error. There was no recipe book and we were going to make mistakes.'[17]

Anglo stood for English capital, while Sanlam's investment arm Sankorp led the charge for Afrikaner capital, with the traditional tensions apparently even emerging within the BEE territory. Rejected by Anglo, Nthatho Motlana, the former activisit, felt that 'that the English were not about to do a deal with the black man.'

Enter Afrikaner capital. 'A few days later, Motlana got the break he was looking for, a chance of meeting with Org Marais, then minister of Tourism in the National Party government, who said to him: "Forget the English. Come and do business with the Afrikaners – ours is Metlife."'[18]

Nail: trying out the conglomerate route

The deal gave rise to Nail, New Africa Investments Limited, which shot BEE into the limelight. Nail's creator, Motlana,* and his co-founder Jonty Sandler, who had started off with a company called Corporate Africa, rapidly built Nail into Sandler's dream of the first black-owned and listed conglomerate. It became the big boy of BEE, drawing into its fold prominent names like the former ANC secretary-general Cyril Ramaphosa, Dikgang Moseneke (later deputy chief justice) and ANC heavyweights like Saki Macozoma.

When I first met them in the early Nineties, Sandler laid out a grand vision of a black-owned conglomerate akin to General Electric – a quite different vision from that of Thebe. Always an expansive thinker, he showed me a web of organograms sketching the envisaged reach of Corporate Africa. They almost succeeded but eventually tripped up, controversial to the end.

White financial institutions acquired shareholding, but without voting rights. This preserved Nail as a black company but distorted the relationship between voting rights (which Motlana and Sandler, through Corporate Africa, controlled) and economic interests (held in the main by white institutions). Ultimately, control rested with Motlana and Sandler, through Corporate Africa and a complex pyramid structure. But the listing also resulted in 11 000 first-time black shareholders and the first ever direct investment by a trade union, Nactu (the National Congress of Trade Unions).

Other initiatives to address black economic marginalisation from the mainstream economy were tried out. But, at the end of the day, nothing quite stuck like the opportunity to acquire corporate shareholding in the commanding heights of the economy. This meant that the BEE space – even for the likes of Motlana – quickly became crowded, with a jockeying for position by an unlikely mix of socialist-leaning trade unionists, often American-educated black professionals, ANC functionaries and other anti-apartheid activists, together with a handful of white businessmen, quick to identify new opportunities and offer their expertise for a share in the rewards.

Ultimately, therefore, Motlana need not have worried about the

---

* Motlana died in December 2008, unfortunately before I could interview him for this book.

ideological impediments to BEE. Once in power, the ANC and many among its allies didn't need much persuading. For some critics, it had seemed as if the ANC had too readily slotted into the slipstream of powerful and entrenched economic interests, dislodging little of consequence.

Those were heady days, ripe with opportunity and enthusiasm. So, what went wrong? The root of the problem is the starting point and not the premature collapse brought about by the Asian crisis. The acerbic American writer PJ O'Rourke provides apposite imagery for top-down economic reforms: 'as if the ancient Egyptians had constructed the Pyramid of Khufu by saying, "Thutnefer, you hold up this two-ton pointy piece while the rest of the slaves go get 2,300,000 blocks of stone."'[19]

The two-ton pointy piece was dangled before black South Africans like the low-hanging apple before Eve. The sale of sizeable business assets, all acquired with debt, encouraged all manner of perverse behaviours. Enrichment, elitism, unproductive redistribution of income and political patronage became the bywords for BEE ownership. The fact that the new black shareholders never carried the financial risk for their investments or got their hands dirty in the operations of business didn't bode well for the creation of a new entrepreneurial culture. It's easy to judge, but why should anyone have resisted? One day you had nothing, the next day you owned a sliver of Corporate South Africa worth multiples of any executive salary. All you were doing was responding to the incentive placed before you.

For a while BEE seemed to be a satisfactory arrangement all round. Ostensibly it provided political insurance to white business as well as some commercial benefit and first-mover advantage to those who saw value in a black partnership – important where state-related business was involved. BEE offered black South Africans the opportunity to accumulate what they had long been denied – the capital necessary to leave the economic ghettos created by apartheid and influence the destiny of the First World economy of South Africa. It appeared so easy, exciting and enriching – and to top it, it was socially and politically relevant.

From zero in 1994 to almost R70 billion just five years later – that was the market value of companies listed on the Johannesburg Stock

Exchange (JSE)* which had transferred to black control, by November 1998 reaching almost 7% of the total market capitalisation of the JSE. Looking a bit further, at companies that had introduced BEE shareholding without transferring control, their market capitalisation edged up to R150 billion. Deals whose values had been disclosed totalled almost R30 billion between 1996 and 1998.[20]

But as with every Quick Fix and Get Rich Fast scheme, we soon find out that a short cut is synonymous with a slippery slope. A wily few can make it through, but most tend not to. This is what happened in the late Nineties, when the full impact of South East Asia's market collapse hit South African shores, bringing to an end the first attempt to establish meaningful black corporate ownership. Financial losses, acrimony, lost opportunities and hopes led to some reflection.

We were left with BEE the paper tiger, and not BEE the antidote to apartheid. The beneficiaries – the emerging black elite – had acquired corporate paper without paying for it. They had risked nothing, built nothing and consumed what they could. BEE had promised to be the distributor of the spoils; or as comedian Pieter-Dirk Uys so aptly puts it, the ANC (A Nice Cheque)[21] of the New South Africa.

The state's defining interventions

As is invariably the case, popular polemic leaves out nuances and makes it difficult to move on, wiser for the experience. It is important therefore to get into the fault lines that marked BEE in those early days, many of which remain embedded.

It is often said that the likes of Anglo and Sankorp defined, activated and controlled BEE. Given the scale of their transactions, they certainly looked like the ones with clout. However, Cosatu and the ANC – and in particular certain individuals – had an understated but profound influence on BEE opportunities. Three interventions prompted by them are noteworthy. The first was the eventual agreement just before the dawn of democracy that some shareholding in the new cellular-licence holders be offered to blacks. The second was the freeing up of broadcasting from state control. The third was the legalisation of gambling, with the issue

---

* Today it is called the JSE Securities Exchange, but will be referred to as the JSE throughout the book.

of licences under the new ANC-led provincial governments.

These three initiatives were crucial in the capitalisation of early BEE players, and for those who used their capital well they provided a cornerstone for building South Africa's largest and most successful black corporations. Importantly, they constituted new industries, with regulatory protection and high growth potential (technically, broadcasting was not new, but under private ownership it amounted to a new opportunity).

Cellphones

Cellular telephony has exceeded all expectations. In 1993, the long-standing trade unionist Bernie Fanaroff* approached the ANC about the award of licences by the National Party government, still in power at the time. 'I approached Jay [Naidoo] and said we can't allow them to give away the people's spectrum; it's like giving away our mineral resources. Jay didn't have a clue what spectrum was, but said if you wanted to fight it, do so.'[22]

The ANC, however, had 'sort of agreed' that the black business representative groups Nafcoc and Fabcos would get some nominal shareholding in Vodacom and MTN (then M-Cell). 'I said this was unacceptable. Because we were in a period of uncertainty and the parties didn't know what attitude to take, this gave us a way of getting in.'[23] Chance also played a role – none of this would ever have happened had it not been for Fanaroff, who had the most unusual qualification for a leftwing trade unionist – a doctorate in physics and astronomy, and thus someone who thought in spectrums.

Fanaroff's actions opened the doors to his union, the metalworkers' Numsa, and others within Cosatu to acquire the rights for some shareholding (5% in each of the two companies who had been awarded a licence). Chance intervened again: Fanaroff joined Jay Naidoo in government to spearhead the Reconstruction and Development Programme (RDP) – and Numsa never followed through. But others in Cosatu stepped into the gap, notably Johnny Copelyn and Marcel

---

* At that time, Fanaroff was with the Cosatu-affiliated trade union, the National Union of Metalworkers, and at the time of writing in 2009 was heading South Africa's bid to host the Square Kilometre Array, the most powerful radio telescope ever, and the construction of its technology-pathfinder telescope, the Karoo Array Telescope (known as MeerKAT).

Golding, then new members of parliament and former unionists in the textile union Sactwu and mineworkers union NUM respectively. They had initiated investment trusts for their unions to participate in the BEE opportunities just appearing on the horizon.

Motlana also edged his way into the cellphone offering. It had been agreed that 30% of the equity in MTN and 5% in Vodacom would go to black shareholders.[24] No one at the time anticipated the scale of value inherent in these licences. MTN was valued then at R500 million, setting the 30% for BEE at R150 million, which seemed an enormous sum at the time. In early 2010, MTN's market capitalisation is around R200 billion.[25] Vodacom's 5% was an initial R100 million option growing at a specified rate and then exercised at R120 million, valuing Vodacom at R3.76 billion against a current market capitalisation of R81 billion.[26]

Broadcasting

Broadcasting provided a good welcome mat to BEE investors too, although nowhere near the scale of the cellphone industry. Also in 1993, the Broadcasting Act[27] was promulgated, starting the process of transformation in the once fully state-controlled sector. This Act placed regulation in the hands of the Independent Broadcasting Authority. It had the responsibility to encourage ownership and control of broadcasting services by historically disadvantaged South Africans.[*]

Driven by ideals at the time, the ANC wanted to see the media freed from state control. Radio stations were thus among the first privatisations, along with the issue of new radio licences and later the issue of a free-to-air television licence for private ownership. Again, no one knew how this market would perform, but at least the assets and licences were acquired at reasonable prices.

Broadcasting offered an important platform for black groups to assume significant, and sometimes controlling, interests in a sector that could not avoid being politically charged. Aspirant broadcasters needed to demonstrate not just a financial interest by historically disadvantaged individuals but also a confirmation of their involvement in making

---

[*] Early empowerment policy included white women and the disabled on the basis that they too had been discriminated against in the old South Africa, and this persisted until BEE legislation was introduced in 2003.

decisions. Licence applications also needed to detail their policies for affirmative action in staffing, training and the development of new and diverse South African talent and opportunity in broadcasting. These 'Promises of Performance' were then made part of the licence conditions, open for review throughout the licence period.[28]

So the stage was set quite early on for empowerment in the corporate sector to encompass more than black ownership. All in all, the regulatory framework successfully changed the face of South African broadcasting, placing black South Africans in control of much of this industry. The bad egg in the pack is that which remained in state hands, notably the South African Broadcasting Corporation – today a shameful example of political interference, inefficiency and corruption. But in the private domain of broadcasting, a number of the early BEE players who rank among the leading companies today have broadcasting interests: MIC (Mineworkers Investment Company) with Primedia; HCI (Hosken Consolidated Investments) with YFM (the Youth radio station) and e.tv; and KTI (Kagiso Trust Investments) with Kagiso Media, which has five radio stations.

Gambling

Gambling provided BEE companies access to an industry that churned out cash. It is in this arena where the biggest and most bruising BEE battles have been fought – HCI's Copelyn outmanoeuvred Johnnic and his one-time trade union colleague Ramaphosa, to gain control of the lucrative gambling assets in Tsogo Sun by taking control of Johnnic (see below). The other major gambling group, Peermont, is under the control of MIC. It's ironic that black workers are significantly invested in gambling, particularly when Cosatu has raised its voice against such investment interests.

But government intervention, using its licensing powers, threw up some red flags that I will come back to later in the book and simply highlight here. One is the creation of new barriers to doing business, often using licensing systems that enable the state to determine who is in and who is out. The ANC had not refined this in the early days, but nevertheless experimented on many fronts. In addition to broadcasting and gambling, a range of obligations and regulations emerged. These not only started to dislodge the old system of business access but opened up a new front for patronage.

The importance of growth

That said, the value of these three industries to BEE lies less in the intervention of the ANC and the state, and more in the high-growth opportunities. As I explore in the next chapter, debt-financed BEE transactions have limited the potential for sustainability in regular- or low-growth industries. In other aspects, where the ANC intervened on behalf of BEE shareholding, principally in the privatisation of state assets, the results were poor.

The early private-sector BEE transactions produced a much more chequered picture than the regulated industries of cellphones, broadcasting and gambling. An early lesson was the importance of having not just a good business asset available to buy, but also at a good price. In the absence of exceptional growth – aka cellphones – the price is crucial. Anglo's initiatives with the 35% sale of the industrial conglomerate Johnnic and a 34.9% controlling interest of the mining group JCI are salutary.

In these, the largest deals at the time, Anglo satisfied its objective to transact commercially. The minority interest in Johnnic went at a 6% discount, while JCI sold at a premium – the outcome of a bidding process that drove up the price. Neither JCI nor Johnnic worked for Anglo politically – and this was undoubtedly a reason for selling them. The JCI deal collapsed soon after. Johnnic has survived but as a shadow of its former self – thinned away through the unbundling of assets in ill-conceived strategic restructures.

Nail, a party to Johnnic, did better with Metropolitan Life (Metlife) – an investment of 30% (over two years) that was much smaller than Anglo's initiatives, amounting to R565 million. The initial tranche of R135 million (for 10%) was financed by the state-owned Industrial Development Corporation. The second tranche was funded through cash raised with the listing of Nail (R165 million) and Sankorp's purchase of a 20% shareholding in Nail (R96 million) and the rest from non-voting preference shares in Nail held by Sankorp. Within two years, the value of the Metlife shares had escalated to R950 million.[29]

Nail's share price also outperformed the market significantly, suggesting high levels of exuberance around BEE companies. Within two years of listing on the JSE, Nail's share price was 27 times higher than its earnings per share (price–earnings ratio, or PE), against an average 15% PE in the industrial holding sector.[30] Neither Nail nor Metlife lasted.

Early investor behaviour

Another fault line in the BEE landscape is the behaviour of BEE investors and what they do with their assets. BEE investors earned a reputation for opportunistic, rent-seeking behaviour.* Many, it seemed, wanted to secure a few million rand to support lucrative lifestyles – hence the derisive label of the Wabenzis tagged to the new black elite for their penchant for luxury cars like Mercedes-Benz. Yet there were others, keen to be the architects of large black corporations even if they started out without business operations, as investment holding companies – Nail, HCI, Thebe, MIC and KTI feature prominently. Some of these companies will be tracked later in the book for creating a positive niche within the BEE domain.

Those early days showed how important it was for BEE companies to normalise as quickly as possible, bringing down debt levels, accumulating capital for reinvestment, and professionalising with an eye to long-term wealth creation. The pitfalls almost invariably occurred when the BEE group was in too much of a hurry to scale up and make large amounts of money at a pace.

The manner in which Nail and HCI each dealt with their cellphone investments is illustrative. Corporate Africa cashed in more than half of their interest in MTN within three months. Motlana had his eye on the black newspaper, the *Sowetan*, which he said would generate immediate cash, as opposed to the long wait expected from cellphones. The BEE commentator Duma Gqubule criticises Nail and HCI for 'a short-term mindset that became the hallmark of many black businesses during the 1990s'.[31]

HCI waited until 2002, when it started to trade its cellphone interests

---

* The *Financial Times* columnist John Kay describes rent-seeking in a way most fitting for BEE as 'a culture in which the principal route to wealth is not creating wealth, but attaching oneself to wealth created by others' ('Uncertain, chaotic and driven by pluralism', *Business Day*, 5 November 2009).

– and only because its financiers insisted. It sold its 5% to other Vodacom shareholders (Vodafone, today the controlling shareholder, and Venfin) for R1.5 billion. It could be argued that HCI also sold too soon, says HCI's Copelyn, but 'we had a business [e.tv] that was losing R1 million a day. We had borrowed to cover these losses, but our share price had crashed and the institutional shareholders were demanding something. Even though MIC and Sactwu were the largest individual shareholders, the institutional shareholders owned over 50% of the shares of HCI. So eventually we agreed to sell Vodacom to pay off the debt and the institutions sold their shares back to the company [HCI] for R2.70.'[32] This is against a share price of some R60 in the recessionary market conditions of late 2009, down from R70 levels a year earlier.

'We bought back 73% of the company, and full control. When e.tv turned positive, it became clear that the institutions had made a bad decision. Then it was assumed that the country wouldn't succeed and investors couldn't envision anything but doom five years ahead. They also made the assumption that trade unionists couldn't manage a business. They misunderstood. That experience changed us. We came to the view that institutions are not always valuable shareholders, particularly if they don't have confidence in management when they enter a shareholding. All these ideas that you can control a company with less than 51% didn't appeal to me after that experience.'[33]

Copelyn had come to a quite different conclusion from Nail. Fancy governance and financial structures to ensure black shareholder control were the trademark of Nail. The economic interest lay in low-voting N-shares,* held by institutional shareholders, while Motlana's Corporate Africa controlled the ordinary voting shares. There was a chasm between the two. In 1999, the N-shares had a market capitalisation of some R7 billion, while the ordinary shares were R350 million. All in all, Corporate Africa controlled a company with a total market capitalisation of R7.5 billion with a stake of no more than R250 million.[34]

This never bothered Sandler – the Oppenheimers had controlled Anglo American for decades with a nominal shareholding. He felt the consternation over control structures was something of a red herring.

---

* This is a special class of shares with low-voting rights. Sometimes companies have A, B, C classes of shares. N-shares was a generic term for low or no-voting shares.

He may have been right, but there were other factors working against him in 1999. Nail's shares had taken a knock with the Asian crisis – after which they traded at a 45% discount to net asset value. And the directors of Nail made the tactical error of getting a bit too greedy at the wrong time – laying claim to some R130 million worth of share options in one of Nail's subsidiaries, African Merchant Bank. Institutional investors revolted in an unprecedented show of shareholder activism. The axe fell first on Sandler, never well liked by the financial establishment, and then Motlana.

Business Day wrote at the time: 'The events at Nail demonstrate just how dangerous it can be to allow people with only a small financial interest in the company to outvote those who have invested a lot more but have only minimal voting power.'[35] As for the BEE investors, they had far more voting power than investment. There was always debate on the contradictions between political versus economic control in BEE transactions.

Subsequent efforts to restructure Nail and give it strategic direction failed, eventually resulting in a sale that can only be described as a corporate raid on its assets – a process that was finally concluded in 2009. 'The trick is not to be greedy,' says Copelyn, who has been no less aggressive than Nail in the pursuit of building his investments, but who dealt with control differently – perhaps most evident in HCI's success in getting control of Johnnic, when Nail failed some years earlier.

Black control in the Nineties was a big issue – hence the preparedness to distort shareholder and governance structures. Unintentionally, it would seem, policy makers have discouraged black control as an outcome of BEE ownership today. Almost all the major BEE corporations that have controlling interests in their investment portfolios are those that emerged in this early period – HCI, MIC, Thebe and KTI. This phenomenon is dealt with in detail in Chapter 2.

For many, however, their interest lay neither in black control nor in long-term value creation. It was easy to be enticed by the free option inherent in the BEE transactional structures. If you are able to trade that option whenever and however, it has significant potential value. The problem with BEE is precisely that tradability. Then – as it still is today – the shareholding tends to be illiquid. For those who got tied up in a form of special-purpose vehicle (SPV)* designed to meet the financing peculiarities of BEE, there was a three- to five-year restraint on sale of shares, dictated by taxation considerations. In addition, the political imperative to sustain black shareholding tended also to result in lock-in periods, usually not more than five years. Practically, this meant that BEE shareholders would not necessarily be able to trade at the best time, and instead be forced to sell at the worst time, resulting in them realising no value – which only serves to underline the popular idioms 'there are no free lunches' and 'nothing ventured, nothing gained'.

All these factors converged to encourage a fairground mentality. Let's juggle – throw as many balls up in the air as you can and thereby improve your chances of at least one or two landing successfully. Of course, this approach 'tended to create an impression that business is about deal-making, and has done little to develop expertise in building businesses organically.'[36]

Choosing BEE partners

Another fault line in BEE at that time was the selection of BEE participants in the transactions and the creation of large consortiums involving all manner of individuals and constituencies. The involvement of important constituents such as trade unions and social groupings made BEE transactions palatable, and helped to soothe the criticism that white business was handpicking the new black elite.

The Johnnic transaction brought together the largest consortium ever, the National Empowerment Consortium (NEC). Most involved felt indelibly scarred by the experience. The NEC became a site of furious politics, which created a strong aversion to future participation in consortiums among many of the participants. Gordon Young, then from the Labour Research Service, had spotted Anglo's announcement to sell an interest in Johnnic, and quickly tested support for trade union participation. 'I went to Trevor [Manuel] and Cyril [Ramaphosa] and they said go for it. After that I approached trade unions directly.'[37]

On the business side, a personality like Mashudu Ramano came to

---

* A special purpose vehicle is simply a ring-fenced legal entity that houses an investment. However, in the first wave of BEE, the SPV became regarded as a specific financing vehicle designed to finance the acquisition of shareholding by black South Africans.

the fore, as the face of black business investor groups. Then Nail came along, after failing to persuade Anglo to deal with it alone. To avoid bidding against the NEC, it joined them, but not without resistance. As Young noted: 'Motlana was seen as a capitalist and was not popular. Later Cyril said we should bring Nail in. But they wanted control.'[38]

Many constituencies and some difficult personalities ultimately resulted in 'deals behind the scenes as part of participation'. But, as one participant recalls, 'the real fun and games started once the deal was struck. The question of financing the deal then arose and Nail engineered that process such that there had to be a financial commitment by every party in the NEC. The NEC as a whole would not be raising the finance. This was designed to eliminate some from the NEC. Nail was safe, as it had already raised its finance. I remember one day, when the group came together to deal with the finance. Dikgang [Moseneke] and not Cyril was chairing that meeting. There were lots of tears as those who had not raised their own finance were bid goodbye. Among them was Patrice Motsepe. He pleaded for more time. Dikgang said: "I'm afraid this is the deadline. Son, there's the door." Patrice gathered up his briefcase. The irony is that today Patrice is wealthier than all of them.'

Lessons were certainly learnt. As my informant went on to say, 'In a large consortium like the NEC, you can't get everyone to have a common commercial purpose. The bickering didn't stop with the deal. As time goes on there are different ideas on what to do with the assets.' For Young, 'this taught me never to get involved in consortium politics. Nevertheless, it was a kind of nursery for many important players in subsequent years. A black-controlled MTN was one outcome.'

There were other variants to broadening the base of shareholders who could benefit from BEE transactions. For the 10% stake in Metlife, Nail deployed some three thousand agents to encourage ordinary black South Africans to acquire shares – the exercise fell way short of expectations with only eight thousand people signing on. Another approach – the most successful to date – was to incorporate many beneficial shareholders into the shareholding structure of a professionally managed BEE company, either directly or indirectly. The Women's Investment Portfolio Holdings (Wiphold), for example, travelled the country to recruit individual women shareholders. Others like MIC and the Women's Development

Business Investment Holdings (WDBIH) were owned by development trusts, with expected dividends to those trusts earmarked for social upliftment programmes. Chapter 6 looks in detail at the many variants of broad-based shareholding.

Adding government muscle

Once settled into power, the ANC government began to add muscle to its BEE intentions, so that by 2000 BEE found expression in numerous legislative, regulatory and policy measures – at least 24 in all. Much of it had nothing to do with BEE ownership and investments. Employment-based affirmative action, black skills training and small business development preoccupied much of the new government's efforts at black empowerment. Still, sectors over which the ANC had licensing leverage, like fishing, began to be shaken up. The state also discovered its buying powers. For example, legislation made provision for a newly established Roads Agency to pay a premium to contractors who showed commitment to social development, and it also had the power to penalise noncompliance.

Later, the state formalised its buying power leverage in the Preferential Procurement Act,[39] which provided the legal framework to accommodate BEE. The Act put forward the first points system for BEE, allowing 10% to 20% of total points to be attributable to BEE, with the rest related to technical, operational and financial capacity. On the surface, none of this appeared unreasonable. Also, the ANC trod softly. Consultation and co-operation, rather than coercive legislative fiat, underpinned its approach to business transformation. Employment equity therefore required businesses to formulate their own plans and targets in consultation with employees and trade unions. This seemed sensible, for it provided the space for companies to take cognisance of their own peculiarities and circumstances.

Learning to use the political veil

Importantly, space had been opened for black inclusion in mainstream business and large state contracts. However, their participation tended to be on the basis of political rather than commercial considerations. This prised open the door for BEE partners, whom white business welcomed on the basis of their political access, the dispensing of patronage by the state and straightforward corruption – a terrain that has significantly worsened over the years. 'In the early days there was limited competition among the BEE groups. This was before the grubby politicians had worked out how they could benefit. Today there is too much underhand stuff,' moans an early BEE investor.

The political flavour of black corporate shareholding, together with the way it was being conducted, led to BEE investors being accused of rent-seeking and unproductive investment behaviours. As the first period of BEE transactions came to a close, a demand for operational involvement of black companies in their investments became a popular mantra. This demand defied the usual limit to shareholder responsibilities; minority shareholders rarely get involved in the operation of their business. However, there was an expectation that BEE should do more than offer the promise of capital; it should also provide the opportunity for black shareholders to learn about business.

The energy in BEE investors' opportunistic behaviour blurred the few positive efforts by some among them to inject gravitas into their business activities. Chapter 2 provides an analysis of the investments of these early groups and the major transactions, showing that there was more commitment to building businesses than has been acknowledged to date.

Political sensitivity stifles debate

The first rush of BEE ended on a very acrimonious note. For those involved in this area, we had learnt that such a transformation was much like being caught up in the turbulence of crashing waves, as South Africans tumbled between the pull of the past, the push of expectations of the day, and the still waters needed to plan and process appropriately for the future.

Political aggression and sensitivity meant that debate got swept away in the backwash. Sasol and Anglo American will not easily forget Mbeki's vitriolic response to their attributions of risk to BEE. In 2003 the oil-from-coal producer Sasol listed on the New York Stock Exchange, as a secondary listing to the JSE. That listing requires an annual submission of the Form F20, in which all risk factors must be recorded. Guided by legal counsel,

Sasol listed BEE among them. This first prompted Brian Molefe, then head of the Public Investment Corporation (PIC) – and Sasol's largest single shareholder – to declare risk 'a four-letter word', 'an excuse not to do things even when you know it is correct they should be done.'[40]

Mbeki followed on, accusing Sasol of seeking 'to communicate to all business people, both domestic and foreign, … that they should view our efforts to address the legacy of racism in our economy as something inimical to good business. Sasol and others that think like this major corporate citizen, which our government has nevertheless not hesitated to support, will have to outgrow an outdated mindset… In the end, they will have to understand that black economic empowerment is in their interest … Sasol and all its kindred spirits must, at last, help to translate into reality the vision that our nation will never again bleed in turmoil, just because some could not free themselves from the chains of bigotry.'[41]

Others got caught in the crossfire. The industrial group Barloworld felt compelled to apologise for their chief economist's[42] defence of Sasol. Just before this fracas, the Anglo American chief executive Tony Trahar felt Mbeki's sharp tongue for suggesting political risks still persisted in South Africa, after which there was a flurried effort to mend bridges.[43]

The *Financial Mail* wrote of the ruptures: 'When economic historians write the chapter covering South Africa's second decade of democracy, the issue that will preoccupy them most will be the ambivalent relationship between white capital and black political power.'[44] Citing the political analyst Adam Habib: 'Behind those attacks [on Sasol] is a feeling in government that capital hasn't come to the party on black economic empowerment or investing in the economy. And this after government believes it has played its part by putting in place business-friendly policies.'[45]

Cracks remained, as a later outburst in parliament by the minister responsible for the mining sector at the time, Lulu Xingwana, reminded everyone. During a debate on BEE she accused 'rich white cartels' of 'continuing even today to loot our diamonds, taking them to London; that are continuing today to monopolise the mining industry.'[46]

It was in this environment that BEE policy was being formulated – lots of pushes and pulls and not much still water. The white business establishment effectively went to ground. Only after Mbeki stood down in 2008, the Rembrandt chairman Johann Rupert said in an address to the University of Pretoria: 'Tonight I have kept my word to Mamphela Ramphele, who made a speech in Cape Town and said that whites should start speaking out a little bit without having the fear of being branded racists. We can easily reach consensus on our goals. The methods and priorities will need more debating.'[47]

BEE leaders looking ahead: the BEECom

So, in the early 2000s, there was little mood among the emerging black elite for anything but a significant step-up in BEE obligations on white business. They had organised themselves under the umbrella of the Black Economic Empowerment Commission (BEECom). It took almost three years to draft a comprehensive BEE framework that argued for the state to 'play an unapologetic and interventionist role to reduce inequalities.'[48]

The BEECom sought to ensure 'that black people should direct and take charge of a new vision for BEE, a process that until then, had been conceptualized, controlled and driven by the (white) private sector'.[49] The BEECom took a similar line to the Malaysian one, when they adopted their New Economic Policy in 1970. It encapsulated BEE as integral to the country's growth and investment policy, recommending an Investment for Growth Accord. It also envisaged poverty alleviation, and in particular land reform, as an element of BEE.

Government however felt uncomfortable with the strong reliance on state intervention in the report; it rejected BEE as a strategy for poverty alleviation and never really integrated BEE into its macro-economic policy framework. The BEECom researcher and author Duma Gqubule later took issue with government on this, arguing: 'This is nonsense, a recipe for elite empowerment.'[50]

A year later, black business met with government to discuss the BEECom report and what government envisaged doing. By then it was clear that BEE would be framed as a strategy to address transformation within the private sector, with state procurement remaining an important lever to push through change. 'An enabling environment' was envisaged that would provide guidelines rather than prescriptions. 'Utilising the approach followed in the liquid fuels the government will, together with the private sector, design measurable and realistic empowerment programmes and targets for core industries and reach agreement through accords.' [51]

The BEE Strategy of 2003

Against the backdrop of this kind of thinking, policy formulation began in earnest. As this exercise advanced, reservations about state intervention retreated. Under the auspices of the Department of Trade and Industry (DTI), government drafted a BEE Strategy,[52] finalised in 2003. It was the start of pulling together all the strands of preferential policies to reverse black exclusion in the mainstream economy. This report eloquently argued the case for an all-pervasive 'transformation imperative'. BEE is defined as a 'necessary government intervention to address the systematic exclusion of the majority of South Africans from full participation in the economy'.

The Strategy identified some benefits in the first wave of empowerment, in particular the creation of 'a new generation of business leaders', but focused on the limitations: highly geared BEE transactions and inadequate involvement of the new black shareholders in the management of the companies in which they had invested. 'Substantial increases' in black ownership and control of enterprises were envisaged. Further, the push for participation by black women gained prominence, and so did the continuing emergence of broad-based and community investment vehicles.

The Strategy signalled a new course by government in a number of respects. For the first time, government articulated its intention to measure BEE obligations and performance at an enterprise level numerically, through what it termed a 'balanced scorecard' – a measure of more than black corporate ownership that would also include human resource development and employment equity and what it termed indirect empowerment through preferential procurement and enterprise development. It promised to issue the scorecard as part of an envisaged code of good practice in terms of new legislation that would define all facets of empowerment.

Secondly, the Strategy framed empowerment in racial terms – for blacks only. Mining legislation still honours the constitutional provision for affirmative action for any historically disadvantaged South Africans

– which includes white women and disabled – although in reality only blacks are recognised.

Thirdly, the importance and hence the weighting of BEE ownership appeared to be reduced – 20 out of 100 points of the scorecard. The rest is earned by six other elements: management control, employment equity, skills development, preferential procurement, enterprise development and what at the time were termed residual factors (to allow sectors to choose other empowerment issues specific to themselves; this was later limited to one factor only, corporate social investment).

At this point, government had not stipulated the level of black corporate ownership required, or any other targets for that matter. However, the precedent had been set in charters already adopted in the liquid fuels and mining sectors – 25% and 26% respectively. The BEECom had also pegged the minimum black shareholding at 25%. At no point did the BEE Strategy interrogate whether company ownership provided an adequate measure of black wealth and participation in the South African economy. It did not look at ownership and wealth measurements or benchmarks internationally, either in developed or developing economies.

Soon after the adoption of the Strategy, parliament agreed to the BEE Act.[53] This rather skimpy piece of legislation made provision for the adoption of a national code and sector charters – it said nothing of their content. State-related entities would be obliged to implement the code and sector charters, while private companies would be expected to but not forced. In reality, companies had little choice. Failure to abide by BEE threatened business prospects – it would be high risk indeed to ignore BEE, particularly for the larger corporations.

Up to now, established business had said very little, except to express general acceptance of government's Strategy. The Oppenheimer family, of Anglo American Corporation fame, went a step further, with what it called the Brenthurst Initiative. The resulting report had the usual staccato of investor messages to the South African government, in particular the need for certainty with regard to the planned BEE scorecard: 'Once set, investors must also have the confidence that these targets are not changed.'[54] It called for 'realistic targets', but most importantly, that the 'rules of the game' would not change.

It recommended more, however – that corporate tax be traded off against transformation. The better a company performed at transformation, the lower should its tax rate be. A quick and sharp rebuttal came from government, and the Oppenheimers' report has gathered dust ever since.

Charters and Codes make their mark

On the face of it, the BEE Strategy appeared reasonable and measured. Only on the release of the first draft of the BEE Codes at the end of 2004 did the extent of the intended state intervention become apparent. They constituted the single biggest exercise in social engineering seen since formalised apartheid was introduced in the Fifties. (Of course, this one was for a good cause; apartheid was not.)

A precursor to the BEE Codes was the Financial Sector Charter (FSC).[55] Beyond the usual provisions of BEE, this charter required financiers to make available the necessary funding for the acquisition of equity by black-owned companies – so the blockage in capital in the post-1999 period was removed. In fact, in an environment of constrained activity in mergers and acquisitions, the revival in BEE transactions offered financial institutions a new commercial opportunity. The mining industry, for example, envisaged a value of R100 billion for the initial 15% ownership target – much of which would require bank finance. The financial institutions themselves had to transact BEE ownership.

The changed mining legislation and the associated Mining Charter* as well as the FSC and the pending BEE Codes, had immediate and immense impacts. BusinessMap recorded BEE transactions valued at R40 billion in 2003 and R62 billion in 2004, with a slight dip the following year and then up to R75 billion in 2006 – way above the R21 billion peak in the first wave of BEE.

The process of change is always uneven and often messy; it's difficult to predict whether the objectives will be achieved. The following chapters track the impact of the changes brought on by the Codes and associated charters.

---

* The Broad-Based Socio-Economic Empowerment Charter for the South African Mining Industry, 2002, was drafted by the Department of Mineral Resources and the Chamber of Mines, with inputs from other interest groups. It is available on www.dme.gov.za/minerals/mining_charter.stm.

Part 1

Decoding BEE

Part 1
Decoding BEE

> We have spent too much time on codes of good practice and
> sector charters, rather than looking at successful avenues of
> implementation.
>
> – Mathews Phosa, ANC treasurer-general

> BEE is trying to be something of a miracle maker. How
> do you transfer large financial assets to those who have no
> money? We've been trying to build a building from the 5th
> floor.
>
> – Laurie Dippenaar, FirstRand Group

When the first draft of the Codes was released in 2004, I couldn't
help asking myself, 'How on earth did this come about?' The
nuances and complexities in changing South Africa's racially scarred
business environment had been reduced to a series of arithmetic formulas
– transformation by numbers. These formulas touch virtually every
aspect of doing business in South Africa: shareholding and shareholder
relationships, corporate control, management, employee profiles, skills
development, procurement and corporate social investment, along with
a requirement that companies develop other enterprises.

Submissions were called for. My business partner and I battered out
a response and dispatched it to the responsible Department of Trade
and Industry (DTI). Silence until well into the drafting process, when
I got an invitation to meet some of the drafting team. Time was short,
so I homed in on just a couple of really key concerns. 'Interesting,' they

said, to which they added: 'The minister told us we had to meet you.' Their duty duly done, my future efforts to further the discussion were fobbed off.

They felt comfortable, it seemed, with their efforts, and they had reason to believe that the white business establishment would go along with it. Later, when I perused their submissions, I found that they had accepted the Codes, more or less. They complained about complexity, some of the targets and the difficulties that small and medium businesses would have in implementing them. But on the whole they liked the idea of a clear set of rules that fixed the landscape for the next decade. This would provide certainty, they hoped.

None of the submissions probed the rationality of the approach. It was as if, once the frame had been drafted, an internal logic started to play itself out. The context had been fixed; there was room only for tampering at the edges. Therefore, while each draft promised less complexity and more refinement, this translated into reducing the volume of words, taking out some bits, adding in others and tampering with formulas. I'll never forget the penultimate draft, which never became public but which formed the basis of an interdepartmental review on cabinet's instruction. New formulas had been added in. Quite remarkably someone thought it possible to measure 'fronting' numerically – fortunately, it didn't make it into the final draft. But another did. This one had the incomprehensible name of 'continuing consequence', designed to allow some BEE shareholding to unwind before the Codes had run their full 10-year course.

Once the scoring got under way, I began to feel like the New Age Pencil Tester. For those of you who don't know, during apartheid Native Affairs officials were known to put a pencil in the hair of a person of doubtful racial origin; if it stuck, their curls were too tight and they would be designated coloured or African. As a transactional adviser, I found myself pulling out my pencil to count points for black women, broad-based, young, rural, new entrant and so on. God forbid if you are just black, male and entrepreneurial – you might just be shown the door.

Fortunately, I did not have to do this too often. There is now an industry of New Age Pencil Testers – the verification agencies that ascertain your BEE status. Level 1, 2, 3… I cringe when I see the post-

Codes newspaper advertisements of corporations – full-page ads with 'We are BEE Level 3' in huge typeface. What happened to innovation and imagination?

This is not what we intended, some of the drafters say today. 'It's not working as we hoped ... the model we have used is not sustainable.'* I have to bite my lip and avoid the temptation to say, 'I told you so.' An unhelpful posture and a foolish one, for anyone with a working knowledge of BEE and economic transformation knows that there is no magic formula.

The Codes were intended to smooth the rough edges that had surfaced in the first round of BEE transactions. Instead, they have multiplied. Enrichment is the most popular one to finger. It has even inspired the absurd Left-slung suggestion that the many billion rand gains made by Tokyo Sexwale (once a provincial premier and today a cabinet minister), Patrice Motsepe (only ever a businessman) and others should be nationalised.[†]

This book is not a guide to the Codes – an appendix provides a summary. Instead, I spend the next few chapters chipping away at the many fault lines in the Codes. If economics is the dismal science then these chapters confirm it. Much of the critique of BEE skims the surface. My intention is to get beyond this, for two reasons – to make a clear case for a redirection and to provide sufficient understanding to stimulate new ideas and possibilities.

---

* Polo Radebe, in the Thought Leaders panel discussion on BEE, Wits Business School, Johannesburg, 30 July 2009.

† Amy Musgrave, 'Nationalise Tokyo's wealth says union', *Business Day*, 3 November 2009.

1

No burst in the BEE bubble
... just a pop

> Too often transformation has come to be seen as a numbers game of replacing white people with black people, a way of compensating previously disadvantaged people rather than creating opportunities for all citizens to contribute. The compensatory approach to transformation poses the greatest risk to our democracy and sustainable development.
> – Mamphela Ramphele, *Laying ghosts to rest*

> Most of economics can be summarised in four words: 'People respond to incentives.' The rest is commentary.
> – Steven Landsburg, *The armchair economist*

The US sub-prime crisis and its rapid contagion into global financial markets sent shivers down the spine of everyone involved in the BEE investment game – and, rightly so. As Paul Krugman, Nobel laureate in economics, writes, 'I'm tempted to say that the crisis is like nothing we've ever seen before. But it might be more accurate to say that it's like everything we have seen before, all at once'.[1]

BEE, despite a short history of just over fifteen years, had crashed once before, in the wake of the Asian currency crisis in the late 1990s. Yet, a decade later, in 2008, a far worse tsunami brushed South Africa's coastline without uprooting the palm trees. The financial markets weathered the storm remarkably well. Banks and their kind boastfully spoke of their financial rectitude. The government, on the other hand, attested to sound regulation, bolstered with fresh restraints on consumer credit provision just before the sub-prime crash, and of course foreign exchange controls. It was because of the latter and not because they knew better that South African financial institutions had not invested offshore in the securitised assets into which sub-prime mortgages had been bundled.

Even with this mind, it was reasonable to be pessimistic about BEE investments weathering the storm, for two reasons. First, the acquisitions had taken place in a bull market. The JSE had picked up in 2003, sinking in early 2008, but only reaching the bottom a year later – reflecting South Africa's usual 12-month or so delayed impact of global shocks. The All Share Index price–earnings ratio moved in the 15–18 band before falling to 8 in early 2009. This meant high asset prices at just the time when policy changes were forcing an enormous step-up in BEE activity – some R350 billion from 2004 to 2008.[2]

A similar picture existed in the Nineties, except the volume of BEE activity was far less – disclosed values of deals from 1996 to 1998 were an estimated R30 billion.[3] After democratic elections in 1994, buoyancy entered the market and asset prices soared, putting the price–earnings ratio at around 20.

The second justification for pessimism is the heavy gearing of BEE investments – in fact, 'heavy' is not strong enough a word; with few exceptions, BEE is totally debt-financed. Logically, therefore, these investments should have capsized as asset values dropped below their debt levels – placing many BEE owners in negative equity.

Why BEE went pop

There are two reasons again why the BEE deals of the 2004 to 2008 generation popped rather than burst. First, the financial institutions had learnt a lesson from the first BEE crash. At that time, there was a lot of exuberance. South Africa was a brave new world, integrating into the world market while entering democracy – nothing seemed to stand in the way of growth. Amidst this newfound confidence we brazenly went about financially engineering the transformation of the South African economy. A smart SPV blueprint was devised to transfer shares to the ownership of black South Africans, funded by willing financial institutions which banked on a good debt return, along with what we liked to call 'equity upside'. All in all, everyone was supposed to win: black investors would get shares without having put down money to pay for them, and the financiers would get enhanced returns.

The problem is that the SPV was designed for favourable market conditions whereas, shortly after these instruments were put in place, the market turned bad. My former business partner, Renée Marais, a financier at the time, always argued that the funding structure had been underpriced. If priced for the heavy debt levels and the absence of collateral (except for the equity itself), then the deals would never have been done – the interest rates would have been unthinkable. But there was a political imperative to bring black South Africans into the top echelons of the corporate sector, and so, according to Marais, the banks went ahead.

At the end of the day the financiers took the losses, as the defaults made them owners of equity that was worth less than the debt – poor security indeed. They wondered why they had assumed all the risks, when the companies selling the equity (the vendors) were the ones who really needed the BEE investors. Not surprisingly, once they had mustered up the courage to finance BEE deals once more, they shifted the risk to the vendors by requiring a good measure of guarantees.

The second reason why the deals went pop can be attributed to the BEE Codes. Companies are expected to have BEE shareholders not for a day or a month or a year, but 10 years. If a deal unravels, companies lose BEE credits. Therefore, add the risks companies assumed in the financing of their BEE partners – usually in the form of guarantees – and the potential penalty if they lost their BEE shareholders, and you can see why companies did what they could to stop transactions unwinding.

On the surface, therefore, the Codes had a positive impact: they prevented a repeat of the Nineties. However, a lot more needs to be said about the above scenario and the role of the Codes before reaching too hasty a conclusion.

Creating black capital

Let's start with the crux of the problem – the absence of capital among BEE investors and their subsequent reliance on debt to buy their shares. Firstly, BEE ownership and the manner in which it is financed are based on the principle known as moral hazard. This is because it are premised on borrowed money and, as Krugman notes, 'Borrowed money is inherently likely to produce moral hazard.' Why? The term refers to 'any situation in which one person makes the decision about how much risk to take, while someone else bears the cost if things go badly wrong'.[4] This is BEE in a nutshell.

It's helpful to wend our way through this issue, which is not unlike a game of snakes and ladders. Let's say I'm an aspirant black business person wanting to lose the 'aspirant' label and become a real player. I have no money but I know you, a company, are willing to sell me shares for a billion rand. We do a deal and go to the banks, which agree to provide a billion rand loan as long as you, the vendor, are willing to stand guarantor, which you do. So I sign up for the loan. My shares are held in an SPV, which is ring-fenced. This means that if I get into other deals and they go bad, no one can make a claim on my shares in this SPV; this saves you, the vendor, from waking up one day and finding that you no longer have me as a shareholder but instead a bank which has secured my investment in you to cover my other investment that had gone under. Equally, no claim can be made on any of my other assets to cover a default in our SPV. So we have a neat, tightly contained investment vehicle that gives me ownership of a billion rands' worth of shares, and in which there is a billion rand loan for which I am not liable in the event of a default – *you* are. If the investment performs, good for me; if it goes bad, I just wave goodbye and you pick up the cost. Having done the deal, got the money and avoided the risk, I am certainty ahead – up the ladder I go.

The Khumalo factor
However, you, along with many other vendors, got wise. You had been watching the manoeuvres of Mzi Khumalo. He had been first in line in the BEE queue, acquiring one of the early mega–deals, JCI, for almost R3 billion. He was also among the first to watch the sad demise of those early BEE investments. But Khumalo is smart and he learnt fast. So he picked himself up, dusted off his coat and put the speculative spark back into BEE: he aimed at the arbitrage opportunity in BEE transactions. He got shares at a discount to market price (usually on offer to make BEE deals more financially sustainable), and sold soon after at an even higher market price than when he transacted; if that extra juice wasn't there, he

could afford to wait a bit longer until it was.

Of course, this made absolute sense to Khumalo, who has yet to show remorse for accumulating large amounts of capital, even if he reinterpreted his contractual obligations. After all, wasn't this the purpose of BEE: to put capital in black hands and let them get on with the task of becoming black capitalists? However, companies who had transacted with him were understandably shell-shocked by his behaviour. One day they were BEE compliant, the next day they weren't. This meant that they had to go and conclude another BEE deal, exacting yet more transactional costs (which I will discuss later).

Khumalo therefore didn't do me, still an aspirant black capitalist, any favours. You, along with many other companies, put in protections against the Khumalo factor and imposed the proverbial golden handcuffs, popularly called the lock-in. This may be as much as a 10-year sentence, coinciding with the measurement period of the Codes. Or it may even be much longer. The market crisis and the resultant restructuring of BEE finance that dominated 2009 pushed out the repayment periods, which are not infrequently linked to lock-ins. Therefore, after this latest crisis, the financial terms of BEE deals may be significantly harsher with lock-ins potentially extended well beyond 10 years. This is black empowerment in suspension, and a story unlikely to end on a happy note.

To get back to Khumalo, whom you have been watching very closely. You realised that I could get round my exit constraints by simply breaching my shareholder's agreement in some way, thereby forcing you to buy back my shares – a common provision of such agreements. You also realised that I would be highly motivated to do this just when my shares are priced right. So you threw in a large disincentive – a 30% discount to market price if I breach our agreement.

So now I own a billion rands' worth of shares, but I can't sell them for a decade or maybe even longer, and if I try to wangle my way out I face a hefty discount on the value of my shares – that's a snake, and down the board I go. The hazard doesn't look so morally skewed any more.

The hazards of policy makers

But that's not the end of the story. Our policy makers, gathered in DTI's

Pretoria offices, were ambivalent about the principle of moral hazard, unconsciously at least. In their early drafting they envisaged the Codes being informed by 'sound economic principles', of which one was the 'risk and reward relationship, where there is a particular reward, it is commensurate with the risk assumed'.[5] If upheld, this would have removed any suggestion of moral hazard in BEE.

However, in the same document, they put forward a brand new and unique measure of BEE that stretched the risk–reward relationship wide apart. After I'd waited 10 years to realise value from my equity, the policy makers had wanted to ensure that I got my full economic due and that the value of my equity would not be lost entirely on debt servicing. Their motivation dates back to the first wave of BEE and the disintegration of equity values after the Asian crisis. The question they wanted answered was how to prevent a repeat of this. The answer is that you can't: people buy and sell shares all the time and they make wrong choices often and markets go belly-up less often. That's life. The best you can hope for is an improved access card – open up opportunities to black investors and look for a framework that tries to ensure a fair deal. But that didn't seem the right answer at the time. Black South Africans needed, in fact had to, own a share of the economy if the country wanted to secure its future.

A bit like an act of faith, the policy makers devised a new principle called 'realisation' or 'net equity value', which said, 'Thou shalt invest and receive thy full due.' It works like this: today my billion rands' worth of shareholding has no net equity value, as it is matched by a billion rand loan. Over the next three years, however, the Codes expect that I should have earned sufficient dividends to repay some of my loan and leave me with a net equity value of 40%. In years five and six, my net equity should be 60%, in seven and eight it's 80%, until by year nine I should have what the Codes term 'ownership fulfilment' – which sounds orgasmic, but isn't. It's like having landed on the ladder again, but in fact I am betwixt and between a snake and a ladder.

Things are not what they seem
The reason is not difficult to fathom. On a visit to the DTI team in late 2005, I took along a financial model to demonstrate my point. In terms of this model, I assumed a 25% BEE equity acquisition, fully

debt financed, with the interest rate priced in accordance with the risk, and normal company performance growing consistently over 10 years at GDP plus inflation. The financing term is 10 years. At the end of this period, the model states that the BEE investors will have to sell 60% of our shareholding to pay off the debt, leaving us with a 10% equity interest at the end of the day. To realise full economic value for the 25% holding, as required by the realisation principle, the companies selling to BEE investors would have had to sell their shares at a discount of around 65% to 70%. This outcome is simply a consequence of financing equity with debt.

A 70% discount gets you close to giving away the shares. Yet there has never been a suggestion from government that it expects anything like this. Instead, there has been an expectation that the terms of BEE deals will be softened, to help make BEE ownership more sustainable. This softening process is called facilitation and is a composite of measures such as price discounts, loan guarantees and favourable financing terms. Companies may choose one or more. They constitute a cost to shareholders which, once accountants have calculated their aggregate effect, tends to gravitate to around an effective share price discount of between 20% and 30% – far short of the discounts that the realisation principle implies.

If we punch a 30% price discount into the financial model, with all else being equal, BEE shareholding will settle at around 17.5% of the initial 25% shareholding in 10 years' time – better than the 10% with no facilitation.

What happens when full realisation is not achieved? Fortunately, I, as a BEE shareholder, am not responsible – but you, the vendor company, are. So, there is definitely no *voetstoots* clause in BEE. If my investment in you, the vendor company, is not successful enough in terms of satisfying the realisation principle, you pay the penalty – a loss of points on your BEE scorecard, which could be as much as 40% of the 20 points allocated to BEE ownership. So, you are now responsible for something you don't own, and whose performance you can't possibly guarantee given your lack of control over so many factors that impact on investments – interest rates, foreign exchange fluctuations and economic downturns, to name a few.

Worse still, you are likely to score less in the bad times than in the good times, given that the value of your company's equity is likely to drop under difficult market conditions, bringing down the BEE net equity value with it. For example, I acquired a shareholding worth R100, with a R100 loan. By year three the loan has been reduced to R95; but in the same year three there is an economic downturn and now the equity is worth R90. In terms of the Codes' scorecard, you should have a net equity value of 40%, whereas there is negative equity, giving you a zero score. So the scorecard penalty is being exacted just when you can least afford it and could do with some relief from BEE obligations. There could be a knock-on effect: lower points could result in loss of business – failure to qualify for a state tender due to reduced BEE status, for example. This would hardly be fair to any of the shareholders, including BEE.

Misplaced incentives

What behaviour is the realisation principle encouraging? The first one is noncompliance. I have yet to find a company willing to pay the costs associated with this principle. Companies therefore tend to offer the standard package of facilitation and then identify where they could compensate for the points that they are likely to lose in the 'net equity' column of the scorecard. They would do this by making sure that they get their full points – and bonuses – by having the right quota of black women, broad-based investors and new entrants in their BEE investor grouping. This would enable them to forfeit all their realisation points and still get a 75% BEE ownership score. This should not be a problem, since there remains the possibility of picking up good scores for the other elements of BEE. So, once all these scores are aggregated, a shortfall in ownership may not matter.

Another response, if you are an unlisted company, could be to massage your company valuation figures, thereby enhancing the value of the BEE shareholding and increasing the differential between the equity value and the debt. This, of course, would improve your net equity value score.

It would not be difficult to put an optimistic figure to your company's value. The Codes place a lot of faith in 'standard valuation methods', but this belies the fact there is a huge room for variance. Valuation models can produce many plausible numbers, depending on the assumptions made. Any challenge of the numbers would be costly and most unlikely (unless there is an obvious fiddling of the figures).

The debt-financing conundrum

There is an important consequence of debt-financed equity acquisitions. As in the financing model, once all debt is cleared, actual BEE shareholding is likely to reduce from 25% and possibly settle somewhere between 15% and 20%. Policy will appear to have failed. How might I and my BEE colleagues react to this? It is too early to say, but a backlash is a probable response. Since shareholding is used to indicate success or otherwise in transferring economic wealth to black South Africans – like a proxy of black wealth in the economy – I suspect that 15% or 20% black corporate ownership, in a society where 90% of the population is black, will be viewed in a very dim light. For that matter, as long as corporate ownership has this proxy status, it is unrealistic to expect even 25% to satisfy expectations. Quite possibly there could be a demand for even more BEE ownership – and where would that take the South African economy? This raises the question: why implement a policy measure that is unlikely to be met and what might be the alternatives? This subject is addressed in Part 3.

How else might the Codes, and the realisation principle in particular, motivate me, a BEE investor, to behave in my investment activity? Since I am not responsible for the successful outcome of my investment and I have no money committed, it is quite likely I won't make considered investment choices. I may sidestep a due diligence and economise on the time and money needed for a professional negotiation. All in all, I may not scrutinise the business or the deal sufficiently, leaving the door wide open for you, the seller, to determine the terms. Later, when I find that my expectations are not being met, I cry foul and my relations with you deteriorate. Unfortunately, this is a highly probable scenario; it is one that I, as a transactional adviser, have experienced time and again, and have seen confirmed many more times in media reports that pick up BEE scandals from disgruntled shareholders.

Still, even if I feel a little aggrieved, I could argue that the concept of net equity value definitely had the benefit of encouraging companies to provide softer terms than in the Nineties to ensure that the deals would be more sustainable and less vulnerable to collapse. So, even if the transaction doesn't give me everything I wanted, I may still get something – there is a ladder, after all, but just not as long as I would like.

What's good for me may not be good for the country

But there are ladders and ladders – mine, which is there to put money in my pocket; and the nation's, which is there to enable large numbers of black South Africans to get into the game and participate in the mainstream economy.

If my responses here are a reflection of the behaviour of the majority of BEE investors, what kind of black capitalists or entrepreneurs are we creating? In not having to commit any money to their acquisitions, they are getting a free option that provides the promise of infinite returns no matter what happens as long as it is positive. But there are always snakes in the grass – who knows how big or small the return will be once debt has been serviced? It makes sense, therefore, to chase as many deals as possible to be reasonably assured of some wealth. As a black entrepreneur, therefore, my attention span is fairly short: I'll attend a few board meetings if I have to, but never take my sights off moving from one deal to the next as quickly as possible. Getting involved in the detail of running a business was never really on the agenda. Fundamentally, the promise of easy money doesn't build character; those of us on the BEE carousel are just not spurred to be productive investors.

There is no better commentator on this than the architect of racial preference in corporate ownership, the former Malaysian prime minister Mahathir Mohamad.* Disappointed after the Asian crisis, when his cronies (as they became known) came back for more support when he believed he had given them enough, he said: 'In business, the vast majority regarded the opportunities given them as something to be exploited for the quickest return. Very early on, they sold off their opportunities to become sleeping partners in an arrangement cynically known as "Ali Baba", in which Ali merely obtains the licences, permits,

---

* Mahathir Mohamad was prime minister of Malaysia from 1981 to 2003, all in all for 22 years.

shares or contracts and immediately sells them off to non–Malays … They learn nothing of business and become even less capable of practising it and earning an income.'[6] If we think about the amount of money pumped into BEE transactions – more than R500 billion – unproductive investment behaviours matter enormously. The next chapter deals with just this issue.

As a final point on the realisation principle, we should note the lack of reaction of established business at the time the Codes were drafted. Given the serious implications of the net equity requirement, one would have expected some protest – at least a raised hand. There was nothing of the sort. I suspect business didn't pay enough attention to the detail, as they tried to mediate the political tetchiness that accompanied any criticism of BEE policy. However, their silence has come back to bite them, specifically in the mining sector.

In 2009, unbeknown to the mining industry, the Department of Mineral Resources (DMR) published a sector code in the *Government Gazette* that may or may not usurp the Mining Charter.* A mishmash of the charter and the DTI's Codes, it produced a miscarriage of the realisation principle. The consequences are very serious: there is a two-year grace period before net equity becomes relevant. After this, it would seem, net equity must be fully realised, since there is no provision for marginal realisation over time as we find in the DTI's Codes. The mining companies will be caught between a rock and a hard place – virtually to give away equity or face the risk of losing their mining rights. This catapults investment risk in South African mining into the stratosphere. This would be a very long snake indeed, unless this provision is changed – as is being discussed between the DMR and the mining industry at the time of writing in 2010.

Yet more policy pitfalls
Now I want to approach the Codes from another angle. A good portion of BEE investments will always be sub-prime or sub-optimal. This arises because all companies (with a few exceptions) are expected to sell shareholding to BEE investors. This presupposes that all companies are

---

* At the time of writing, the status of the Mining Charter and the Mining Codes was up in the air, awaiting a review by the DMR.

worth investing in, which is patently not true. There are many companies of sub-optimal performance. Ordinarily, around 30% are probably not worth considering, if we think of company performance along the bell jar curve. However, when we add the overlay of debt finance to equity acquisitions, many more companies, even sound ones, may become sub-optimal for BEE transactions.

If you recall from my financial model, the performance of an average growth company is not enough to service the debt fully. So, a below-average growth company becomes a very poor investment choice indeed – yet BEE is expected to be transacted even here.

There are also certain types of companies that are ill suited to bringing in third-party shareholders. Family-owned businesses are the most obvious. For the entrepreneur Vhonani Mufamadi, these businesses should be treated as a class apart: 'Once I invested in a family business. They just continued to run their personal expenses through the books, regardless that they had outside shareholders. Government is misplaced to force BEE on family business. They do it for the tenders, but it builds up a lot of resentment between the founders and the black shareholders.'[7]

The problems cut deeper. Once you have external shareholders, a range of governance issues raise their head, like board meetings and formal reporting procedures that are rare to find among shareholders who are family members. Also, some owner-managed businesses have seen perverse opportunity in BEE ownership. It has provided them with a chance they might otherwise not have had, to sell shares or even exit entirely. Valuing such businesses is testing, to say the least. The potential to massage figures is enormous.

So, here I am again, still an aspirant BEE investor, and I come across such a business. The existing shareholders put on the table a value for the company – which I am in no position to interrogate – and offer a generous 'discount'. Ah! A sweet deal; I'm in. Of course, I have no idea they have overvalued my shares in the first place, and that they are still overpriced even with the discount. Anyway, the business is not very big; I don't need hundreds of millions, or even billions of rands, like the headline-catching deals. I can put in a bit of cash and get some extra funds from the bank if I offer my house as surety. This is BEE done, and soon to be undone, as experience has shown many times.

So many snakes. FirstRand's Laurie Dippenaar is right. Trying to sell equity to those with no capital is like building a house from the fifth floor. Miracle making indeed.

The commercial contortions of policy

What do we really want to achieve by requiring most companies to have 25% BEE ownership and keep it that way for a lengthy measurement period? The commercial interests of business seem ill served by this requirement.

Company shareholding changes for two reasons: first, through buying and selling, and second, by issuing new shares to raise capital for growth. The potential to buy and sell is influenced by the liquidity of a share. When there are lots of buyers and sellers, as there may be in listed stock, liquidity is high, and a liquidity premium gets factored into the share price. Equally, low liquidity will discount the price. This brings us back to the BEE lock-in I spoke about earlier. The lock-in means BEE investors cannot sell and hence they lack liquidity, which depresses the value of their assets. When markets are buoyant, they could well be stuck, unable to realise value from their investment activities. Equally, they could be required to sell at a time when the markets are at their worst.

The former ANC leader and businessman Cyril Ramaphosa believes that lock-ins 'offend the spirit of empowerment. It could be argued that in the last year lock-ins have depleted black wealth and reversed black advancement because black people were uniquely prevented from realising value when markets indicated that a measure of profit-taking was prudent.'[8]

The problem arises because BEE ownership is expected to be retained over a long period. The Codes make some allowance for black shareholding to unwind, but limit the ways. Companies are still penalised in terms of the BEE scorecard if they lose some of their BEE shareholding and don't transact anew. When they have to do that, they have to facilitate the BEE deal again; this means further costs again – both in terms of financial facilitation and management time. Therefore, despite the limited scope to unwind shareholding, companies are disinclined to contract for this with their BEE shareholders, and prefer instead to impose a blanket lock-in – any decision later to release the handcuffs is the prerogative of the vendor.

Retaining BEE ownership

The matter of rights arises when companies issue additional shares to raise capital and current shareholders have the right to buy in proportion to their shareholding. This is particularly difficult to deal with in a BEE environment, when most black investors will not have the capital available to follow their rights and acquire the additional shareholding on offer. The practical consequence of this is a dilution of their shareholding. So, if a BEE entity holds 10 shares in a company that has 100 issued shares, and the company issues an additional 50 shares but the BEE investor does not take up the shares it is entitled to buy, its shareholding drops from 10% to 6.7%. In terms of the Codes, the company that has issued the shares will be less compliant (having allowed the dilution to occur) and will be penalised with a lower BEE score.

The mining industry, however, is a special case. It is the only industry where there is a legal obligation to have a 26% BEE shareholding; mining companies are at risk of losing their licences if they do not retain that level. Yet a rights issue would, in all likelihood, result in the 26% being reduced. There is no clear solution to this dilemma.

Government policy is certainly opposed to dilution. The mining industry is faced with officials who are particularly stubborn on this issue, and who have been known to postpone the issue of licences until dilution clauses[*] have been removed or softened in shareholders' agreements – in their view, dilution of black shareholding should not be an option.

Interestingly, trying to retain a specified level of preferential shareholding, regardless of rights issues, is a problem that Malaysia never resolved in almost forty years of affirmative action – until last year, when it removed rights issues from any policy obligations.

South Africa also had a way of dealing with such matters before the Codes were adopted. The Financial Sector Charter (FSC) took a different approach: as long as deals were transacted in terms of agreed

---

[*] These clauses in a shareholder's agreement may, for example, state that other measures of raising capital will be implemented without affecting the BEE shareholding. These are extremely complex clauses and highly problematic.

principles, such as financial facilitation and meaningful participation of black investors, transaction could unwind.[9] If that happened there would be no further requirement on a financial institution to sell further equity in terms of their BEE obligations. The principle coined for this approach is 'Once empowered, always empowered'. But the drafters of the Codes did not like it, and at the time of writing, the financial sector was under pressure to conform to the Codes.

The regulation and codification of BEE ownership has resulted in commercial contortion. Some of it might have been avoided if policy objectives had been limited. Instead, there is conflict between objectives.

If we had simply looked to BEE shareholding as a means of black capital accumulation, which black South Africans could then apply to building businesses and expanding their activities in the mainstream economy, the requirement to retain BEE shareholder levels over the long term would not be necessary.

However, another objective, to promote broad-based redistribution of economic assets, makes some sense of fixing BEE equity ownership and restraining the sale of shares. Without this, people would simply sell as soon as they could to realise much-needed income. This would open up the risk of shareholding reverting back to the original or similar shareholders or becoming concentrated in the hands of a tiny black elite.

Which is our preferred objective? In terms of policy, none – we should have both. So, we have a BEE landscape replete with unintended consequences – as slippery as snakes. Could we have avoided this? In part, yes. Langburg's four words, 'People respond to incentives', are a valuable policy guide. If policy makers had really thought through all the incentives that are inherent in the measures they proposed, they would surely have come up with a different policy construct. Instead, as implementation has faltered, we see shoulders shrugged and two words, 'unintended consequences', uttered a lot.

The consequences we see, however, may be unwanted – and in that sense unintended – but many are not unknown. They were already evident in the Nineties. The trouble is that even having a good grasp of incentives may not ensure policy success. When we are trying to change so much, particularly in a short period of time, we cannot possibly predict the outcome of the complex interactions that take place. As the economist and author Paul Ormerod writes, 'There are too many factors that determine the outcome and whose relative importance alters over time, for the complete picture ever to be grasped.'[10] Incentives therefore matter. But, as a further complication, we have no assurance that people will respond to them in a rational or consistent manner; this makes predictability extremely elusive.[11]

I have delved into a few aspects of the Codes to expose some design faults that will make it difficult to meet policy objectives and to position South Africa for future challenges ahead. There is a default button in the Codes that reverts to the past – redressing black exclusion through wealth redistribution rather than staying with the future – ensuring an inclusive economy with black South Africans very much part of creating wealth.

In the following chapters, I continue to explore the implications of trying to achieve economic transformation through a codified system of compliance. Here are two comments that set the tone for further analysis of the Codes. The *Financial Times* commentator John Kay sees 'regulation by rules' as inviting 'compliance with the rules rather than the objective of the rules, and the more extensive the rules the easier it is to lose sight of the objective.'[12] South African academic writings pick up a similar theme: 'In current international practices of auditing and certification, it is perfectly possible to match procedures, indicators and management goals and at the same time openly fail to match the "spirit" of the basic principles upon which a certification system is built.'[13]

2

Form over substance

Another weakness in the empowerment programme is that it has been focused on transfer rather than transformation. By 'transfer' I mean the ceding of existing assets to individuals in a manner that does not in any way alter the economic structure. By 'transformation' I mean the creation of new markets, new investments, new drivers of domestic demand in the economy.

– Kgalema Motlanthe, Deputy President

BEE has always walked through brambles, consistently scratched by criticism that has left some persistent scars. Much of the critique is good but has failed to range widely enough to touch the nuances. Looking further, there are some surprises to be found.

My focus here is on black ownership as a means to create economic wealth as opposed to personal enrichment, which is undisputedly an outcome of BEE. Policy has tried to travel the dual path of redistribution and productive investment, but ultimately it has failed to mediate the tension between them. Redistribution dominates – unfortunately, too often with the look and feel of the spoils of war being divvied out.

The ANC picked up on this tension just as the Codes were being drafted. A discussion document at the time talks of the 'difficult issue' of BEE financing that does 'not necessarily raise productive investment levels in the domestic economy [and] is therefore a drain on scarce capital assets and will impact on the medium term investment level. This is just one example where policy decisions in South Africa sometimes contradict each other resulting in failure to meet our most important objectives.'[1]

Concerns about productive outcomes kept emerging as the Codes took shape. The businessman Chief Lediga drew attention to the waste of 'black talent', too 'focused on deal-making, spawning a generation of people whose only mission is to buy into existing white companies.'[2] The *Financial Mail* editor, Barney Mthombothi, pinpointed the absence of 'ingenuity' and 'innovation' in the deal-making mix. Instead, 'we seem to regard the state as the vehicle to riches'.[3]

Even well after the Codes had been adopted, the former ANC policy guru Joel Netshitenzhe still finds that 'we have shareholder capitalism as opposed to entrepreneurship'.[4] This is despite the Codes being framed with the explicit intention that 'substance should take precedence over legal form'. The drafters had wanted to encourage real black ownership, not black faces fronted as shareholders; they wanted to see real economic value emerging out of BEE transactions and real black businesspeople taking charge of their economic destiny.

Here's one surprise. Contrary to perception, more of the real thing occurred in the first wave of BEE than in the period after the adoption of the various BEE policies, Codes and sector charters, all of which took shape from 2003. The reason, you will see, is directly attributable to the design of the Codes. The Mining Charter and to a lesser extent the Financial Sector Charter, both of which preceded the Codes, have similar flaws, but for the purposes of my argument here I deal with the Codes only.

Policy intentions

Let's look more closely at the policy intentions. Unfortunately, they are not self-evident on reading the Codes. We have to go back to the first version, as subsequent drafting resulted in much abbreviation in an effort to reduce complexity.

This first draft[5] defines BEE, in part, as 'increasing the number of black people that manage, own and control enterprises and productive assets'. The objective is to create 'new enterprises undertaking new forms of economic value-added activities'.

The policy makers also intended to guide BEE beyond capital accumulation and ensure that 'the proceeds [from the benefits realised] are re-invested in the South African economy'. Black shareholders also needed to be afforded the right 'to determine strategic and operational policies of an enterprise'. *

Although the Codes make no mention of entrepreneurship, except in the definitions, Philisiwe Buthelezi, who led the initial drafting, says: 'We expected entrepreneurship to happen within the ambit of the Codes. We persuaded white corporations to support new black-owned firms through [the element of] enterprise development. With this, we were no longer talking about blacks getting a stake in white corporations.'⁶ The practical outcome is quite different.

Policy impact on productive investment

In Chapter 1, I considered capital accumulation and its curtailment due to debt financing. Here I look at the other side of the coin, how capital is invested, and test whether government has created the kind of rules that will encourage money to be well spent.

Let me say upfront that I am not disputing that there is a value to BEE ownership that falls outside commercial considerations. There is a political side to empowerment that frames long-term economic prospects. As Mamphela Ramphele points out, 'Political power without economic power is unsustainable.'⁷ Quite simply, business worldwide needs sound governmental relations and it is impossible to imagine South Africa's private sector having these without black South Africans visibly in the driving seat. But of course deracialising the workplace will take much more than tampering with ownership.

More than fifteen years on, it is time to place economic imperatives at the centre of BEE, and in particular focus on productive results. Too much money is going into changing the country's shareholder profile for us not to be concerned about its efficient use. It is not good enough to promote black capital accumulation, which, studies show, is not sufficient for economic growth.⁸ How we put our capital to work matters

---

* In some instances companies contracted with their BEE shareholders to meet certain participatory commitments, such as assisting in marketing or facilitating government interactions. These 'performance contracts' never gained widespread appeal. Too often they became a source of contestation in negotiations as BEE investors tried to secure large 'fees' for loosely defined participation; and too often, expectations of participation by vendor companies and their BEE investors never aligned. As such, by the time the Codes were introduced, there was a low level of expectation within established business of so-called strategic, business-orientated BEE companies adding any more value than a passive, broad-based shareholder like a community trust.

enormously. So, it is important to know whether BEE investments are enhancing productive activity or simply tying up large amounts of capital in asset swaps. Also, what kind of black business investors are being encouraged – asset traders or productive entrepreneurs?

Let's look first at productive investment. There is little information available on what BEE companies are doing with capital already accumulated. Further, many are still awaiting returns. I have therefore chosen a proxy by which to assess productive outcomes. That proxy is black shareholder control, based on the assumption that control will encourage black investors to become engaged in their investment and make strategic decisions that have productive implications. I envisage such investors as productive black entrepreneurs, be they individuals or legal entities.

There are of course shortcomings to this proxy. For example, BEE investors may exercise control but still behave like an investment holding company that devolves much or all of the strategic decisions to management. One of the reasons the investors may do this is because they carry little or no financial risk.

There is considerable discussion around the absence of financial risk in BEE and its negative consequences on business behaviours. It seems counterintuitive to think of non-risk-taking entrepreneurs. As Robert Shiller, a leading international academic in entrepreneurship, succinctly puts it: 'Indeed, risk-taking is what entrepreneurship is all about.'[9] But in the case of BEE it's difficult to make risk capital a requirement, since one of the purposes of BEE is to redress the absence of black capital.

Whither black shareholder control?

So, what picture emerges when we look at black shareholder control? I reviewed the major BEE transactions* from 1995 to 2008, divided into two periods, the first up to 2003 (which I call the pre-Codes period), and then from 2004, when new BEE policies started to be drafted and

---

* My research considered on average the top 10 deals per annum. In the pre-Codes period of lower deal flow, the top 10 deals could constitute up to 80% of the disclosed values of BEE transactions, while post-Codes, when deal flow escalated significantly, the top 10 deals tended to constitute between 30% and 40% of disclosed values. The deals were drawn from the research conducted by BusinessMap up to 2006, and from the Ernst & Young mergers and acquisitions reports, 2007 and 2008.

implemented (post-Codes period). As soon as the new BEE frameworks became evident and the drafting of the Codes began, business went ahead on these terms. The Codes therefore started to define the structure of BEE transactions long before they were gazetted in February 2007.

The first surprise is the much stronger emphasis on black control in the first wave of BEE than in the post-Codes period. Almost 30% of all major deals in the pre-Codes era transferred control to black investors, while this figure is 10% for the post-Codes period. Where the shareholding threshold is raised to above 25%,* then the pre-Codes figure shifts up to 38% of transactions against 15% post-Codes.

In the pre-Codes period, there were a number of factors that motivated black shareholder control, not least an interpretation of the political imperatives of the time. As the former Anglo American Corporation director Michael Spicer says, 'political liberation needs to be accompanied by economic liberation' – and the absence of black capital meant 'there had to be an artificial intervention'.[10] Anglo American envisaged this as black people acquiring controlling interests within the corporate sector in much the same vein as it had done some forty years earlier for Afrikaner empowerment.

Further, as South African conglomerates re-entered the global economy, they needed to unbundle non-core assets. This provided an opportunity to place sizeable corporate assets in the hands of black South Africans, satisfying both political and commercial imperatives.

A former chief executive of MIC, Clifford Elk, also says of that period: 'The businesses that embraced us were the more forward thinkers. They saw the competitive opportunity. It's different today when everything is about compliance.'[11]

Broad-based performs better

The second surprise came when I looked at the profile of the leading investors in the major BEE transactions. I considered those who have dominated the top echelon of activity, participating in three or more top deals throughout the 15-year history of BEE ownership. I profiled their investments in terms of the level of black shareholder control

---

* For mining, the compliance level is 26% and this was applied to mining transactions.

within their portfolios;[*] some have a high proportion (although not necessarily the majority of their portfolios) of controlling stakes, while others have just a limited number. I also considered what type of BEE investor they are – individuals (dominance of black professionals, business people and/or ex-political figures); controlling broad-based investors (large grouping of individuals or an investment entity that represents a broad spectrum of black South Africans, such as trade union members); and significant broad-based investors (above 25% but less than 50% of large groupings or entities). I also cite those who have started new ventures.

What is interesting about this profile of BEE investors is that, on the whole, they do not fit the general perception of a small grouping of 'usual suspects' playing at enrichment rather than empowerment – although a few may fall into this category.

Of the 15 companies that feature here, 40% have a high level of shareholder control in their investment portfolios, which rises to 80% if limited control is included. Most of these companies are broad-based investors or have significant broad-based shareholding and most were founded in the first three years of BEE. In addition, the companies with strong broad-based shareholding have been more inclined than the individual BEE investor groups to invest in new ventures.

I also broadened the analysis of BEE companies and their investment portfolios to include those who have become prominent but haven't featured as the top deal makers. All the companies with some controlling interests were established in the pre-Codes period and were a mixture of broad-based and individual. Companies that emerged after the Codes have not acquired controlling interests.

In summary, therefore, the evidence suggests that earlier black corporate shareholding initiatives provided a basis for productive investment outcomes. The Codes stalled this trend. Further, investment companies with a strong broad-based shareholder flavour display a type of corporate entrepreneurship that is barely evident among the individual BEE investors. This runs counter to the perception that broad-based investor groups are primarily interested in cash flow from

---

[*] I excluded from consideration those subsidiaries that BEE companies create to house minority BEE investments.

BEE entities in major deals	Shareholder profile	Investment portfolio profile	New ventures
African Rainbow Minerals	Individual	High black control	Yes
Brimstone Investment Corporation	Individual	Limited black control	No
Eyesizwe Mining/Coal	Individuals & significant broad-base	High black control	No
Fabcos Investment Company	Controlling broad-base (which represents small black business)	No controlling interests	No
Hosken Consolidated Investments (HCI)	Controlling broad-base & listed (trade union trust)	High black control	Yes
Kagiso Trust Investments (KTI)	Controlling broad-base (social trust)	High black control	Yes
Mineworkers Investment Company	Controlling broad-base (trade union)	Limited black control	No
Mvelaphanda Resources	Individual	Limited black control	No
Peu	Individual	Limited black control	No
Royal Bafokeng Holdings	Controlling broad-based (community)	Limited black control	Yes
Sekunjalo Investments	Significant broad-based	High black control	Yes
Shanduka	Individual	No controlling interests	No
Thebe Investments	Controlling broad-based (social)	High black control	Yes
Women's Development Bank Investment Holdings	Controlling broad-based (social)	No controlling interests	No
Women's Investment Portfolio Holdings	Significant broad-based (women)	Limited black control	Yes

their investments and therefore lack the necessary long-term horizons needed to build businesses.

It is important to distinguish the broad-based companies that feature here. They are professionally run on commercial principles, but provide a special case of social business, as the KTI chief executive JJ Njeke highlights: 'A key ingredient has been our strong value system. The profit motive is not the only reason for our existence ... We are part of a bigger cause, creating something that will be there for generations ... We took to heart the advice of one of our board members, who said it would be sad if BEE was only defined by investments and we didn't learn how to run companies.'[12]

In any review of the Codes, these successes need to be recognised and understood as a platform from which to construct improved policy. Interestingly, the BEE companies achieving high levels of black control in their investment portfolios are also those who put at risk some of the capital they accumulated – usually not a high proportion of the investment, but enough to make the seller feel their BEE partner has skin in the game. As Njeke notes, 'You don't take your investments as seriously as you should without financial risk and you are not taken as seriously by your partners.'[13] This early idealism may lie at the heart of why some leading companies have operated in defiance of the rent-seeking incentives offered by BEE ownership. What they also show is that there is a case for a more nuanced criticism of BEE.

No escape from ownership

Some of the policy makers have suggested (politely) that I am being unfair in focusing on the ownership element of the Codes. Ownership is just one of seven elements – 20 points out of 100. As Buthelezi says, 'Ownership doesn't excite me. What really excites me is where black people take control or put in milestones to achieve control, working in partnership with others.' Two elements of the Codes, preferential procurement and enterprise development, are relevant in promoting black business and achieving Buthelezi's goal of black control. The problem is that black shareholding is still the main gauge by which a company may qualify for preferential procurement and enterprise development. Nowhere in the Codes is it said that these black owners must do more than just be shareholders.

Essentially, a company is expected to have 25% BEE ownership within its own shareholding, to procure from suppliers who have a minimum 25% BEE ownership and to support the development of enterprises with at least 25% BEE ownership. This more than doubles the effective weighting for ownership.*

---

* The total score for preferential procurement is 20 points, of which 12 points are attributed to goods and services acquired from companies that have a broad-based BEE recognition level. Given that BEE ownership constitutes 20% of that recognition level, I have assumed that 2.4 points of the 12 can be attributed to ownership. An additional 5 points under preferential procurement are directly related to black ownership of suppliers; I have therefore attributed 7.4 of preferential procurement's 20 points to BEE ownership. I have attributed the full 15 points for enterprise development to BEE ownership, as this is the only criterion that a company must

There are only a few escape points. Micro enterprises up to R5 million annual turnover are exempt, and small businesses with a turnover of less than R35 million can choose four of the seven elements by which to be measured – so ostensibly they could leave out the three elements where ownership is pertinent. Multinationals, too, may be exempt from having to bring in black shareholders if they can meet certain stringent conditions, electing instead to do an equity equivalent (a development-related programme, for instance). Finally, listed companies with institutional investors (such as pension funds) may score these shareholders at 10% BEE out of the required 25%. Overall, however, by far the greatest portion of productive activity in the economy is captured by the Codes and required to have or promote black ownership.

The total value of BEE transactions testifies to just how important ownership is. Between 1996 and 2003, the value of disclosed transactions is some R90 billion, whereas this figure escalates to around R350 billion between 2004 and 2008. If the 25% ownership milestone is to be reached, some observers have estimated that a further R700 billion of equity may need to be sold to BEE entities[*] – although this could be much less, around R450 billion, if we consider that 10% is already covered indirectly by institutional investors.

Do the Codes really help enterprise development?

There will also be a substantial amount of money chasing enterprise development. The Codes require that companies must develop other enterprises which are 25% black-owned or more. At worst this could cost a company 3% of net profit after tax (NPAT) per annum or at best 3% of one year's NPAT spread over five years, depending on the measures chosen to develop these enterprises.[†] Further, the contribution need not be cash; staff time given to developing another enterprise may be

---

apply when selecting enterprises to develop. As such, 22.4 points need to be added to the 20 points directly attributable to BEE ownership, giving a total of 42.4.

[*] Martin Kingston, chief executive of the South African office of Rothschilds, speaking at a panel discussion on BEE in July 2009 at the Wits Business School, Johannesburg, gauged that 25% shareholding in the private sector is an estimated R1200 billion.

[†] For example, a five-year loan to an enterprise may be included in your scorecard count each year for five years, as the loan is recorded in your accounts each year as a contribution to enterprise development. A grant, however, is once off and may only be recorded in the year it is provided.

included, but it is nevertheless a cost to the company.

Drawing on corporate tax revenues for 2009, a 3% NPAT would be an estimated R12 billion; and, as a guesstimate, probably 75% of that nationally aggregated sum is produced by companies required to comply with the Codes. Enterprise development could thus require a commitment of as much as R9 billion.* Some of this would be contributions in kind – staff time to mentor enterprises, for example – but the figure is still likely to be enormous.

To see the scale of the task, consider the fact that it took the National Empowerment Fund, now headed by Buthelezi, five years to disburse R1 billion of funding up to 2009. Anglo American's small business initiative, Anglo Zimele, invested some R300 million over a 15-year period to 2008. The longstanding investment company Business Partners advanced just over R300 million in 2008 to black entrepreneurs and start-up businesses. So, it's not so easy to spend large amounts of money on effective enterprise development. As Anglo Zimele's Nick van Rensburg emphasises: 'You can't just create a business without a market. If the market is not there to service all that enterprise development money, then what?'[14]

And there is good reason to worry that the money may not be well spent. The design faults in the Codes are too weighty – as illustrated in the rest of this chapter.

The ownership ceiling

The first flaw is that the 25% marker for black corporate shareholding has effectively become a ceiling. In October 2002 the Department of Minerals and Energy (now called the Department of Mineral Resources (DMR)) wrote the first draft for the Mining Charter that required 50% ownership by historically disadvantaged South Africans across all mining companies. Never before had government signalled an intention of this kind. The value of listed mining stock plummeted by R56 billion in just two days, while the JSE lost R99 billion[15] in the following week. Both the industry and the DMR hurriedly assumed a short-term mask of mutual co-operation to present to the world and thereby hopefully recover the losses.

---

* This figure could be overstated, as I have also assumed the actual tax rate and not the effective tax rate.

Evidently 50% was not feasible. The compromise of 25%, a level at which certain minority shareholder rights kick in,[16] seemed the next best option. And 25% looks eminently reasonable, since 90% of the population in South Africa is black.* As Tokyo Sexwale (now earmarked by his own political allies for nationalisation of his wealth) says: 'Let black people become a minority in their economy. That's what the government policies are. Any other government would have gone the other way in its own country – it would have demanded everything.'[17]

The effective ceiling exits because there is no incentive to exceed it. There are bonus points for bringing in rural people, broad-based groups, co-operatives and new black shareholders, but no bonus for selling more than 25%. Interestingly, the penultimate draft of the Codes allowed for a black-controlled company to skip to a higher BEE performance level; if rated Level 4, it would record Level 3, potentially giving it an edge when bidding for business. None of the policy makers I spoke to could explain why this provision had fallen away; perhaps it was omitted in the last-minute review ordered by cabinet.

The two elements, preferential procurement and enterprise development, have an explicit objective of promoting black-owned and -managed businesses. However, even they fall short in achieving this.

Under preferential procurement, a company – while itself only needing 25% BEE ownership – may require its suppliers to have a controlling black interest in their shareholding. However, the incentive to push for black control in the supply chain is not strong. Only 15% of a company's preferential procurement score is attributable to procurement from black-controlled firms, which translates into 3% of the total BEE scorecard.

For enterprise development, there are two categories of business that qualify. The first is micro and small enterprises that are more than 50% black-owned, for which there is a points enhancer in the scorecard. The second is any other enterprise that may be 50% black-owned or more than 25% black-owned as long as the latter meets certain BEE recognition conditions, which are not particularly onerous. It would be possible for a company to support enterprises with 25% black shareholding only and secure a reasonable score.

---

* I use the Code's definition of black to cover African, coloured and Indian South Africans.

Voices within black business circles are starting to cry foul as they observe corporate South Africa's reluctance to overreach the 25% marker. Some actually insist that 25% should be a minimum. But even one of the drafters of the Codes, the legal adviser Kevin Lester, says this cannot be the case. When drafting, he says, they thought that 25% could be a guideline. They sought legal opinion, which found that the Constitution makes provision for variation from a basic right, such as advancing the interests of previously disadvantaged people, only when this is done by statute. 'Government has got itself in a difficult spot,' he concedes.[18]

What chance for black control?

But let's ask again, why not 50% or more black ownership? It is only untenable when there is a requirement on almost everyone to transact BEE ownership – clearly, you cannot demand that almost everyone gives up 50% of their shareholding without courting a market revolt.

During my research in Malaysia, a policy specialist touched on just this issue: 'I hope you don't make the same mistakes as us. Our objective of 30% [Bumiputera] shareholding was a national figure. The initial intention was not to ensure that 30% of each company was held by a Bumi. Our problems started when they [the government] began to enforce the policy at the micro level.'[19] What could I say? We were making the same mistakes.

The Codes have also failed to achieve what is termed 'negative control' by BEE shareholders. In terms of the Companies Act, minority shareholders with 25% plus one vote are able to block shareholder resolutions on certain specified matters – but the provisions only kick in when the shares are voted in one block. The Codes require voting rights of 25% + 1, but they don't require that this shareholding is voted jointly. And in fact the Codes have unintentionally encouraged the opposite – the division of black shareholding into small portions so that no single BEE investor has sufficient shares to achieve negative control.

The reason lies in the diverse BEE investor profile required. If you are a BEE investor, it's not good enough to be black; 40% of your shareholding needs to be held by black women and 10% by broad-based entities. Furthermore, if part of you qualifies as a 'new entrant', so much the better. To present the right profile, you either create a company with the required black shareholders or construct a consortium of separate groups that together give the right look. So, complex shareholder relationships are created from the outset.

The alternative approach is for the company in need of BEE shareholders to construct its own grouping. In recent times, an increasingly favoured approach is to divide BEE ownership into small parcels of equity, shared between disparate groupings of BEE investors, each exercising their small portion of voting rights as they see fit.

Add up all these design flaws and we have a set of rules that discourage the creation of productive black businesses and entrepreneurs. The only alternative is to scurry about for a slice of the cake. It is therefore not surprising that we are seeing more rent-seeking and opportunistic behaviour than ever before.

Enterprise development: the new hope

For those disillusioned with BEE ownership and its deal-making activities, enterprise development is the next hope to deliver the real thing – black owners who get their hands dirty in business operations. But here again, enterprise development is fraught with faulty assumptions. The notion exists that companies are equipped to help other businesses develop. It is hard to imagine why, since there are few compelling success stories to prove it. There is some history of South Africa's largest corporations getting involved in enterprise support, usually among firms in their supply chain. Anglo Zimele is the most notable initiative, seen today as best practice. Unlike most, however, these corporations have deep pockets and can commit large resources. Even then, success tends to be elusive.

Quite unrealistically, the Codes require all companies with a turnover of more than R35 million to get involved in enterprise development – this means that thousands upon thousands of small- to medium-sized companies are obliged to carry the burden of developing other businesses, when the task of simply running their own business is already onerous enough. Not unexpectedly, a new industry of intermediaries is emerging, promising to take over companies' obligations for enterprise development.

Another flaw is complexity and the loopholes for avoidance. Qualifying activities could be any of the following: cash contributions; commitment of effort, such as mentoring and employee time; facilitating access to finance; improved credit or payment terms; and payments to intermediaries that specialise in enterprise development. Even the development of a new project in which a commodity is further processed in South Africa may qualify. Monetary contributions are easy to verify; non-monetary contributions are wide open to manipulation.

To add to the complexity, there is a benefit factor matrix which determines whether the value of a contribution may be scored at 100% or at a discount. A grant provided to an enterprise may be counted in full, whereas only 70% of the value of a loan to a micro enterprise at market-related terms will be recognised – and deciding on the discounts, I am told, was something of guesswork by the drafters. There are 16 different categories in this benefit matrix.

This is compliance at its best. But, as Anglo Zimele's Van Rensburg says, 'If you, as a company, do enterprise development and run it according to a set of rules, it won't work.'[20] Ticking scorecard boxes fits poorly with the grit of entrepreneurship. And it doesn't help when the task is handled by the human resource and corporate social investment departments in companies.

Allon Raiz, himself an entrepreneur who runs business incubators, gives a taste of just how wrong things can go. He says the selection of enterprises is too often based on the 'five usual suspects: the cleaning, garden, guarding, driving and canteen services.'[21] What's the pattern? Raiz put it like this: Mary, the cleaner, is approached by her employee to become a cleaning service. She can't say no because he's the boss. At the month end, Mary doesn't get paid. She goes to her bosses, who tell her that she failed to provide an invoice. She is then told how to draw up an invoice and submits it. Now she must wait 30 days for payment, and the creditors are knocking on her door. December arrives. In the past she relied on her Christmas bonus. Now her bosses tell her she is self-employed – no bonus; and worse, the company is closed for 15 days during Christmas – no pay for those days.

Another unintended consequence is the perception of enterprise development as the mini-terrain of BEE ownership, with all the rent-seeking behaviour associated with it, only on a smaller scale. As one intermediary says, 'Some black businesses are figuring out that this is another way of getting a share of value from white companies – it's a blank cheque, like BEE ownership.' Says a member of the drafting team, Kevin Lester: 'Rather than looking at the ownership status of the enterprise, we should have looked at what we were trying to achieve.'

This brings us back to the same story as in the ownership element of BEE – the act of creating black businesses does not imply productive, growth-orientated or innovative entrepreneurship. In his award-winning research into entrepreneurship, Scott Shane found that 'firm productivity increases with firm age. This means that, at least in the United States, the average new firm makes worse use of resources than the average existing firm, which is not what you would expect if economic growth benefits more from the creation of new firms than the expansion of existing ones.'[22]

I return to this point constantly. If we want a strong, strategic presence of black owners in the mainstream corporate sector, then established black companies must get more support. Some of the 'usual suspects' may be just who we need to take BEE to another, more productive level.

3

Lessons of the past

The more things change, the more they stay the same.
— Jean-Baptiste Alphonse Karr

At the close of 2009, banner headlines declared the government's intention to ban trucking on certain roads in an attempt to divert freight to the flagging state rail service.[1] This threw me back to childhood and growing up immersed in the local economy of a sugar mill in Natal. Company trucks moved constantly between the rolling fields and factory, stacked with cane cut by impoverished Pondos,[*] while rail tracks webbing the landscape carried trains loaded with processed sugar for export. Etched in my memory is my father's exasperation with the National Party government's control over how the company conducted its business – only state-owned rail services, and not trucks, could transport the sugar outside the boundaries of the sugar estates. Permission had to be sought for company transport to operate; the rail service was inefficient and decisions difficult to extract. This was only one of many state edicts that proliferated and hampered productivity in those years.

Among my classmates at the whites-only village school I attended was a minority group – children of railway workers. They were poor, Afrikaans, inarticulate and alienated. An alternative apartheid existed between them and us, children of blue-collar workers, factory artisans

---

[*] The Pondos are a Xhosa-speaking people from an area in Eastern Cape called Pondoland, the traditional recruiting ground for cane cutters. Working in unbearable humidity and searing heat they wore sackcloth, guaranteed to chafe the toughest skin.

66

and managers, none of whom were poor and all from an English-speaking community. The railway children lived outside the sugar estate in ramshackle state housing. Invariably they attended school wearing only half the regulation uniform, faded and frayed. Their meagre resources seemed unbecoming of the status accorded them by the Nationalist government. Uneducated Afrikaners employed by the government translated into a badly run state – or so it seemed.

The unashamed preference given to Afrikaners during Nationalist rule rooted out Afrikaner poverty, ensured quality education in Afrikaans and created Afrikaner capitalists and corporations of world-class standing. The Pondos are still impoverished, hailing from an area that ranks among the poorest in the country. So, when I took a leap from childhood to 1994, when the political arena changed and the scope for black opportunity widened, I saw logic in the baton of affirmative action being passed on from Afrikaners to black South Africans.

The prominent commentator Mamphela Ramphele writes: 'Established English-speaking business people took steps to empower Afrikaners, facilitating their access to economic resources and encouraging them to play an active role in wealth creation. This was considered essential to social stability.'[2] She was therefore surprised when, as a managing director of the World Bank, private sector lobbyists approached her to persuade the Bank to exert pressure on the ANC government to step back from BEE.

But, putting aside such compelling logic, I also hear voices from the past who found fault with many a consequence of Afrikaner affirmative action – a policy that could not but succeed given that an entire state apparatus focused on enhancing benefits to a very small section of the population, while escalating the exploitative system of cheap black labour.

Every era has its myths. Johann Rupert, whose Rembrandt empire was born amidst the stridency of the Broederbond's economic movement, believes the efficacy of Afrikaner empowerment is one of these pipedreams. Dispelling black aspirations of quick fixes, he insists that Afrikaner capitalists had not risen off the back of a sympathetic government that took the sharp edge off business risk. In the Fifties, his father built his business 'by selling shares from farm to farm and in the trains … It was not until 1978 that the company became cash positive. It is never easy in business.'[3]

He disputes the notion that Afrikaner unity was another underpinning to protect their business growth. 'Forget about Afrikaner empowerment. In 1982 I went to Volkskas [for money], and they pulled my lines [of credit].' At the time, Rembrandt held 30% of Volkskas stock, 'so forget about Afrikaner solidarity.'[4]

Meeting the Malaysian parallel

Malaysia is the best and closest parallel of positive discrimination to draw lessons from – the economic affirmation of a majority that also controls political power. As the South African government was stepping up its interventions, the Malaysian prime minister Mahathir Mohamad[5] questioned his own affirmative action effort, the Bumiputera policy – or at least the part that had cushioned the Malay business elite in patronage. That elite, mostly in leadership positions in the ruling party, had become Ali Babas, selling licences to Malaysian Chinese businessmen in the foyers of Kuala Lumpur's luxury hotels.

Clearly, Malaysia deserved a visit. Within hours of arrival I encountered two vignettes that made me feel pretty much at home. On telling my driver of my purpose, he declared without prompting: 'I am a second-class Bumiputera; I'm from Sarawak* and we've been ignored. The government takes our oil and uses the benefits for Malays.' Shades of South Africa's coloured (mixed race) population – never white enough under apartheid, not black enough under democracy; thus, locked into second-class status.

I proceeded to an island retreat for a spot of pleasure before work. A diving enthusiast, I wasted no time in finding the local dive centre. I was greeted by a young woman with Malay features and a clipped English accent.

We're closed.

When will you be open?

We don't know. We don't have any diving instructors.

---

* Bumiputera is translated as the 'sons of the soil' and refers to the Malays at the time, largely rurally based poor farmers, and indigenous groups of the Sabah and Sarawak, part of the island of Borneo, where most of Malaysia's oil and gas fields lie offshore.

What?

Actually, we have been forced to shut. Yesterday the police raided us for employing foreign diving instructors without work permits. They fled, and so we have no diving instructors. We are told we are not employing enough Malays as diving instructors and in senior positions.

Aren't you Malay?

Yes, my father is, but my mother is British. So I am not regarded as a true Malay.

So, this is the reason for raiding you?

No, our permit to operate here expires in a few weeks. We have applied for renewal, but the hotel management supports a Malay businessman replacing us.

She directed me to the other side of the island – a mere few hundred metres away – to another dive centre, where the diving instructors who had earlier fled her centre were now gainfully employed, apparently perceiving no threat to working without the necessary permits.

On leaving a couple of days later, I heard that the dive centre fracas was resolved. The young woman cheerfully informed me, 'We're open. Padi* refused to give the Malay businessman a licence. He didn't qualify to run a dive centre.'

Thirty-six years of affirmative action, and Malaysia is still locked into racial economic tussles. Is this what South Africans have to look forward to? It raises the question: When does positive discrimination become negative discrimination with all its unwanted consequences?

My visit to Malaysia in 2008 was at a time of long-overdue political change. The hegemony of the United Malays National Organisation (UMNO) had eventually disintegrated. The multiracial opposition coalition Pakatan Rakyat (PKR)† had begun sniping directly at the Bumiputera policy, although this was done with caution as it still created political discomfort to challenge a policy that people had become accustomed to.

In Kuala Lumpur I found a modernised economy throbbing with

---

* Padi is the major international dive certification authority.

† PKR is an informal political coalition formed to oppose the ruling party in the 2008 general election. The coalition comprises a group of Malaysian political parties: the People's Justice Party, the Chinese-based Democratic Action Party, and the Pan-Malaysian Islamic Party. In the 2008 election, about half of the Malays voted for PKR.

commercial energy and people open to discussing the shortcomings of affirmative action – sunset clauses that never set; too great an emphasis on Malay entitlement to corporate shareholding; the absence of an entrepreneurial culture among Malays; far too much corruption and patronage; racial polarisation.

But education had opened new doors for Malays, creating a large middle class, and rural development reforms had softened the edge of poverty in Malay communities. These reforms were also integral to preferential policies first encapsulated in the New Economic Policy (NEP) in 1971.

So much the same, yet so different
Afrikaner, Malaysian and black empowerment feel and look alike in many ways. Yet there are differences, some of which matter enormously. In all three cases the government, sooner or later, stepped in and used the power of force that only a state has at hand. But South Africa today operates in a very different world from South Africa in 1948, when the National Party (NP) assumed power and institutionalised racial policies; and from Malaysia in 1969, when bloody race riots led to the NEP that favoured the Bumiputera.

In the rest of this chapter I will explore lessons drawn from Afrikaner and Malaysian affirmative action that bear on South Africa's reassessment of its own policy choices. There are three focal areas. The first relates to the difficulty of repaginating economic structures and patterns of ownership. The second deals with differences in the starting points, in particular the economic context and availability of resources, both financial and human, to support the NEP. The third area is unintended consequences.

Afrikaner ownership
First let's look at Afrikaner ownership of economic assets. Under NP rule, Afrikaner control of companies on the JSE grew from less than 10% in the late 1970s to 20% by 1990.[6] Mapping the period from 1948 to 1975, Dan O'Meara, a renowned author on what he terms *volkskapitalisme*, calculated Afrikaner control of the private sector to rise from 6% to 21% – a 15% shift in 27 years. The mining sector's proportion of private

sector ownership increased from 1% in 1948 to 10% in 1964 to 18% in 1975 – a 17% rise, largely due to the acquisition from Anglo American Corporation of General Mining and Finance Corporation by Afrikaner capital. The percentage growth in participation is fairly consistent for other key sectors. Liquor and catering escalated from 20% to 35%; finance from 6% to 25%; and manufacturing and construction from 6% to 15%.[7]

The state sector, on the other hand, grew significantly. O'Meara writes: 'NP statism also involved the creation of literally hundreds of new state and semi-state bodies and institutions.'[8] State capitalism resulted in a more than doubling of the public sector share of the economy in the first 25 years of NP rule. If state corporations are included in the count of Afrikaner economic participation, industrial output under Afrikaner control rose to some 45% by 1975.[9] It seems reasonable to count them in, as they indisputably constituted an important form of economic control and participation for Afrikaners. Their boards and managements were almost entirely Afrikaner, and they were managed in terms of NP interests.

Malaysian shareholding patterns

A similar pattern is evident in Malaysia. There, the government ruled that 30% corporate shareholding should be held by Malays and other indigenous groups by 1990. This was off a base of 2% Malay corporate shareholding in 1970, while foreign investors owned almost 70%, with the Chinese owning much of the rest.[*] The 30% target, the Malaysian government has insisted, has never been achieved, with the figure being consistently around 20% since 1990. But government measurement, using the Malaysian stock exchange Bursa Malaysia as the proxy for Bumiputera share ownership, is disputed. The first point of challenge is the use of the par value of shares and not their market value. The second is the exclusion of government-linked companies (GLCs) and unlisted companies from the tally.

The Malaysian government attributed the 20% listed shareholding to individuals and trust agencies. The latter were a key government

---

* The calculations were based on the par value of the shares – that is, the value given by the company when the shares are issued, unrelated to the market value. Listed and non-listed companies are included in these calculations.

instrument used to initiate a shift in ownership patterns in the Seventies, and have continued to play a significant investment role to this day. Trust agencies were created, effectively to warehouse shareholding on behalf of the Bumiputera (and Malays in particular), with the intention that they would acquire unit trusts once they had the capital to do so, and with banks encouraged to assist. Trust ownership includes various funds, including pension funds, with the largest fund manager being Permodalan Nasional Berhad.

At the head of government-owned corporations is the oil multinational Petroliam Nasional Berhad (Petronas), which has a foothold in South Africa with an 80% shareholding in Engen Petroleum. State governments, through their economic development corporations, also own equity.

The acquisitions of trust agencies and GLCs were aided by the 1975 ruling that earmarked 30% equity for Bumiputera ownership. This provision resulted in equity being offered at a discount on any new listing or rights issues, and became an important platform for the creation of a Malay business elite. The latter were further helped by Mahathir Mohamad, who 'selectively distributed government-created concessions to a small group of businessmen, who would inject these assets into the stock market as a means to help them swiftly develop their corporate interests.'* These were his popularly labelled 'cronies', giving rise to the term 'crony capitalism'.

The GLCs are significant economic players, who, it is argued, represent Bumiputera economic interests. In 2005 the GLCs constituted 36% of the total market capitalisation of Bursa Malaysia, with government-controlled institutions having a majority stake in seven of the top 10 listed companies.[10] The combined assets of these companies constituted more than half of Malaysia's GDP. If the GLCs' equity interests are included in the Bumiputera ownership count, Malay participation in corporate shareholding amounted to an effective 45% in 2005, according to research by the Kuala Lumpur-based Centre for Public Policy Studies.[11]

---

* 'Corporate equity distribution: Past trends and future policy', Centre for Public Policy Studies (CPPS), 2006; this paper triggered much controversy at the time of its release, with the government denying the figures presented. Subsequently, the author, Lim Teck Ghee, lost his job at CPPS.

Recalculating South Africa's ownership figures

In the previous chapter I argued that black corporate shareholding was likely to level out at between 15% and 20%. This number excludes institutional shareholding that may be attributable to black benefit. However, there is a case for counting black interest in retirement fund investments as well as in other third-party-managed funds, as Malaysia did. This is a matter for Chapter 10, but suffice it to say here that such indirect black ownership has a significant impact on the measure of black ownership. If both direct and indirect black shareholding are counted, conservatively it could already be around 25% and optimistically closer to 40% – the expectation is that certainly within the next few years 40% or more is most likely.

Affirmative action's own glass ceiling

There is a remarkable confluence of numbers – a 20% marker for direct shareholding, whether it is in Malaysia or South Africa today or forty years ago; and around 45% when we factor in other forms of economic ownership that are relevant to the interests of those being affirmed. This may be a coincidence. Equally, it may suggest something more. Perhaps there is a threshold to the benefits of policies of the affirmative action type: at some point, the negative consequences overtake the positive, and the anticipated advances stall in things like shareholding. So, affirmative action may have its own glass ceiling.

Also relevant may be a pattern of corporate ownership in middle-income emerging markets – where Malaysia and South Africa qualify. Foreign and institutional shareholding, along with corporate cross-holdings, may leave not much more than 20% or so of listed stock available for individuals and private entities.

There are two further points on the measurement of ownership that I want to touch on here. The one relates to what would best constitute a measure of wealth. Fazilah Abdul Samad, a professor in finance at the University of Malaya, disputed reliance on share equity, and instead argued for a measurement of wealth in all its forms, which includes assets like property and land.[12] A composite measure of economic assets would provide a different and more realistic picture of economic participation by marginalised groups, allowing for better policy responses.

The second relates to a form of broad-based ownership, apart from institutional ownership, that has emerged under the BEE mantle. It is the direct shareholding by legal entities such as investment trusts that represent a broad spectrum of black people or interests and did not feature in Malaysian or Afrikaner empowerment. Broad-based ownership offers an alternative to the cronyism and enrichment that is associated with the usual equity ownership initiatives. Part 2 is dedicated to this broader form of ownership.

A different economic context

The next area of exploration that we should look at is the conditions under which Afrikaner and Malaysian affirmative action unfolded. The economic context is crucial. Both experiments took place at a time of economic protectionism. Globalisation did not exist, import substitution was an acceptable economic strategy,* and large states prevailed. As O'Meara highlights, 'The nature of the international economy has profoundly changed since the 1940s. In the context of globalisation, the space for state intervention to protect and support an emerging "national bourgeoisie" is much smaller. And today, capital is more than ever a global (rather than national) institution, throwing into doubt the possibility of there existing a "patriotic capital."'[13]

Within this context, Malaysia rolled out an interesting growth strategy. It was already at the head of the curve of changing international economics. It had never in fact been a closed economy, reliant on protectionism, either pre- or post-independence. It had a large trading sector with no capital controls and large foreign investment in rubber and tin. This probably earned the country credits that enabled it to restrict foreign ownership without impacting negatively on foreign participation in the economy. A little-known fact is that the NEP also sought to increase Malaysian Chinese and Indian ownership to 40% (which meant only a slight rise from where it had been already). Foreign ownership thus shrank from some 63% in 1970 to just under 30% in 2004, but still

---

* Import substitution policies are designed to encourage the local manufacture of goods that are otherwise imported. High tariffs are often placed on such imports to make locally manufactured goods more price-competitive. Import substitution is seen as an inward-looking policy; in the Eighties it gave way to export orientation, where countries focused on developing industries whose products would be exported.

with sizeable foreign direct investments as a result of the growth of the economy. Malaysian Chinese equity continued to rise through the NEP decades, from an estimated 27% in 1970 to 40% in 2004.[14]

This dual strategy of encouraging and restricting foreign investors worked both because of the economic context and because the Malaysian government followed a macro-economic policy of 'conservative pragmatism'[15] that assured high growth. In the twenty years of the NEP, Malaysia ranked as the world's tenth fastest-growing economy.

Afrikaner nationalism a pillar of affirmative action

Strong nationalistic and cultural assertions underpinned the economic rationale for affirmative action by and for Afrikaners. Afrikaners had a history of mobilising savings among their own, underscored by a patriotic fervour for self-reliance. For example, the life assurer Sanlam emerged in 1915 under the motto 'Born out of the Volk to serve the Volk.' Many years later, in alliance with the NP government, Sanlam became the most significant receptacle of Afrikaner capital, helping to fulfil what was identified as three 'powers' of the Volk: savings power, labour power, and buying power.[16]

The savings mobilised by Sanlam found their way into Federale Volksbeleggings, formed in the late Thirties, which effectively became the venture capital fund for Afrikaner entrepreneurs. As Sanlam was a mutual society, its policyholders shared in the returns from investments in Afrikaner businesses. In this sense, Afrikaner empowerment was fundamentally broad-based.

Collective savings of the Volk therefore created the platform for emerging Afrikaner business and, after assuming political control, the Afrikaners running the state provided much of the buying power. Afrikaners did not build their corporate muscle from shareholding made available by English capital. The much-cited case of Anglo American's offer of General Mining has created a misconception; the gesture did not set a trend of Afrikaner ownership through share transfers and asset trading – far from it. Apartheid's main architect, Hendrik Verwoerd, eschewed the deal for attempting to 'co-opt Afrikaners', who were much more inclined to create their own businesses, immersed as they were in their own culture, pursuing innovation and new production with patriotic zeal. Out of this emerged some extraordinary technological advancements and business operations. The most notable is the production of oil from coal by the then state-owned Sasol, in a complex of plants that stands as an engineering feat even by today's standards.

Yet I do not want to suggest that Afrikaner affirmation did not also reflect patterns of patronage, corruption and inefficiency similar to those found in Malaysia and current-day South Africa. The manoeuvres of the secret Broederbond,* interlaced with state patronage, brought special benefit to many. Examples of Afrikaner favouritism were the allocation of fishing quotas, mining and liquor concessions, government contracts and all sorts of valuable inside information.

Malaysia draws on culture and religion

Malay nationalism became the motive force of the NEP, underpinned by the constitutional description defining a Malay. Someone is a Malay if they profess the religion of Islam, speak the Malay language (Bahasa Melayu) and practise Malay custom. More recently, Islamic fundamentalism has asserted itself with the adoption of a dual judicial system – civil law and Sharia laws. Consequently, racial polarisation is now said to be at a level that may threaten to become racial conflict. Many Malays are themselves unhappy with the fundamentalist direction, which they feel is being used for political purpose by the ruling party.†

The Malaysian government, like the Afrikaner one, sought broad impact aimed at poverty reduction and economic restructuring. The latter sought to bring Malays into mainstream economic activity through preference in equity ownership and employment. Unlike the Afrikaners, the Malay people did not have financial self-reliance through collective

---

* The Broederbond existed from 1918 until 1994 as a secret and powerful organisation to advance Afrikaner interests.

† 'Malay custom' was not elaborated in the Constitution, but its meaning is understood. Malays have rituals that encompass a way of life relating to marriages, social norms, etiquette and so on. Some of these customs are Hindu in origin, some animist and some linked to the practices common in Java and Sumatra. In some instances, they are distinct from Islamic practices. However, with Islamic fundamentalism increasing, it is said that some of the Malay customs are being marginalised. There is a term Ketuanan Melayu, roughly translated as 'Malay supremacy', that has gained greater currency within the ruling alliance and is being used to promote Islamic fundamentalism – Muslim Malay supremacy. The Islamic party in the opposition coalition does not subscribe to this concept, which is seen as divisive and offensive to Malaysia's Chinese, Indian and indigenous populations of the Sabah and Sarawak islands.

savings that could be mobilised to build their economic base. However, they had control of a state with valuable resources at hand to fund the NEP activities.

Money and education to underpin empowerment

Both South Africa and Malaysia had the benefit of natural resources to fund their aspirations. South Africa's rich mineral endowment ensured plenty of money to buttress Afrikaner social upliftment. In the beginning it was easy: Afrikaners were always less than 12% of the population. Education was available as another important resource. Afrikaners started off disadvantaged, but only as regards access, not quality. Afrikaans- and English-speaking scholars received comparable education, unlike black South Africans, who had an inferior system of 'Bantu education' imposed upon them. The NP government quickly ratcheted up the availability of education to Afrikaners, establishing and expanding Afrikaans-speaking schools, universities and colleges, supported by an extensive state bursary system.

Malaysia, too, had rich resources: oil, tin, timber and palm oil. At the time, the prime minister Abdul Razak made it clear that 'we were not going to rob Peter to pay Paul' – a phrase I heard time and again during my visit to Malaysia more than 35 years later. There had to be a growing economic cake, without which there would have been 'disruptive redistribution', notes the economist Mohammed Ariff.* The numbers also helped. At the time, Malaysia's population was less than some ten million, with Malays constituting 52%, followed by the Chinese at around 36%. Today, higher fertility rates among Malays together with emigration of Malaysian Chinese have pushed up the Malay numbers to about 60% out of a population of 26 million.

The Malaysian government's approach to education was similar to the Afrikaners'. Malays had access to the same education as other ethnic groups, but many never managed to get to school. Today, Malaysians pinpoint education as one of the NEP's great successes but there is ongoing dissatisfaction with the results. For example, I found consistent

---

* This point was made in an interview with the author by Dr Ariff, executive director of the Malaysian Institute of Economic Research, June 2008. It is pertinent to South Africa's redistribution objectives.

concern about the loss of fluency in English and a belief this may disadvantage Malaysians on the global stage.

BEE on a different footing

The starting point for black empowerment was quite different. The ills of apartheid had long caught up with the country. Inferior black education amidst skills shortages had set a limit on economic performance. The new South Africa did not – and still doesn't – have the economic fat that had been available to Malaysian and Afrikaner nationalism. Importantly, the numbers are quite different: 90% of a 40-million population have a justified claim to economic redress. Educational resources are also sorely lacking. We need advancement in both the quality of education and access for black scholars to ensure enough human resources to finance a turnaround in black disadvantage. Today, the government has achieved significant improvement in access to education, but results point to a national crisis: the quality of education is poor indeed, with far too high failure and dropout rates. As it stands, education may well become the Achilles' heel of BEE.

Negative consequences proliferate

My final area of focus is the negative consequences of Afrikaner and Bumiputera preference. A whole category of these emerged out of the shift in policy focus from broad-based preference to disproportionate benefits for a small elite. Here, I want to concentrate on the Malaysian experience, given its influence on South Africa's approach to black corporate ownership.

The period of the NEP under Mahathir Mohamad is one that South Africa has drawn from the most. When Mohamad came to power in 1981, he sought to create a heavy industrial sector under government sponsorship. This saw a rapid expansion of GLCs and privatisations. But he also wanted this new industrial thrust to catapult Malay business into the top echelons of the economy. To achieve this, he handpicked individuals for favoured support – his popularly known 'cronies'. They had preferential access to privatised assets, state contracts and licences, and secured bail-outs after the East Asian crisis of 1997/8.

The costs of the programme and its inefficiencies weakened the country's macro balance, culminating in the first economic crisis in 1985/6. But it was only after the next economic trauma – more than a decade later – that Mohamad threw his own policies into question. After the Asian market collapse in 1997/8, he became deeply disappointed in the Malay business elite, who came to him, hat in hand, for yet more support: 'It is easy enough to promote affirmative action, not easy to implement it ... Today, they can lean on the crutches of Malay privilege, but crutches invariably weaken the users.'[17]

But these were his cronies, of his creation, spoilt by preferential access to lucrative assets and targeted lending via the largely government-owned banking system – the incentives for efficiency and competitiveness were just not there. A core weakness lay in the high levels of debt used to sponsor their business expansion. Even with cheaply acquired assets, many couldn't avoid the pitfalls of debt. The words of Malaysia's Centre for Public Policy Studies are worth remembering: 'Growth through debt, rather than through equity and reinvestment of profits, is evidently not the basis on which to develop a modern economy.'[18]

Nevertheless, individuals got very rich and income disparities persisted despite positive NEP results in terms of poverty reduction and the emergence of a reasonably sized Malay middle class. In 1970 the Gini coefficient* stood at 0.47, dropping slightly in 1990 to 0.43, and again increasing in 2004 (0.45) – yet Malaysia still has one of the worst Gini coefficents in South East Asia. The economy also suffered the consequences of a large drain of highly qualified Malaysians, largely Chinese and Indians, who emigrated to neighbouring Singapore, the United States, Australia and elsewhere.[19]

Immersed in patronage and corruption

However, most criticism is levelled at the underbelly of political and business enmeshment – the cronyism, patronage, corruption and poor transparency making up what one source, who had participated in formulating the NEP, called 'UMNOputera' policy. It spawned a business class outside the realm of governance and accountability. Vested interests became entrenched, making it difficult to challenge policy and

---

* The Gini coefficient is a measure of statistical dispersion, used as a measure of income or wealth inequality. The measure is between 0 and 1, with one being highly unequal.

impossible to remove or moderate it. As the Malaysian historian Lee Kam Hing told me, vested interests prevent sunset clauses from working and so the intended temporariness of the policy becomes permanent. The Bumiputera are incentivised 'to play around with the figures', making it 'difficult to stop or to check the negative consequences' of such policies.[20] It has taken almost forty years – and a political crisis in UMNO – for the sun to start setting on racially defined policies. Not surprisingly, the starting point is in the area most criticised: Bumiputera equity ownership. But much is needed to change the character of Malay business that has become dependent on preferential access to government contracts and licences without transparent bidding. This has, Malaysians say, lulled Malays into believing their successes have been achieved on merit. Good governance, too, is said to be absent in many Malay-run businesses.

Reforms at last

Reforms in 2009 removed the 30% Bumiputera equity requirement for new listings. Instead, a Securities Commission regulation says that half of the 25% public-shareholding spread must be reserved for the Bumiputera. Effectively, therefore, corporate ownership by the Bumiputera has been reduced to a minimum of 12.5%. But even that level is not immutable, for it applies only to initial public offerings and not to subsequent rights issues or to earlier holdings.

The Malaysian government, however, remains committed to what it called a 'macro target' of 30%, meaning that the aggregate value of all corporate shareholding – listed and unlisted – should be 30%; and 30% of all listed equity should be owned or held by Bumiputera. When making the announcement, it offered no clarity on the measurement of this 30%. Other reforms lift restrictions on foreign ownership, but only for a narrow sub-set of industry. Services are a new focus for growth and there is government concern that ownership restrictions will inhibit the success of this strategy.*

Bumiputera policy, therefore, has outlived its usefulness. In recent

---

* Malaysia's prime minister, Najib Razak, just ninety days in office, provided the new broom. Interestingly, his father Abdul Razak, as prime minister, had spearheaded the Bumiputera 30% equity provision.

years, Malaysia has found it increasingly difficult to compete with the new 'Asian tigers' of China and Vietnam. The heart of its growth strategy, manufactured exports, has stagnated. In part, the reason lies in the success of affirmative action in creating a large Malay middle class, which raised wage rates well above those of new competitors.

Further reason may be found in an inherent weakness in the policy – the failure to create a productive Malay capitalist class. Joe Studwell, in his book *Asian godfathers*, explores this malaise as not just of Malaysia but South East Asia, in contrast to the North East countries like Japan, Taiwan and South Korea. The relationships that evolved between the political and economic power elites impacted directly on the character of economic development. North East Asia nurtured a homegrown manufacturing sector – what we might call hardcore business, where competition is sharp and returns are tight. The North East Asian countries also 'maintained relatively small public sectors and intervene in their economies in ways that do not require direct government control of resources'.[21] In South East Asia political patronage defined business and government relations, spawning a capitalist class spoilt by high returns from the easy business that governments sent their way. The manufacturing of goods for export was therefore left to foreign multinationals, which today are moving to different shores. What evolved were companies that 'don't have strategies. They do deals.'[22]

South Africa courts similar risks

South Africa is at risk of a similar malaise, as Chapter 2 showed. The emerging black business establishment has taken on many of the characteristics of the South East Asian 'godfathers'. Yet BEE has emerged amidst a strong domestic manufacturing sector that provides a basis for emulating the North East Asian example. Can we expect business leaders, born of nonproductive investment activity, to appreciate fully the value of a homegrown industrial sector and get involved in its development? It is quite possible that implicitly they see little room for themselves to be active in manufacturing and much more space for white participation. Interestingly, in Malaysia a case was made against following the North East growth path of domestic-led industrialisation for fear of this favouring Malaysian Chinese.[23]

Malaysia's NEP centred on one objective, to reduce inter-ethnic differences and create national unity. Against this measure it is difficult to determine the level of success. In almost every interview and conversation I had with Malaysians, reference was made to increased racial polarisation. As Ariff commented, 'Everything is seen in racial terms. Even political parties are racially based. The system is embedded. We have an identity crisis.'[24]

The apparent stability in Malaysia, many argue, is deceptive. There are serious concerns about the consequences of increased racial polarisation that combine with massive corruption, the absence of a free press and an independent judiciary; and the ruling party that remains is jittery about its hold on power. In addition, regained competitiveness and a new economic model must be found.

However, education and the emergence of the Malay middle class, along with the emergence of Malay entrepreneurs, may offer counters to the concerns about ongoing stability. Many among them have emerged without access to the privileges enjoyed by Mahathir Mohamad's business elite. It would seem that economic growth and subsequent NEP policy (post-1990) gave increasing space for Malay entrepreneurs to emerge and develop real commercial relationships, in contrast to the 'rent-a-Bumi' practices that characterised equity partnerships. 'Partners in these business enterprises appear to be equally competent, implying a decline in "Ali-Baba" alliances.'[25]

The question often asked is how much of this may be attributed to economic growth and how much to the Bumiputera policy. It is difficult to say. Malaysia certainly went against the trend of lower economic performance in ethnically heterogeneous countries when compared to homogeneous societies. Perhaps affirmative action provided the plaster necessary for Malaysia to counteract the debilitating fractures that prevail in multi-ethnic societies. Without the NEP, 'Malaysia's growth rate could conceivably have ended up looking less like Singapore's and more like Sri Lanka's.'[26] It is interesting, too, that the Malaysians avoided the curse of resource-rich countries – bloody conflicts over the spoils.

Yet evidence suggests South Africa today should be very cautious about drawing on Malaysia or even the affirmative action experience of the Afrikaners. Malaysians I spoke to often cautioned against using their country as a model to justify BEE. Instead, they believe it offers many tips on mistakes to avoid.

The journey of these affirmative action experiences is something like the race between the tortoise and the hare. The historical imperative is to sprint, making a laggard out of the private sector as transformation starts out. But the limitations of the state and the many unintended consequences created by its interventions eventually strain the policies of racial preference. The hare loses stamina. The trick is to discern when to change direction.

4

If you're black and you're BEE, clap your hands

O Lord, won't you buy me a Mercedes-Benz?
My friends all drive Porsches, I must make amends.
Worked hard all my lifetime, no help from my friends,
So Lord, won't you buy me a Mercedes-Benz?

In 1970, four days before she died, Janis Joplin recorded this song, her commentary against materialism. It resonates in present-day South Africa, reminding us of the WaBenzi – the black elite aptly named for their conspicuous consumption and easily identified by their Mercedes-Benzes and other luxury cars.

From the start, BEE has been marked by criticism about enriching an unproductive elite. More recently, however, a darker side has emerged with the increasing abuse of the state's resources. The ubiquitous ANC Youth League leader Julius Malema provided the latest and largest hook on which to hang the wrongs of corruption and political patronage. His exposed excesses, taken up with relish by the media, appear even more distasteful against news of violent protests by residents in townships and squatter settlements who had taken to the streets over the failure of municipalities to deliver basic services. A justification for their outrage may be linked to an admission by a local mayor: 'I'm a part-time businessman and full-time mayor.'[1] Or, as a young ANC member cynically told the columnist Jacob Dlamini, 'The National Democratic Revolution ended a long time ago. It's now the Tender Distribution Revolution.'[2]

Malema was exposed for advancing just this kind of revolution.

Notoriously abusing even senior party members, he flaunted a lifestyle an ANC salary could patently not support. A wily operator, not even the pull-no-punches Debora Patta could wedge him into a corner as she interrogated him on e.tv's *3rd Degree* progamme about his expensive tastes.[3] Malema played the race card: Why shouldn't he have Louis Vuitton belts? Can only white people have them? Failure to tighten those belts became his downfall as their source was eventually exposed by a leak – a bank account reportedly containing many millions of undeclared rands.[4] Allegedly benefiting from state contracts dispensed in his home territory,[5] Malema was characterised by Jacob Dlamini as 'a cunning thug who is the nexus of a patronage network based in Limpopo but which cuts across provincial boundaries.'[6]

Herein lies the positive side to the Malema story. Press freedom enables the exposure of political misdemeanours, and divisions within the ANC ensure that enough sources are willing to 'share' information for whatever reason. But many still express concern the ANC is moving towards moral bankruptcy. And there are too few leading figures within civil society and the ANC willing to take a public stand. Because of this, a statement by Bobby Godsell, chairman of Business Leadership South Africa, in support of his counterpart in the union movement, Cosatu's Zwelinzima Vavi, is an important intervention. Never shy, Vavi earmarked what has become popularly known as 'tenderpreneurs' as 'the new enemy of our movement, not the Congress of the People or Helen Zille's Democratic Alliance. It is crass materialism which is the most formidable enemy that we must confront and defeat.'[7]

Godsell joined in, portraying the tenderpreneurs as 'a form of economic terrorism, imposing a cost and conferring no benefit. It is a form of theft actually. We don't need that.'[8] He backed Vavi's quest for lifestyles audits, arguing they should apply equally to the corporate and the political elites, who are too often undeserving of the large sums of money they lay claim to. Memories were fresh. A messy conflict in the state-owned electricity provider Eskom between Godsell as chairman and the chief executive Jacob Maroga ended with Godsell resigning and Maroga making a nationally derided legal claim of R85 million for his own dismissal.

Despite the ANC identifying corruption as a priority concern, it tackles the task lethargically. The *Financial Mail* editor, Barney Mthombothi, pinpoints a credibility gap in the leadership, calling Jacob Zuma 'our ethically challenged president'. Commenting on Zuma's announcement that he wanted to initiate a national dialogue on a moral code, Mthombothi wondered whether the president 'said this with a straight face'.[9]

But the problems run deeper – and they are vast. It is not my intention here to highlight individual characters but to focus on what is germane to BEE. Of particular relevance are the ANC's own BEE companies which benefit from state-related tender business and its financial dependence on the rent-seeking character of BEE and associated political patronage.

The nature of the beast

It is important to understand the concepts we are dealing with here. In much of the voluminous media reportage, little distinction is made between legal and illegal activity. The perception is one of a generally parasitic system in which enrichment, rent-seeking and corruption are merged.

A wide spectrum of the population see something undeserving in a black elite becoming excessively enriched without being productive. This is what rent-seeking is about – merely redistributive activity that absorbs resources and results in rent, a profit exacted and unrelated to any productive activity. It is not necessarily illegal but, against the backdrop of widespread poverty and joblessness, it appears ethically indefensible.

Political patronage is another facet of BEE-related business activity that deserves attention. Such patronage may be envisaged as a patron–client relationship. The Wits academic Jonathan Hyslop points out that 'a patron may often be able to help a client in ways – personal donations or recommendations for instance – that do not involve violating rules or procedures.'[10] Again, therefore, it is not illegal in itself. However, the intertwining nature of relations developed between business and the ANC political establishment may at the very least be defined as 'disguised corruption'[11] or 'legal corruption', which, according to the World Bank, occurs 'where a politician has close connections to the private sector and both exploit such connections for mutual benefit.'[12] The divide between legality and illegality tends to be crossed when with 'fierce conflicts over scarce resources it is unlikely that a patron who is unwilling or unable to break the law will retain his or her client base.'[13]

Corruption differs from rent-seeking and patronage in that it is generally understood to involve illegal or unprocedural activity. Hyslop notes that it is 'notoriously hard to define' and, as the prosecuting authorities find, even harder to prove. Transparency International simply describes it as 'the abuse of entrusted power for private gain'.[14] But it also distinguishes 'political corruption' as 'the manipulation of policies, institutions and rules of procedure in the allocation of resources and financing by political decision-makers, who abuse their position to sustain their power, status and wealth.'[15] It is this latter form of corruption that has become associated with many within the ANC.

Another troubling area is conflict of interest, where individuals or entities are 'confronted with choosing between the duties and demands of their position and their own private interests.'[16] The ANC have resisted seriously addressing such conflicts. They have, on numerous occasions, defended the right of their office-bearers to be involved in business. To manage the potential negative consequences, the ANC introduced requirements on members of parliament and government leaders to disclose their business interests and economic assets. This, it would seem, has had marginal impact, if any.

How bad is it?

Transparency International's *Corruption perceptions index* scores South Africa in the medium corruption range. However, its ranking in relation to other countries has deteriorated significantly in the past decade, from 34th position in 2000 to 55th in 2009 out of 180 countries.[17] (This survey is not an objective measure of corruption and is based on the perception of individuals in business across the world.)

Some in the ANC and government may be harsher judges. The deputy president, Kgalema Motlanthe, has expressed his dismay at the prevalence of corruption in the public service: 'The rot is across the board ... Almost every project is conceived because it offers opportunities for certain people to make money. A great deal of the ANC's problems are occasioned by this. There are people who want to take it [the ANC] over so they can arrange for the appointment of those who will allow them possibilities for future accumulation.'[18] The auditor-general, Terence Nombembe, indicated in his 2008 report that state corruption was far worse than originally feared, and that even when it is identified the government does not have systems in place to deal quickly and decisively with offenders.[19] His office found that significant numbers of senior public officials had awarded contracts for hundreds of millions of rands to themselves, their family or associates.

A government report also implicitly offers good cause for the regular eruption of community protests against local governments. With surprising frankness the report says: 'A culture of patronage and nepotism is now so widespread in many municipalities that the formal municipality accountability system is ineffective and inaccessible to most citizens.'[20] Sue Brown, the former editor of the *Transformation audit*, notes that competition for councillor status and access to resources is so acute that factions within the ruling party 'expect automatically to replace incumbents connected to other factions, whether capable or not'. With that, she argues, the country is 'threatened by the spoils system'.[21]

There is a discernible difference between the abuses we are seeing today and those in the Nineties. Private-sector BEE deals then were the principal arena of enrichment activity. Many companies sought out politically well-placed BEE partners to reposition them with the new government and improve access to state business. Usually, this constituted a broad expectation that did not necessarily translate into an understanding that specific state contracts or licences would in fact be successfully delivered.

Today, however, most BEE activity has shifted to the public sector, for several reasons. Firstly, the biggest and the best BEE deals in the private sector have almost all been done, so the search for rich pickings has extended to the public sector. Secondly, the private sector's BEE transactions could not accommodate everyone. Many failed to gain access to these deals and then applied whatever influence they had to leverage off state resources – the lower down you go in government tiers, the more abuse is uncovered. Thirdly, it took the ANC some years to exercise power across all spheres of government. In the early years, its focus and energy went on the gargantuan task of state restructuring.

Finally, anyone involved in corruption needs time to get good at it – as with everything, experience counts, and after fifteen years many with leverage over state resources are now highly skilled at manipulating the system.

As a consequence, it matters enormously to companies to identify precisely who will determine the outcome of tender decisions and how to construct a BEE partnership that will encompass the 'right' people; those who will deliver specific state business. It is simply no longer good enough to take on a politically well-positioned BEE partner. Time and again I hear business people, black and white, declare their lack of interest in bidding for state contracts and licences. In their view, too many tender outcomes are predetermined, making the tender itself merely a means to legitimise the suspected distribution of state resources – what Brown calls 'the ritual of open competition'.[22] As an Institute for Security Studies (ISS) report notes, 'The tender process used to be a tool to foster transparency and prevent corruption in procurement ... However, the frequency with which public officials are embroiled in tender controversies unfortunately marks the end of the road for the tender as a reliable antidote to corruption.'[23]

Established business also carries responsibility for what has evolved. As Steven Friedman, director of the Centre for the Study of Democracy, comments: 'Many white-owned companies have chosen black parties not on the strength of their acumen or ability, but on connection with government. For much of established business, BEE has not been about building a non-racial business class, but about seeking the favour of the post-1994 government. It is hardly surprising, then, that some politicians might assume that leadership of the ruling party also means a right to benefit from BEE – and to freeze the losers out.'[24]

Consequences of history
Should we be surprised? Perhaps not. Every victor in war ultimately has one unambiguous focus – the redistribution of the spoils. It would be strange indeed if the new black elite left the economy in the hands of whites, satisfied with a few corporate morsels thrown its way. That said, a democracy requires a different approach to wealth redistribution – an equitable process matters. Allowing elites to help themselves to the

spoils, regardless of others, doesn't fit with hard-won ANC principles or the South African Constitution.

In part, the ANC has become entrapped by a history that has made the shift from the old to a new system of patronage and corruption quite seamless. And, as time has passed, corrupt behaviours have found a self-sustaining energy that the government will continue to find extremely difficult to contain.

Hyslop sees the historical legacies of both the apartheid regime and the ANC as being important for understanding current developments. On National Party rule, he sketches three distinct periods: the high tide from 1948 to 1972; the efflorescence of corruption until 1984; and then the looting of the state until 1994. In the first period, rent-seeking was pursued 'within the bounds of legality'. There was 'relatively little evidence of overt corruption in the top ranks of bureaucracy', an echelon that 'has been informed by a genuine, if misplaced, sense of mission'.[25]

In the second period, large numbers of Afrikaners enjoyed 'unprecedented prosperity' as new middle and capitalist classes emerged. The ideological grip of the Afrikaner weakened and 'a scramble for personal enrichment began'. This was also the time of the emergence of bantustan governments, with significant administrative malfunction and corruption. It is relevant that those provinces in which we find the worst records of corruption and administrative failure – Mpumalanga, Limpopo and the Eastern Cape – incorporated the bulk of these bantustan administrations after 1994. As Hyslop notes, 'The incompetence and corruption of the old statelets was simply carried over into the new era, with the difference that the civil servants now often enjoyed the patronage and protection of ANC leaders.'[26] I am reminded here how successful many were at currying favour; in particular, Bonile Jack, a former head of a Ciskei bantustan department, who engineered the removal of the Land Bank's chief executive, Helena Dolny, widow of ANC leader Joe Slovo.[27]

In the third period, once the grasp of the security establishment had weakened and political reforms made it clear that white rule was coming to an end, 'there was a rush to grab as much in the way of spoils as possible before the curtain came down'.[28]

Less attention has been paid to corrupting influences within the

ANC during the liberation struggle. Hyslop identifies the large sums of money from foreign donors for anti-apartheid activities as an occasion for poor accountability. Security difficulties were bypassed by entrusting well-regarded resistance figures with 'substantial quantities of cash to dish out on an ad hoc basis; proper records were not kept.' Hyslop also notes, 'A cavalier ethos in the handling of money and a sense of being above mundane processes of accounting were fostered amongst some who rose to positions of power in the transition.'[29]

I had personal experience of how life in exile might edge open the doors of corruption. Monies intended for underground activities could easily be diverted when criminal and underground networks intertwined as weapons, money and people were sneaked across borders in or out of South Africa. I was therefore not surprised when some names emerged later in press reports on corruption or suspicion of state tender manipulation. The nature of exile and underground work also created 'an overriding ethos of loyalty' that acquired a value transcending all else. This, argues Hyslop, was carried into the post-apartheid government. 'Such loyalties can easily be transmuted into patronage networks.'[30]

ANC as a source of political corruption

A noticeable portion of the ANC's active and leading members certainly appear to understand the benefits of Pieter-Dirk Uys's ANC (A Nice Cheque). But the problem reaches beyond the dishonesty of individuals. There is evidence of the ANC as an organisation extracting financial benefit from its leverage over state resources. A case where firm evidence emerged was the 'Oilgate' scandal, in which the BEE company Imvume Management – and in particular its principal shareholder, Sandi Majali – diverted R11 million of public money from PetroSA to the ANC, apparently to help it fund its 2004 election campaign. Uncovering the scandal, the *Mail & Guardian* found that the state-owned oil company had 'irregularly paid R15 million' to Imvume 'as an advance for the procurement of oil condensate. Then, when Imvume diverted the funds to the ANC instead of paying its own foreign suppliers, PetroSA had to cover the shortfall by paying the same amount again.'[31] The ANC adopted a stolid silence; it would appear the intention was to pay back the money before anyone spotted its disappearance – but it never did.

Such an incident could have happened regardless of BEE. What BEE policy has provided is the mantle under which state resources and licences may be legitimately redistributed. Both this legitimacy and the large scale of redistribution have provided a cover for the widespread abuse of the system. The ANC itself is immersed in this in two respects. Firstly there are the traditional mechanisms of political patronage, where party loyalists – after 'deployment' in business – are expected to provide financial sustenance to the ANC in return for access to state resources. In the past, ANC treasurers have said as much. This was well illustrated in the R6 billion Telkom sale of shares and is ongoing in the allocation of mining-related rights, which I address below. Secondly, abuse happens when the ANC's own BEE investment companies are assured of access to valuable state tenders and licences. Here, the merging of the ANC's interests with the use of state resources is direct – although the ANC has tried to hide this linkage.

The centrality of the state to BEE, with the ANC intertwined, 'has led to the common charge of cronyism, influence-peddling and the creation of a black aristocracy against a backdrop of increasing poverty.'[32] Further, 'the values of solidarity and mutual protection of the struggle years can become distorted in the context of access to public resources.'[33] Let's look at specific examples.

Telkom as a site of patronage
After the 'Oilgate' scandal, another exposé in 2004 centred on the state-controlled telecommunications company Telkom as a result of the 15.1% sale of equity by its US and Malaysian shareholders in the Thintana consortium. This transaction gives a vivid view of the intricacies of the patronage network in action. What really piqued the media's interest was the curious involvement of Smuts Ngonyama – then head of Thabo Mbeki's office in the ANC – as a facilitator of this transaction. He had never participated in anything like this before, so the obvious question was why now and why in Telkom? Although Telkom is a publicly listed company, the state is the controlling shareholder and had pre-emptive rights over Thintana's 15.1% share offering. This means that the government needed to waive its rights to acquire these shares and make way for another buyer, whom it had the right to approve.

The smooth-talking Andile Ngcaba, having just ended his term as director-general of the department responsible for Telkom, got in first. He secured endorsement from his former minister of Communications* for his consortium, Lion, to acquire the shareholding; one newspaper report suggests that his exploratory work had started even before leaving government service.[34] This was unbeknown to Ngonyama, who had paired up with another consortium, Leopard, led by Gloria Serobe of Wiphold, also closely associated with Mbeki. Ngonyama got the ANC treasurer-general, Mendi Msimang, to write a letter to Thintana, stating that the ANC and Mbeki supported Leopard. Thintana, however, pointed out that Ngcaba already had government support. Mbeki then stepped in by proposing that both consortiums join forces. The two consortiums then created an umbrella consortium, Elephant.

After that, the Public Investment Corporation (PIC), which administers state pension funds, became a party to the deal by agreeing to warehouse the shares while Elephant tried to raise the necessary finance after its first attempt failed. By then, however, the public outcry had become so great that the PIC decided to keep some of the shareholding to sell later to broad-based groupings – this, it was hoped, would placate critics like Cosatu, which had condemned the transaction as 'the very worst form' of empowerment 'which benefits only a tiny elite'.[35]

But the media kept digging. Ngcaba, Serobe and Ngonyama consistently refused to disclose all the members and beneficiaries of their consortiums. Ngonyama was particularly evasive about what he was due from the deal – when pushed, he once responded: 'I did not struggle to be poor.'[36] In 2009 the *Sunday Times* named two company shareholders in Leopard which it claimed were holding the ANC's stake.[37]

ANC's own BEE companies
The ANC has also sought to benefit from BEE opportunities through its own companies. The Youth League's Lembede is a shameful example of mismanagement, absent governance and dubious associations, not least with Brett Kebble, the slain mining magnate. Kebble courted political favour with aplomb and large sums of money. Forensic investigations

---

* Ivy Matsepe-Casaburri was the minister of Communications for ten years until her death in 2009.

93

into Kebble's estate uncovered records of well over R25 million that he paid to the ANC and its structures,[38] and he dispensed far greater largesse again through the many BEE deals he sponsored.

Of more concern is the ANC's own company, Chancellor House Holdings, registered in 2003. The Institute for Security Studies and the *Mail & Guardian* jointly conducted an extensive investigation into party funding through corporate fronts, and Chancellor House (the ANC's investment company) in particular.[39] Later on, the former ANC businessman and close ally of Mbeki, Saki Macozoma, acknowledged Chancellor House as a 'badly kept secret'.[40]

The sole shareholder in Chancellor House is a trust[41] that is vague in its purpose, allowing for 'involvement in all economic and political sectors of South African persons and entities which have been historically disadvantaged'.[42] In short, trustees may donate funds to whomever they like. Chancellor House has acquired interests in just those sectors where state sanction or leverage is relevant – mining and energy are important. The ISS report gives a blow-by-blow account of how Chancellor House acquired an interest in valuable manganese reserves in the Northern Cape. It is the first public account I have found which reveals the complicity of the Department of Mineral Resources in the promotion of politically aligned figures to gain access to the country's mineral reserves and in the untoward allocation of licences. In addition, Chancellor House has a 25% interest in Hitachi Power Africa – a subsidiary of Hitachi Power Europe – which has secured two Eskom contracts, valued at almost R40 billion, to supply steam generators to two new coal-fired power stations. The second contract did not go out to tender.[43]

Even the reputable Standard Bank group found, unbeknown to itself, that the ANC had become a beneficiary of its BEE transactions through a trust in one of the BEE consortiums. Exposed in the *Sunday Times* with a banner headline of an 'ANC payoff scandal', the BEE consortium in Stanlib – in which Macozoma's company Safika is the lead party – paid R9 million to the Zandile Trust, said to be linked to Chancellor House.[44]

The exposure of Chancellor House reminded me of a transaction in which I had advised. Two leading ANC figures – one in the cabinet – approached one of the company's directors with a proposition: Make us your BEE shareholders – no one will know. We will use trusts as conduits to disguise the true beneficiaries. There was an implied sweetener – a large state contract which my client intended to bid for and which the two politicians were in a position to influence. Tell them to go away, I advised, which my client duly did, but not without concern that they might not secure the tender (which they didn't).

How could these two individuals risk their political careers making a potentially corrupt proposition, just after Zuma had been removed from office on allegations of corrupt relationships? One interpretation – which Zuma promoted – was that the real reason for his demise lay in political agendas and not corruption. Then the news of Chancellor House as an ANC company emerged and I wondered whether the approach to my client was a clandestine attempt to get the ANC in on the deal.

Who sanctioned Chancellor House or the other initiatives? This is a question the ISS report does not answer. Even the ANC's secretary-general, Motlanthe, didn't know of Chancellor House's existence until phoned by the *Mail & Guardian*. The treasurer-general at the time, Mendi Msimang, is identified as the front man. As one of the president's men, could he have done this without Mbeki's sanction?

Redistribution of mining rights

Since 1994 no other sector has gone through such significant restructuring as mining. In 2002, new mining legislation[45] removed private ownership of mining rights. Government wanted to stop what it perceived as 'hoarding' of rights by the large mining houses and to promote a more competitive mining environment, particularly the provision of opportunity for black South Africans and junior mining companies, known for their entrepreneurial pursuit of new opportunities. The state assumed what it called 'custodianship' of the country's mineral resources. Companies with what were popularly referred to as old order rights had to apply for their conversion to new order rights. To convert the old order rights to new rights, the Mineral and Petroleum Resources Development Act (MPRDA) introduced new requirements on empowerment and social and labour contributions, among other things. However, the reallocation of mining rights probably constitutes the most significant and dubious redistribution of the spoils in post-apartheid South Africa.*

With the conversion of existing rights in mind, the MPRDA led to the Mining Charter,[46] which set two ownership milestones: 15% ownership to historically disadvantaged South Africans by 2009, necessary for companies to convert their old order rights;† and 26% BEE ownership by 2014, necessary to retain those converted rights. The charter made provision for ownership to be offset against beneficiation, the processing of minerals. To date, however, the DMR has never exempted a company from its full BEE ownership obligations as a result of it beneficiating a mineral. No one quibbled with the empowerment objectives, which sought to 'promote equitable access' to all South Africans; to 'substantially and meaningfully expand opportunities' for blacks, and women in particular; and to ensure that mining companies contributed to the socio–economic development of communities in which they operated.

In the granting of new rights, two categories are relevant: mining rights, applicable where mining is taking place; and prospecting rights, for specified areas where there is believed to be a presence of mineral reserves but where economic viability has yet to be determined. In the latter case there has been widespread redistribution to BEE companies, mostly shelf companies (devoid of any business operations). These companies have no purpose other than to hold the rights, and more often than not they are owned by a handful of individuals who have no capacity of any kind to prospect for minerals. As a result, once rights are acquired, the holders then start the process of trading their rights with established mining companies. If successful, transfer of the rights takes place (in terms of Section 11 of the MPRDA) either directly to other mining companies (as long as they have the requisite BEE ownership) or yet again into a new company where the BEE entity and the mining company enter some form of joint venture, with the latter agreeing to

---

* New mining legislation conformed to the constitutional provision for historically disadvantaged South Africans, meaning that white women and white disabled qualified. In practice, though, black ownership has prevailed.

† Each mining company must achieve 26% historically disadvantaged South Africans' (HDSA) ownership of its mining industry assets within ten years, with the mining houses facilitating HDSA participation to the value of R100 billion within the first five years (the computation implicit in the R100 billion is 15% HDSA ownership within five years – a percentage not stated in the Mining Charter but referred to in statements by the minister and the Chamber of Mines).

do the exploration. Mining rights may also be transferred between BEE entities and mining companies, but this is less common and tends to be between established mining houses and black-controlled companies involved in mining operations. Many complexities emerge in this process, but the intention here is simply to provide a broad overview of how rights are being traded.

A couple of problems have emerged in the implementation of the new legislation. One is the absence of transparency; and the other is abuses by DMR officials (some legal, some not) that have been allowed to go unchecked for years. Mining companies have preferred to acquiesce in demands of officials, afraid that if they don't, they will be blacklisted and hence denied access to new reserves.

The mining specialist Manus Booysen, of the law firm Webber Wentzel Bowen,[47] argues that a key problem lies in poor information disclosure on rights applications and the rights holders. The amended Mining Title Registration Act did away with the legal obligation for government to provide a public record of mining rights – perhaps because technically the holders of the rights do not own the title. Interested parties now have to bring applications on the basis of the Promotion of Access to Information Act to get information on mining rights, with long delays (usually beyond legally permissible timeframes). As a result, there is no comprehensive information publicly available, like a Google map of the country's registered mining and prospecting rights and their holders. Most extraordinary is the DMR's system of publicising applications made for rights. It physically pins the notices on a public board at its regional offices, where anybody could remove them. This has enormous significance since applications are supposed to be processed on a first-come, first-served basis. If a notice goes 'missing', where is the proof of who applied first? There are even reports of companies seemingly removed from first place in the queue.

This lack of transparency has resulted in a veil of secrecy over the allocation of licences. How can the process of granting prospecting and mining rights be fair if information is not publicly available? What seems to be taking place is a selective provision of information by DMR officials to BEE groups, with widespread suspicion that politically well-placed individuals are being favoured. Such individuals have an advantage in getting ahead of the queue, but even more worrying are reports of DMR officials allegedly waiving the first-come-first-served provision in the allocation process – only possible because of the shortcomings in disclosing information.

Both black and established mining companies are disadvantaged. One of my clients lost a number of rights to BEE entities, most of them shelf companies, after it had applied first and the DMR was aware it was transacting an agreement with another BEE group to develop a new black-controlled mining company as a joint venture. Why did DMR not recognise this BEE group instead of allocating the rights to groups with apparently no intention to develop mining operations? The listed BEE group HCI has also bumped up against a similar obstacle in its coal-mining subsidiary, HCI Khusela Coal. It questions 'the inexplicable granting' of a key portion of their prospecting right to the newly established state-owned African Exploration Mining and Finance Corporation, which resulted in HCI Khusela Coal having to redesign mine infrastructure and amend environmental approvals.[48]

The ISS's Chancellor House report suggests that DMR had acted unprocedurally in the allocation of some licences. The Russian mining multinational Renova had agreed to partner with Chancellor House, along with two others, Dirlton and Kalahari. But amidst a disagreement with Dirlton, and on the day that Renova terminated that relationship, the DMR approved the allocation of the manganese prospecting licence to Pitsa ya Setshaba Holdings, a company less than a month old, when the other three had lodged their applications months earlier. Ultimately Chancellor House and Pitsa, also involving individuals highly placed politically, became the joint holders of the prospecting licence, together with Renova, creating UMK (United Manganese of Kalahari). According to the ISS, 'UMK got eight farm portions, more than anyone else did, even though on five of those portions neither Chancellor nor Pitsa had put in the first applications.'[49]

The system of licence allocations that has evolved is designed to encourage rent-seeking behaviour among BEE companies. There are two reasons for this. First, there would appear to be widespread redistribution of rights to individuals who have no demonstrable interest in developing productive mining companies. Second, the rights that they receive are often not commercially viable without being part of a larger reserve base. Let's take the experience of another client who was considering a major new mining operation that had the backing of the government as strategically important for the country. The mining company had a large portion of mineral reserves for which it had reapplied. The DMR approved only some of its applications, giving the other rights to a number of unknown BEE groups that applied to patches of reserves located amidst the planned mining operations. As such, these reserves had no value for the BEE parties except to trade with my client, who did need them – rent-seeking in its purest form.

Besides this process adding an extra cost to mining with no productive outcome, such redistribution also introduces fractious negotiations with the potential for racial antagonism. BEE parties find themselves trying to trade something of uncertain value, but which may be known to the mining companies. Invariably, the BEE groups will be influenced by their expectations rather than any objective assessments based on solid information. They are thus always at risk of overplaying their hand. Yet another experience: a mining company had reached agreement with two individuals who held an exploration right for a consideration of R5 million. After signing, the two had second thoughts and came back with a demand for R50 million. My client didn't have an absolute need for this particular reserve, but how could these two individuals know this or believe my client?

Another big problem area is the abuse by DMR officials of their powers; something that has become quite pervasive in the absence of any pushback from mining companies. Mining houses argue that the DMR's power of sanction is too high – they worry about being denied access to new rights needed to expand their businesses. But I would argue that acquiescence has worsened the problem.

Distrust between the DMR and the established mining houses resulted in protracted and difficult discussions on what DMR required of them before it would grant licence conversions. Personalities mattered here. Particularly problematic was the DMR official responsible for overseeing licences, Jacinto Rocha, originally from Angola. He fulfilled everyone's image of the apparatchik, engaging aggressively with the mining companies and patronisingly with BEE companies. He knew, it seemed, what was best for everyone – and he left no one who dealt with him in any doubt that they'd better listen to him. As one source told me, he was intolerant of any legal challenge of his interpretation of the MPRDA, reportedly telling someone that the law needed to be interpreted as he'd intended in the drafting of it. In early 2010, however, he suddenly resigned for unconvincing reasons, saying he was 'tired' and his thirteen years at DMR had been 'stressful'.[50]

I never had a client who did not have difficulties with DMR and Rocha in particular; their experiences matched others I have since learnt about. I am sure that DMR has many justified complaints about mining company behaviour. But, in my area of work – the sale of shares to BEE entities – I have met a number of reasons for concern about official actions.

Abuses of power may not necessarily be illegal and may be motivated by good intentions, even if misguided. Nevertheless, DMR officials venture into territory that is not appropriate for a government department to enter. Officials rule over minutiae in transactional agreements and social and labour plans. They are said to regularly reject the proposals submitted by mining companies, which get worn down by the repeated revisions required of them. Section 11 transfers have got caught up in this, says Manus Booysen, with delays of up to eighteen months – and 'when we tell foreign investors about these delays, they often decide to pack their bags and invest elsewhere.'[51] In another case, a company was told that a programme for early childhood development had to be removed from its social plan – the DMR official processing their application did not see this as a relevant or worthwhile social intervention. Did government really intend this level of micro-management in company affairs? Hard to imagine it did, but such interventions persist. When government officials believe they are entitled to interfere in operational decisions of such a nature, the door inevitably opens to abuses of power.

Once that happens, it is only a small step to unprocedural or illegal abuses. Where large sums of money are involved and the opportunity for political patronage is so high, it is difficult to imagine misconduct stopping at the level of petty interference – experience and the little evidence that has emerged suggest it hasn't. For example, DMR officials are known to intervene in the selection of BEE partners, which has enabled them to dispense state patronage to the emerging black elite and in particular those with political standing. I recall a client's unpleasant interaction with Rocha at a workshop at which he was considering conversion of mining rights. My client was therefore expected to present the details of its BEE transaction. Prior to this, we had been negotiating with three BEE parties to acquire shareholding. Two originated from the local community and one was a leading BEE company, headed by someone politically well placed. Negotiations with the company had broken down. However, we went to the DMR meeting with the two other parties, who we had agreed would take up the shareholding of the third. But Rocha refused to consider the transaction – he had been lobbied by the excluded party and demanded they be brought back into the deal. Until that happened, he said, my client's application for licence conversion would not be heard.

In another instance, I had been asked by a mining house to structure a transaction that would be to the benefit of communities within their mining areas. Previously the company had agreed on the sale of shares to two other BEE groupings led by personalities aligned to the former president, Thabo Mbeki. DMR officials wanted a portion of the shareholding earmarked for communities to go to individuals aligned with the new ANC leadership – they gave them some names to choose from. The company acceded and communities lost the benefit of shares valued at some R1 billion.

The Chancellor House report quotes the director-general of DMR, Sandile Nogxina, as seeing 'nothing untoward nor conflicting' about introducing mining companies to BEE parties. In fact, he believes that the MPRDA makes provision for the minister to 'facilitate assistance to any historically disadvantaged person'.[52] But national legislation is never drafted with the intention of supporting or promoting specific individuals. There are companies that ask DMR to recommend BEE parties; but this is not always the case. Proof of undue interference is difficult to attain, as companies report that discussions are always verbal and officials usually propose more than one BEE group or individual to choose from – thus protecting themselves from accusations of advancing the interests of a specific company or person. Preferences, however, may be implied.

All in all, the reallocation of rights to BEE parties has undoubtedly led to extensive rent-seeking activity and also forms of political corruption and patronage that need investigation. A good start to resolving the problems would be improved systems of information disclosure and transparency, with mining companies prepared to take a stand, insist the rule of law is upheld, and ensure the procedurally sound management of highly valuable national assets – the mining houses are not as powerless in the face of officialdom as they may believe, but commitment is required.

The consequences

It does not follow that corruption and rent-seeking will block economic growth. East Asia has many examples of corrupt political systems and spectacular development. I don't want to enter into a debate as to what may differentiate South Africa from Asia. There are enough grounds for concern that an extensive network of political patronage and rent-seeking is taking root and is profoundly unproductive. Because of this, I wish to draw attention to two conclusions reached through academic research, finding that rent-seeking is likely to inhibit growth. First, such activities 'exhibit very natural increasing returns' – they become self-perpetuating. Second, rent-seeking, particularly among government officials, 'is likely to hurt innovative activities more than everyday production. Since innovation drives economic growth, public rent-seeking hampers growth more severely than production'.[53] Innovation is both a concern and a focus of policy makers in government.

What struck me in my research is how much the ANC has come to rely on the worst consequences of BEE policy to support its financial needs. The renting-seeking character of BEE allows a company like Chancellor House to scan for opportunities that require nothing of themselves but their political standing. When Chancellor House's involvement in state contracts became publicly known, there was a whisper from within the ANC that the party would review the company's participation in state-related business. As yet, nothing has come of that, and I suspect it might not: Chancellor House would be an empty shell without the offering of access to public resources, and the ANC would be deprived of much-needed investment income.

The ANC also has a high expectation and need for significant party donations from its black business constituency, in particular those 'comrades' it claims to have 'deployed' in business. Not everyone is willing to give, as Msimang once said in this rebuke: 'We ... have to express our dismay at the sleight of hand that has greeted our appeals from comrades deployed, we want to stress the word *deployed*, in the civil service and private business.'[54] If the ANC stops dispensing political patronage, it would be difficult indeed to find generous contributors. BEE, as we have seen, provides an extensive and legitimate platform for patronage activities.

The risks are high. The ISS report also argues that the likes of Chancellor House 'raise the spectre of government actions being shaped by party interests rather than the public interest.' Democracy is placed in jeopardy: 'If state power is abused to direct resources to support political parties, the basis of fair political contestation is undermined. Access to the democratic decision-making process is put up for sale, which not only undermines the management of political parties but also the overall governance project at national level.'[55]

There are no easy solutions. But at the very least, party funding needs to become a matter of national debate. As Friedman emphasises, 'We have no laws which compel disclosure of donations to parties, let alone any which regulate them. The international evidence shows that no society can sustain an effective democracy unless it regulates control of the political system by the moneyed.' As long as funding remains unresolved, the ANC will remain financially dependent on an ill-conceived BEE policy and its ability to extract financial benefits from state resources – and it will lack the necessary political will to act forcefully against patronage and corruption, and to review the current BEE policy construct.

5

Sailing amidst a whirlwind

> Yet a man who uses an imaginary map, thinking that it is a true one, is likely to be worse off than someone with no map at all; for he will fail to inquire whenever he can, to observe every detail on his way, and to search continuously with all his senses and all his intelligence for indications of where he should go.
>
> – EF Schumacher

If we pause to review our lives, a collage – as opposed to a draughtsman's drawing – is likely to appear. Plans, probably ill conceived, will be laid over random events, which may or may not be of importance; bad decisions might be partially obscured by a huge dose of luck. We all know life rarely runs according to plan yet self-help books advising how best to organise our lives regularly top the best-seller lists. Clearly many of us believe if we simply adhere to rules and measurements we might engineer control over our lives.

History suggests nation states like to harbour similar hopes. In our lifetime we have lived through monumental exercises in social engineering, matched in scale only by their failure. The collapse of communism in the Soviet Union is an obvious example while less obvious is the whittling away of the socialist order in China and Vietnam.

In South Africa, despite lessons that should have been gleaned from the failure of a Nationalist government hellbent on control, the inclination is increasingly towards more, not less, state intervention. The BEE Codes are a gargantuan attempt to engineer transformation within the business environment. But the ANC is envisaging more than that as it articulates its concept of the 'developmental state', underpinned by state corporations that will ultimately serve its goals.

As South Africa tries to put the global crisis behind it, BEE has emerged from the difficulties with even more questions about its suitability as a means of economic transformation. The climate therefore is favourable for a policy rethink, but the ANC leadership may not take the opportunity. The reason is not because there is nobody in the Zuma government who would support different policy choices; but because the many factions that have emerged within the ANC may make it impossible to reach a consensus about charting a new or revised course. Also, as this book went to press, the ANC was being buffeted from all sides – politically, in large part because of the disruptive posturing of its youth leader Julius Malema, socially as black communities protested poor municipal services, and economically. Under such pressures the ANC could easily revert to a defensive posture, which typically inhibits new and innovative thinking. The inclination may well be to push harder for more of the same rather than to open up to new ideas.

Two scenarios look most probable. One is to resort to higher targets and even more measurement of BEE. The other is keeping the status quo with reliance on political muscle, behind the scenes, to redistribute the economic spoils further to the black elite. Either way, South Africa seems likely to follow the path of formula-based social engineering, currently captured in the BEE Codes but with a potentially growing layer of political patronage determining the distribution of resources.

Simplifying society
Perhaps we should not be surprised. This is the 'comfort zone' of states, James C Scott, in his book *Seeing like a state*, so eloquently discusses. Scott concludes that in general a central government wants society to be legible and simplified, to be achieved by using measurements where possible. Only then does it feel able to exercise power and control.

There are good and bad reasons for a state to simplify the country it is trying to run:

State simplifications such as maps, censuses, cadastral lists, and standard units of measurement represent techniques for grasping a large and complex reality … If we imagine a state that has no reliable means of enumerating and locating its population, gauging its wealth, and mapping its land, resources, and settlements, we are imagining a state whose interventions in that society are necessarily crude. A society that is relatively opaque to the state is thereby insulated from some forms of finely tuned state interventions, both welcomed (universal vaccinations) and resented (personal income taxes).[1]

In this context, BEE Codes make sense. The South African government has fixed its approach with the right motivations: a clear set of rules by which everyone is measured. This seems fair. But, as Scott argues, the problem starts when blanket measurement interferes with productive social relations and reconfigures society to its detriment. We can see this happening with BEE Codes.

Engineering empowerment

So far, I have delved into the detail of the Codes, finding fault with specific measures and teasing out a number of the many unintended or unwanted consequences. I now wish to look at the BEE landscape with a wide-angle lens; to put in broad focus the principle of (well-intentioned) state interventions to engineer societal changes. Few would question the principle of affirmative action or black empowerment when circumstances cry out for economic justice. Yet Malaysians I spoke to with experience in this area invariably said: 'Good in principle, poor in implementation.' This is equally true in South Africa.

The problem, as Scott highlights, lies not in trying to effect social change but in trying to do so using sweeping measures. He argues that one of the great paradoxes of social engineering is that it is at odds with experience: 'Trying to jell a social world, the most striking characteristics of which appears to be flux, seems rather like trying to manage a whirlwind.'[2]

Societies are simply not easily malleable. The idea of the 'rational agent' that underpinned so much of economic theory for decades has been all but discarded. We now talk of 'bounded rationality'.* Economic psychology has emerged as a new domain of theory developed to understand how people respond to the workings of the world. The more we globalise (and hence endeavour to homogenise societies across boundaries) the more aware we become of intangible factors that impinge upon economic dynamics – like human behaviour, cultural legacies and local knowledge.

Not only governing states have a monopoly on 'utilitarian simplifications'. Scott notes, 'Large-scale capitalism is just as much an agency of homogenization, uniformity, grids, and heroic simplifications as the state is, with the difference being that, for capitalists, simplification must pay.' But he adds, 'What the state does at least aspire to, though, is a monopoly on the legitimate use of force.'[3]

It is not surprising that South Africa's business establishment had very little to say against the codification of economic transformation; this fell within its comfort zone as well. It is equally unsurprising, therefore, that the only public intervention from the business side – that of the Brenthurst Initiative[4] under the auspices of the Oppenheimers (South Africa's wealthiest dynasty) – endorsed the Codes but sought a tax rebate should a company fulfil its BEE obligations.

No room for nuance and local practices

Scott's unique contribution is in the area of local knowledge. He refers constantly to *metis*, a Greek term typically translated into English as 'cunning' or 'cunning intelligence'. 'Broadly understood, *metis* represents a wide array of practical skills and acquired intelligence in responding to a constantly changing natural and human environment.'[5] He argues that social engineers are intolerant of *metis*, as it flies in the face of standardisations and simplifications inherent in programmes under state control. When I was looking at the transformation of the Cape fishing industry this term acquired particular relevance.

---

* Herbert Simon, the economist, political scientist and psychologist, is thought to have coined this phrase, but it is the Nobel Laureate Daniel Kahneman who developed the concept into a model to overcome the limitations of the rational agent on which traditional economic models are premised.

Kalk Bay loses to BEE

I focused some of my research in 2009 on Kalk Bay, a small fishing harbour on the Cape Peninsula. It is unique in being perhaps the only place in South Africa where middle-class white residents happily coexisted with working-class coloured fisher folk throughout the apartheid years. They maintained ties despite determined attempts by the Nationalist government to enforce a racial divide and relocate the coloured community.

Kalk Bay harbour, coming up to a century old in 2013, is home to the traditional *chukkie*, a timber-deck fishing boat whose presence speaks of hard-fought livelihoods caught between apartheid and the dark waters of False Bay. Most of the boat owners are coloured fishers with an instinctive knowledge of the sea – their *metis* born of generations of fishing families. 'We used to learn from our parents – there are no better hand-line fishermen in the world than those born in Kalk Bay,' says one among them.

Up to 2007, crowds would gather along the quayside awaiting the *chukkies*. The vessels routinely disgorged an abundance of tuna, yellowtail, snoek and the occasional octopus, which went on sale in a cacophony of bargaining. Sadly, all that went. Today, boats leave the harbour only occasionally and the haggling crowds are gone. Visitors to Kalk Bay, unaware of the change, might find themselves questioning the price or provenance of a former frozen fish.

The reason for such misfortune lies in a far-reaching restructure of the fishing sector. In 2007 the Department of Marine and Coastal Management (MCM) decided that quotas for all fishing sectors had to be reallocated, with certain key objectives in mind: improved management of a depleting marine resource, increased investment in a lagging sector in the economy, and black empowerment.

There are 19 fishing-specific policies. I focus here on one, the traditional line-fish sector, affecting the Kalk Bay fishing population as well as many other communities along the west and southern Cape coasts. For them, the term transformation is synonymous with loss. Ironically, an unlikely person supports their viewpoint: Horst Kleinschmidt, the former head of MCM and leader of the restructure that effectively decimated their livelihoods. Kleinschmidt cannot escape the daily visual reminder of his policy measures – he lives down the road from the harbour. 'I thought if I could not dispense an egalitarian dispensation, to be Robin Hood would be second best. But even that fell short of what I had hoped for, even though the fishing industry is blacker than any other as a result of quotas giving government a stick that it could wield.'

Kleinschmidt may not have achieved his objectives, although the massive restructuring effort was far better than similar initiatives in other parts of government – a comparison of little comfort to the Kalk Bay fishers. 'There are traditional fishermen who have fished for forty years or more and didn't get a single licence. Then there are people who have never fished before who have huge quotas. How does this work?' asks a perplexed Sulaiman Achmad,[6] who overcame illiteracy to build a profitable fishing business, patiently acquiring his fishing quotas over decades. A well-established Kalk Bay boat owner, Jacobus Poggenpoel, adds: 'We have a crayfish quota, which is used up in two months. Then we tie up the boats until the following year. We used to support 12 fishermen, and now that's gone.'[7]

New licence allocations

How could a seemingly well-designed policy and system of licence allocations ultimately disempower those earmarked as beneficiaries of transformation? The first restructure, the allocation of medium-term (four-year) commercial fishing rights, took place in 2001 and 2002. Before then, fishing rights were allocated on an annual basis, which resulted in 'an unstable fishing industry and a generally unattractive economic sector in which to attract capital to finance small and medium-sized enterprises, particularly of black entrepreneurs,' according to Kleinschmidt.[8]

The medium-term rights provided a test run for the later long-term allocation of rights, which were finalised in 2006. The problems that emerged then could be smoothed over with the promise of resolution in the next round. But the long-term allocation was bound to set off flares. Ill-conceived measures or mistakes would destroy livelihoods, for a lost opportunity on this round could not be reversed for many years – quotas were anything from eight years for traditional line fisheries to 20 years for the capital-intensive deep-sea trawling.

Few fishing rights for Kalk Bay

Some 75% of the Kalk Bay fishing fleet failed to secure medium-term rights.[9] Freddy Vorsatz had the misfortune to be hit by a taxi and break both his legs at the time the medium-term rights were due for processing. MCM refused to consider his case as special. Instead he was told he could still apply for a long-term quota, but as a 'new entrant.' Since he had failed to secure medium-term rights, he was not recognised as an official participant in the sector, despite having been a fisherman for more than fifty years. Unsurprisingly, the label 'new entrant' jarred. The Kalk Bay Boat Owners Association objected: 'Fisher folk with 50 years experience at sea, and who come from families that have been fishing for centuries, had their licences removed in 2003 and given to newcomers … The traditional fisher folk, with all their experience, are now forced to beg for a right under the heading *New Entrant*!'[10]

Kleinschmidt and his team were aware of the risks associated with an inadequate allocation process for long-term rights, and set about drafting policies and deploying an extensive application and allocation machinery from 2004. In 2005, the MCM and its advisers travelled the coastline to consult through *imbizos* (community meetings). Draft policies were presented, oral submissions from 1700 fishers were documented and some 330 written comments were processed. Mindful of potential abuses and corruption – in particular, what became known as 'paper quotas' – the verification of applications was managed by a team of independent auditors called the Rights Verification Unit. As Kleinschmidt explains, 'We couldn't only look at the ownership in an application. We found that lawyers had got very smart in hiding white interests, creating mirage structures. We had to go to the next layer or even a triple layer to identify the real owners.'

In August 2005, numerous centres along the coast handled the distribution of applications. More than a thousand applicants registered. Once the information had been processed an advisory committee headed by Kleinschmidt and comprising mostly independent professionals assessed each application. Scores and weights were attributed to criteria by which applications would be assessed. After this, the MCM published the provisional assessments, including the scores. Applicants could then comment on the scores and request a review of their assessment.

It is difficult to fault MCM in its efforts to create a transparent and consultative process. As described in the previous chapter, this had been completely absent in the re-issue of rights by the Department of Mineral Resources. So what went wrong?

Traditional ways ignored

A key omission lies in the failure to understand and accommodate how the traditional fishers organised their operations and their underlying social relations. In the past, fishing licences were awarded to vessels. Fishers boarded boats as freelancers, jockeying for those with the best skippers to improve their chances of a good catch. There was no such thing as a guaranteed minimum wage or employment benefits, making the life of a fisher open to exploitation.

Poggenpoel, who recalls his grandfather catching whales in False Bay, vehemently disputes this. 'Find me a fisherman who was exploited by a Kalk Bay boat owner. Forty percent [of the catch earnings] went to the boat owner – and we paid all the expenses – and 60% went to the fishermen. This was based on trust. A fisherman would say, I have earned R5000, and I would say, okay, give me my 40%.' Other boat owners were not so ready to claim little conflict between themselves and the fishers.

MCM also found this trust unconvincing and stopped the allocation of quotas to boats, giving the fishing rights to individual fishers, with each simply giving details of the vessels they intended to use. This approach also opened up access to black African fishers who had a limited history in the sector. But, as Kleinschmidt notes, 'the preferences afforded to whites and coloureds [in the Western Cape only] under apartheid could not be maintained after 1994. I had to give to blacks and to women, the latter of which quadrupled the numbers who felt that they had a right to have access to fish. I faced Hobson's choice.'

Two problems arose from removing rights from vessels. The first is commercial in nature. By awarding the rights to individuals, the asset (the fishing right) was separated from the investment (the boat). This injected uncertainty into the investment, effectively making a liability of the boat, instead of it being an asset joined at the hip with a fishing right. 'I spend money [building my business]. When transformation came, people who have never been in the fishing game were better off,' laments Achmad.

111

The second problem relates to the organisation of the Kalk Bay fishing community. Achmad's description is along these lines: When fish are running, we boat owners have to go to the homes of fishermen and drag them drunk from bed into the boats. They sleep off the alcohol on the boat and we wake them up when we have reached the shoals. It is these fishers who now own the fishing quotas.

Put another way by the Kalk Bay Boat Owners Association: 'The true Traditional way does not conform (to the requirements of MCM) in that the Fishers are essentially freelance and migrate from boat to boat. This is a non-discriminatory free entrepreneurial methodology preferred by the Fishers ... This is a true informal sector.'[11] Kleinschmidt points out that heavy fines had been paid by Poggenpoel and other Kalk Bay boat owners for poaching – some R5 million in all. Boat owners could not have served their purpose well with that record.

What was expected of boat owners in the application requirements? Fishers had to demonstrate that they procured supplies or services from black South Africans and contributed part of their income to charities or community organisations; they needed to get letters from their suppliers and charities as proof. They were also asked if they contributed to medical aid and pension for their employees, and provided safe working conditions. All of this was required of fishers whose mean annual income came to under R150 000. Such expectations were an absurdity – but are a normal requirement of formal business. This shows the difficulty presented in a one-size-fits-all policy. Fortunately sense prevailed and these criteria were not used in assessing the application; only registration with the South African Revenue Services applied.

Standardising society

Using Scott's analysis, policy was working on the basis of 'standardized citizens', who 'have, for the purposes of the planning exercise, no gender, no tastes, no history, no values, no opinions or original ideas, no traditions and no distinctive personalities to contribute to the enterprise'. This, he adds, is not an accident or 'oversight; it is the necessary first premise of any large-scale planning exercise'.[12]

The MCM was not unaware of such issues. It had before it a report commissioned earlier that pointed to 'local and indigenous knowledge' being 'rarely afforded any status' in natural resource management, with 'little room for local people to set the agenda and pace' of policy and planning.[13] However, says Kleinschmidt, the department had received legal advice 'not to accommodate local deviances, as this could set precedents that could not be defended in a court of law.' So, they set three conditions for hand-line fishing which applied to everyone: historic involvement, dependency on fishing for a livelihood, and catching the fish yourself.

Also, he adds, 'tradition was denied in favour of another imperative.' One was to open up fishing to previously excluded black Africans. This may explain the high proportion of new entrants (some 20%) along the Cape coasts, and it confirms the perception within the Kalk Bay community that, as several people put it, 'we were not white enough under apartheid, and not black enough under the ANC.' In fact Poggenpoel complains that 'I've been told that I must give a share in my boat [to black Africans]. That's rubbish. I worked for this boat. I didn't get it for free. Why involve myself with people I don't know? Government gave me nothing, what I have got today I worked hard for ... this whole black empowerment thing is a hand-out story.' Yet the policy explicitly endorsed support of 'black traditional line fishers' and the allocation of 'a fair proportion of rights to applicants based at fishing harbours that are historically associated with traditional line fish catches'.[14]

There were other obstacles to registering the traditional knowledge of the Cape fisher folk. One, it would appear, was the MCM's scientists – white, usually of the old regime, seen to be conservative in both political and scientific outlook – for whom the Kalk Bay boat owners have only vitriolic comment. Leftwing politics also intervened. Kleinschmidt recalls a conversation with Andy Johnson,[15] who represents subsistence fishers: 'He said to me: This is not a socialist state and I am organising these people as part of the political task to achieve that.' As such, Kleinschmidt said, 'it was difficult not to be suspicious of the motives of some of those who lobbied me.'

Tradition also got a slap in the face when modern ski-boats were included in the traditional line-fishery policy. Kalk Bay boat owners protested loudly: 'It must again be stated that the Ski-boat is NOT a Traditional fishing boat and should be dealt with separately, and

CONTROLLED MORE SERIOUSLY.'[16] But for MCM, this did not suggest that fishing from the traditional boats didn't need to be controlled either.

Too many unintended consequences

There is good reason for the fishers' dislike of ski-boats. These boats tend to be white-owned, often by former state officials from the police, harbours and railways who, when retired from government service, use their pension or retrenchment packages to acquire boats and large SUVs to haul them. Ski-boats are highly mobile. All it takes is a cellphone call to report the presence of a good shoal along the coast, and a ski-boat is hauled from the water, latched to a vehicle and rushed to the best fishing location. The *chukkies*, on the other hand, don't have this mobility. 'It could take us eight hours or more to change course and head for better waters. As long as we are not using modern equipment, like sonar, we can't deplete the resources like the ski-boats can,' boat owners told me time and again.

Of the 30 boats in Kalk Bay, only three are still working in the traditional line-fish sector. The boat owners note that only one among them was successful as a 'new entrant' in the long-term allocation, whereas 59 vessels along the west and southwest coasts were allocated to new entrants. They claim most of these are ski-boats: 'Something is *very* wrong somewhere.'[17]

The massive communication and consultation process was a first by a government department and nothing similar has been done since on such scale. Yet it failed the Kalk Bay fishing community. Poggenpoel doesn't mince his words: 'The *imbizos* were the biggest load of crap under the sun.' Why? 'Deloitte & Touche did this. What do these people know about fishing? There were umpteen meetings where they spoke to people; they did not listen to people.'

With a department of scientists and consultants with audit and legal backgrounds, perhaps 'being spoken to' was inevitable. How do we step away from the 'we know better' syndrome in a society where education is low and poverty is rife? We can also often mistake and romanticise the notion of community, assuming a unity of interests – which is often not the case. The disintegration of communities is another issue. Kalk

Bay is probably the most coherent, but many community members have dispersed, often to former white suburbia. Since 1994, fishing communities have trebled in size, as people from the impoverished Eastern Cape have migrated to the wealthier Western Cape. A cheaper source of labour, they have replaced many of the traditional coloured fishers.

The MCM envisaged its responsibilities as limited to fishing with socio–economic considerations not seen as its remit. Yet these have proved crucial to the successful redistribution of fishing benefits: 'If you give someone a quota, they also need an extension officer to help them build and administer their business. Whites are buying quotas back especially where people have got themselves into business trouble.' Kleinschmidt adds: 'There are many chances for whites to buy back black quotas. So, I do believe that there is 60% black ownership on paper but in reality more like 40% actually fishing and getting the economic benefit of the licences.'[18]

At the end of the day, he admits, 'the poorest fishing communities were left out.' Other fights are therefore brewing. I have not dealt with subsistence fishers, whose cause is currently championed by the socialist firebrand Andy Johnson. More recently, the MCM offered to resolve the subsistence fishers' lack of access to inshore resources by awarding them a cut from the quota for recreational fishers, in what is termed interim relief. This was like a red rag to a bull – and akin to what Zanele Mbeki refers to as 'dealing with the poor by exemption'.[19] The poor, in her view, are deserving of policies that are specifically tailored to their needs and conditions, instead of being carved out of mainstream policy.

Where lie the answers?

Problems are easy to identify. Solutions are not so evident. I look again to Scott, who talks of the need for a 'great deal of respect for the diversity of human actions and the insurmountable difficulties in successfully coordinating millions of transactions'.[20] Or in the words of the economist Albert Hirschman there is a case for 'a little more "reverence of life", a little less straitjacketing of the future, a little more allowance of the unexpected – and a little less wishful thinking.'[21]

What to do practically? The starting point for Scott is 'taking small steps'. If we cannot know the consequences of our interventions then it makes sense to 'take a small step, stand back, observe, and then plan the next small step.'[22] In South Africa's case, this hardly seems politically feasible. Ninety percent of the population want decisive change in their economic status – incremental steps are seemingly an impossible demand.

Another of Scott's suggestions is to 'favour reversibility'. In other words, 'prefer interventions that can easily be undone if they turn out to be mistakes.' Unfortunately, under the former presidency, reversibility never seemed an option. Thabo Mbeki's style was to dig himself into a corner, notably on Zimbabwe and HIV/Aids, leaving no room to concede error. BEE too seems to be caught in a trap of irreversibility. And in fishing, some have argued that 'the deteriorating managerial and scientific capacity at MCM' means that 'corrective measures are unlikely to happen in the interim'.[23]

Scott also suggests we 'plan on surprises'. Choose plans that allow 'the largest accommodation to the unforeseen.' Creating space and allowing 'human inventiveness' is his final advice. He finds surprising how 'little confidence' social engineers have in the 'skills, intelligence and experience of ordinary people', despite 'their quite genuine egalitarian and often socialist impulses'.[24]

Operating in a global environment in a structurally rigid economy, there is a high requirement to be nimble and innovative in our thinking – if we don't, we will always be playing catch-up. This remains relevant even in the allocation of fishing licences.

Part 2

Empowerment to the people

Part 2
Empowerment to the people

Once a perception sticks, it is extremely difficult to dislodge. So it is with the view of BEE having become little more than a playground for the elite. When the deputy president Kgalema Motlanthe officially launched the BEE Commission in 2010, his comment that 'only a few benefited again and again' reflected a general sentiment.[1]

BEE ownership most certainly excludes most black South Africans. The net is only cast as far as the private sector can reach – it can never extend far enough to capture the nation. But, of those who have been fortunate enough to fall within its ambit, there is more diversity in the role players than we might think. In fact, it could be argued that the pendulum has swung at last towards broad-based ownership schemes and investment companies.

This part of the book covers what has become a vast new facet of investment in South Africa, some of which has the makings of what you could call a new asset class of social capital. It certainly differentiates South Africa's current empowerment from the earlier efforts of Afrikaners and Malaysians.

Today there are broad-based investment companies that provide an example of what BEE needs to be. They occupy strategic positions in some sectors, invest productively and have occasionally even started new ventures. This in itself is a good outcome, but there's more; the returns that are earned by these broad-based shareholders are put to good causes. Added to that, some try to use their influence as shareholders to prod companies to transform their employment practices and relationships with society at large. Importantly, they are professionally run, with portfolios large enough to enable them to spread their investment risks.

For want of a better name, I call them social corporations. But they are a diverse group, and not what you might expect: shareholders are drawn from socialist-inclined trade unions, a small community in the northwest of the country, and NGOs. These I deal with as being among the best that BEE has to offer.

But they are the exception, and their existence should not imply that broad-based ownership is a panacea. Some models have proved themselves unworkable – too much complexity, too many conflicts between competing groups and (too often) too little investment knowledge to ensure a fair deal. Corruption has crept in here as well, as just the smell of money tends to distort expectations and relationships.

The early experiments of large unwieldy consortiums have given way to a variety of models: employee ownership schemes, social investment trusts, and share offering to the black public. None are free of financial or political risks, as even these investors have to borrow to acquire their shares.

But perhaps there is no greater risk than in the mining sector, where usually remote rural communities are offered shares in the mining operations in their area. I trace the experiences of two very different communities, one on the west coast and one in the east. I am left with a deep discomfort about the belief that equity ownership, acquired as per usual with debt, is a valid way of empowering poor people. These communities are almost invariably poorly advised, if at all, with their hopes vested in just one investment, the mine located on their land. Who knows whether they will have paid a reasonable price for their shares; whether the mine has good reserves or whether it has much life left; or, once having paid back the loan, whether there will be much money left over. The risks are enormous and I suspect much of this story will not have a happy ending. Hence, these concerns that such investments could become BEE's powder keg.

For communities such as these, BEE ownership is fundamentally about the redistribution of wealth. But ownership is a poor tool that has emerged from a paucity of thinking on the issue of redistribution. There are international experiences that could have guided us – I touch briefly on the most far-reaching economic transformation of our times, that of the former communist countries of the Soviet Union and Eastern

Europe. We are very different from each other but their efforts to place shareholding in private hands have important lessons.

If, as Motlanthe says, the need is for the 'productive participation' of black society, then we need to review policy. Broad-based ownership is favoured by many not because considered thought has been given to this as an appropriate means by which to redistribute wealth. Rather, it is preferred as the alternative to enriching small numbers of individuals. So, if you have to do BEE ownership, rather do it broad-based. But that still doesn't suggest that what we are doing is the right thing. That issue needs interrogation. Also, we need to start discriminating between what is working and what isn't, and redirect policy accordingly.

6

Mass appeal

There isn't as much support for the proposition that
poverty causes crime ... However, there is a much stronger
conviction among academics that inequality causes crime;
that the difference between what the rich and poor earn
matters more than the depth of the poverty.

– Anthony Altbeker, *A country at war with itself*

In 2003 the South African multinational Sasol stood accused of
bad-mouthing South Africa by citing BEE as a potential risk to
shareholders in its New York listing. After that, Sasol seemed ripe
for a politically crafted empowerment deal that would smooth ruffled
feathers. Yet, five years later, it implemented the largest empowerment
transaction in the country's history, 10% for R23 billion, and set a new
standard for broad-based black ownership. There were no politically
well-placed black individuals or investor groups among the beneficiaries,
just thousands upon thousands of ordinary citizens and employees given
facilitated access to shareholding.

There was nothing unique in the component parts of the Sasol
deal. Throughout the short history of BEE there have been employee
share-ownership schemes, retail offerings of shares to the black public,
stakeholder shareholding for groups like trade unions, customers,
suppliers and franchisees, and not-for-profit investment entities that
support social upliftment. However, it was the first time that only such
investors had been included in a transaction of such scale. Until then,
BEE companies would participate alongside broad-based shareholding
– and more often than not, in the lead role, with political heavy hitters.

Soon after Sasol, the cellular provider Vodacom surprised the market when it sidestepped the 'usual suspects' and slipped past the political nose to select only broad-based shareholders. Yet another substantial transaction at R7.5 billion, it allocated the greatest share of a 6.5% interest in the company to the black public and employees. Two long-standing, professionally managed broad-based investment companies got the remainder – Thebe Investments, whose origins lie in the ANC but which has maintained a quiet independence during its 17-year investment activity; and Royal Bafokeng Holdings, which as a tribally defined investment group is not on the politically correct list.

Also in 2009, SABMiller totted up the largest deal that year – 8.45% of the subsidiary SA Breweries (SAB) for R7.3 billion – with a broad-based scheme that spoke directly to its commercial interests. Black tavern or shebeen owners along with black suppliers got the largest share of froth, followed by employees and then the company's socially responsible investment vehicle, SAB Foundation.

As these major corporations were transacting BEE shareholding anew, Mineworkers Investment Company became involved in the largest restructuring by empowerment groups yet seen. Two leaders in the gaming and media sectors, Peermont and Primedia, were restructured to accommodate new investors and a leveraged capital structure in the private equity mould,* with the latter delisting as well. From this, MIC emerged as the controlling shareholder in Peermont, and the single largest shareholder in Primedia. Together, the transactions totted up to R13 billion. MIC had already been a shareholder in Primedia and controlled the prime gaming asset that Peermont had wanted. The exercise put a lot of cash in MIC's hands, which enabled the payment of an unprecedented dividend to its shareholder and set a new standard for financial returns to the beneficiaries of broad-based investment groups.

---

* A 'private equity'-type acquisition of a company is based on the concept of leverage. This is done by restructuring the capital base in a company – usually made up of debt and equity (the shares). As much debt is placed in the company as is commercially prudent, which has the effect of lowering the equity value. The investors then acquire equity at a lower value than they otherwise would, and over time the dividends are used to service the debt. As the debt reduces the equity value increases, giving an enhanced or higher than usual return on the investment. In brief, this model allows an investor to buy into a company with very little equity capital, which they later sell at a much higher value because they have used someone else's capital (the debt provider) to finance the growth of the business. However, the success of this model requires high-growth companies.

Among the BEE transactions of leading JSE-listed companies, most of which were done after 2003, I found a higher than expected level of broad-based ownership. A quarter of these corporations had done deals that were entirely broad-based. Half of them had ensured that more than 50% of their BEE shareholding was broad-based.* The market capitalisation of this shareholding amounted to more than R100 billion, calculated in mid-2009 when the markets were low. Being just a limited sample, we may assume that a sizeable amount of social capital is in the making. It is this which makes something unique in South Africa's efforts to address black economic marginalisation. Later I will discuss the next step: to extend the ambit of social capital, drawing on growing international experience and breaking away from the narrow frame of BEE ownership.

Codes try but fail to clip the wings of broad-based investors

The Mvelaphanda Group therefore had read the signals correctly, when it announced its decision to unbundle its assets. A preference for broad-based shareholding had removed much of the remaining BEE opportunities from the individually owned BEE companies. As its CEO Yolanda Cuba says, 'Today the landscape has changed. When we did the Gold Fields transaction in 2003, we were the only BEE partner. We were able to have a bigger participation in transactions that delivered significant value upfront. Now transactions are broad-based ... and you have to ask what value we can add.'[1]

This was precisely what black business had tried to stop when it persuaded the drafters of the Codes to limit broad-based ownership to no more than 10% of the required 25%. White business, they believed, was not acting in good faith, but instead wanted the passivity that diverse shareholding implied. This would leave white control of the corporate sector intact.

The DTI sympathised and restricted broad-based investors from acquiring more than 10% unless they played by some additional rules that imposed a higher standard on them than other BEE groups. The Codes therefore require that broad-based schemes must either have a

---

* I analysed the BEE transactions of 34 listed companies who were leaders in 10 sectors in mid-2009.

'track record' of commercial operations, or evidence of full operational capacity – and the latter means having 'suitably qualified and experienced staff in sufficient numbers, experienced professional advisers, operating premises and all other necessary requirements for operating a business'.

Hallelujah for bad drafting. What is a 'track record' or 'suitably qualified' staff? I'm told by BEE consultants that one year of operations is seen as sufficient for a track record. After that, a broad-based scheme may increase its shareholding without the added conditions.

DTI's response was disingenuous, to say the least. Firstly, there is no evidence to suggest broad-based shareholders are any more passive than their individual counterparts – earlier we saw broad-based companies more active and productive than most.

Secondly, there is certainly no evidence to suggest individually owned BEE companies are any more businesslike than broad-based investors. Too many have no intention of building businesses – many are trading assets off the back of BEE policy while holding down jobs elsewhere in the corporate sector, government or the ANC. Even if engaged fulltime in their investment companies, there are still too many who aren't interested in productivity.

Years of experience in BEE leads me to believe only a minority among individually owned BEE companies are committed to growing new commercial value. The real issue therefore is not how to keep broad-based schemes out of the transactional queue but how to support those black-controlled companies, broad-based or otherwise, that are productive and how to encourage more of them.

Ambivalent policy messages

Business can't be blamed for favouring broad-based ownership. Until the last-minute changes to the Codes, government strongly endorsed the wide spread of black shareholding. The BEE Strategy requires 'an increasing portion of the ownership and management of economic assets' to be vested in community and broad-based enterprises.

Phumzile Mlambo-Ngcuka – much maligned for reportedly suggesting blacks were entitled to get 'filthy rich' – spoke out, when crafting new mining policy, against an 'old boys' [BEE] club': 'Government has an obligation to a broad-based constituency, and we have to service every one of our people. For assets that are state-owned, and in transactions facilitated by public policy, broad-based empowerment is a must.'[2]

The Codes however have never required a high level of broad-based ownership – in fact, no more than 2.5% of the 25% is needed, with there being a bonus point for meeting that target. But until the final draft of Codes there was nothing to stop selling the full 25% to staff trusts or NGOs as long as the beneficiaries were largely black. The message that business took from this was a clear assurance that broad-based ownership was legitimate and credible – before that, there was always some ambivalence about how much of a BEE transaction could be broad-based.

Companies almost invariably exceed the 2.5% level. I have no doubt that some have done so to secure passive shareholders, as black business believes. This might be expected in family firms, for example. In my advisory work, I found different reasons. Corporations had become resistant to the evident renting-seeking behaviour of BEE companies. I found managements decidedly uncomfortable about enriching a few individuals. In their assessment, if BEE was simply about redistributing wealth, then better it go to the most deserving – staff and highly disadvantaged communities. I also found that multinationals more readily accepted broad-based investors – offshore boards understood corporate social responsibility well and, if shareholding could be placed within that frame, the mandates for BEE equity sales became easier to secure.

You could therefore argue that individual black investor groups became their own worst enemy. If you have before you, on the one hand, a few individuals keen to acquire shares in your company but who seem more interested in their lifestyles than adding value to your business, and on the other a credible NGO-owned investment company, who would be the obvious choice?

Many models

Broad-based investment has become an amazing technicoloured dreamcoat, offering a range of investor types from which companies can pick and choose.

There are the first movers, those that survived the Asian crisis in the

Nineties to grow large investment portfolios under professional eyes. Today, they are among the leading BEE investors and tend to be one of two types: representative organisations like trade unions or interest groups for women, the disabled or specific communities; and not-for-profit NGOs with a broad developmental mandate not tied to any specific constituency. Right from the start of BEE, numerous organisations of this type set up investment companies in which they held shares either directly or indirectly via investment trusts. They hoped that over time they would receive a nice income stream that would feed their socio-economic activities.

The second type is companies with a mix between individual and broad-based shareholding. Women's Investment Portfolio Holdings is a notable and innovative early example. They offered a triple whammy of empowerment – race, gender and spread of shareholding. After starting out as a private investment trust, the company changed its strategy in 1997 with a private issue of shares. The core group of prominent black women who had started the company travelled the countryside to encourage individual women to acquire shares – this attracted some 18 000 women, both black and white, since at that time affirmative action polices included all women. Later it listed on the JSE, with financial institutions also investing, but in non-voting shares to maintain Wiphold as a black-controlled company. However, the market collapse in the Nineties stripped bare the expectations that a listing raised, and soon afterwards Wiphold delisted, creating a different share structure with a major financial institution holding a third of its shares, losing its majority broad-based character.[3]

Mega-consortiums
In many of the first large transactions, you would find layers of broad-based shareholding. Take Anglo American's Johnnic sale: 76 parties came together in the National Empowerment Consortium for that multi-billion rand acquisition. Just that number of individuals would make a consortium broad-based. But that wasn't enough. The consortium itself was divided into two parts: business groups on the one side, and trade unions and their pension funds on the other. The business group itself included representative companies such as Nafhold, owned by the black

business association Nafcoc.* Added to that, Anglo also placed a further 6% of equity in a retail vehicle, which attracted 32 000 individual black shareholders.

Via Johnnic, the NEC got what the former Anglo executive Michael Spicer describes as 'a bootload of good assets', like Toyota, SAB, and the leading media group Omni.[4] Yet it fumbled strategically, selling assets and breaking up the group without growing in new directions. Today, there is nothing left of the NEC or the original Johnnic. Many attribute this to the sprawling character of the NEC, fraught with conflicting agendas and bickering – an ill-equipped shareholder, indeed, to exercise control over a large industrial holding company. As one consortium member told me: 'You can't run a railroad like this.'

For those involved, the NEC experience was painful. But as BEE became increasingly tainted by accusations of enrichment, the use of consortiums to broaden the shareholder base has remained attractive throughout the early years of BEE. You would find parties claiming to represent not just thousands or hundreds of thousands of black beneficiaries but millions. The most extreme claims came in the bidding for the third cellular licence. I sat aghast when one bidder, Khuluma 084, claimed to have 10 million direct beneficiaries, whose ID numbers they would most certainly tabulate if they secured the licence – if not, I reflected wryly, why not bid for the task of conducting the national census?[5]

Containing complexity
Broad-based ownership offers a good story, but it is a labyrinth of complexity that promises to test even those most adept at social management. Today, therefore, much effort is directed at avoiding the Johnnic-type consortium and designing simpler alternatives.

Take Gordon Young,[6] who initiated the union participation in Johnnic and made one brief comment on that experience: 'Never again.' He kept his word. Instead, after soothing the bruises, Young developed his own broad-based model. In 2000 he launched Ditikeni Investment Company, together with 22 reputable NGOs that are all not-for-profit – the criterion was that they had to be stable and properly established.

---

* Nafcoc started the Nafcoc Investment Holding Company (Nafhold) in the mid-Nineties.

They provided a little seed capital between them – R2.8 million, which Ditikeni paid back as a special dividend. Subsequently it has provided a healthy return of 40% per annum compounded, although the sums are still small.

Young has sought to manage the complex and often conflicting relationships inherent in broad-based groups by registering Ditikeni as a public company. This places an obligation on it to live according to the rules of good governance and information disclosure. Money, Young also knows, is too often the source of disputes, and so Ditikeni has a dividend policy to pay something each year, no matter how small.

But even Young's model imposes a load of shareholder administration not usually required of small companies. Others have simplified the broad-based ownership model even further. Some NGOs that are large enough or with a well-enough established reputation have created their own investment companies; one shareholder, one investment company, all committed to the same goal, offers a neatly contained broad-based model. An example is Cida City Campus in Johannesburg. It provides tertiary education to those unable to afford fees at a state university and has captured the imagination of many donors (Richard Branson being one). As a private, albeit low-cost, university it is vulnerable to the vagaries of donor money and so established its own investment company with the necessary BEE qualifications. It is now building an investment portfolio to smooth out the lumpiness of donor finance and support the substantial expenses.

But this model is only workable for NGOs that have institutionalised themselves sufficiently. Companies want to know that whomever they are transacting with has a reasonable chance of a future existence.

Company-sponsored social trusts

A similar self-containment is found in social investment trusts created by the parties on both sides of the transactional table – the companies in need of BEE ownership and the companies offering BEE ownership. These may be specialist trusts mandated to deliver one service, such as educational bursaries, or maths and science education or HIV/Aids support – the list can be as long as a society requires. Or they may have a broader socio-economic mandate, allowing them to get involved in multiple developmental activities.

Fundamentally, they are tailor-made by companies, raising the question as to their independence as shareholders. Some have argued that they are merely extensions of corporate social investment programmes, but we should not be too hasty in dismissing them.

Let's say you are a company that needs BEE ownership – remember, in terms of the Codes, your BEE shareholder needs a particular make-up: majority black-owned, of which 40% must be black women and 10% broad-based. Instead of selecting a variety of groups who offer this profile, you create your own. It's not that difficult. All you do is draft a trust deed that satisfies the Codes' criteria for broad-based schemes. These are not onerous. For example, you need a board that is chaired by someone independent of the trust's beneficiaries; and is majority black and 25% black women. Further, the trust beneficiaries must be at least 85% black South African. All this goes into your trust deed. If you prefer, a requirement for a certain proportion of beneficiaries to be black women may be added, and you will have gone a long way – if not all the way – to meeting the ownership requirements of the Codes.

Some of these trusts have the potential to become large sources of social funding – envisage them as potentially evolving along the lines of the Rockefeller or Ford Foundations. I advised on one such trust which focused on closing a serious gap in the health sector. Discovery Holdings, best known for its medical insurance, initiated the Discovery Foundation as one of its BEE shareholders. The Foundation has two objectives: the education of medical specialists and the development of academic and research centres. Discovery financed the share acquisition, meaning that the Foundation will take several years to meet its repayment obligations and start to receive a good dividend stream. In the mean time, limited dividends and Discovery contributions are ensuring the Foundation is operational. Over the next few years, the Foundation is expected to have some R100 million available to train about three hundred medical specialists. The Foundation is professionally managed, with trustees who are medical and development experts. It is a broad-based investment vehicle without the complications of too many decision-makers and interested parties – a seemingly neat solution.

Individually owned BEE companies have followed a similar model.

Instead of being one of many in a transaction, they have sought to structure their own shareholding to reflect the ownership profile required by the Codes. By doing this, they hope companies will only deal with themselves – or at least keep the number of parties involved in a transaction to a minimum. So they create social investment trusts, and possibly black women shareholding within their own shareholder structure. They manage these trusts in much the same way as established companies are doing.

An early initiator of such a structure is the Tiso Group, which established the Tiso Foundation when the company was constituted. The Foundation has a 15.5% shareholding in the group, said to be worth R100 million. Cyril Ramaphosa's Shanduka Group gave away 10.5% of its shares to a black women consortium involving 74 women, among them prominent anti-apartheid figures, on the understanding that they will 'pay it forward' by investing their own money in education and mentoring programmes for young women.

There needs to be a word of caution on investment trusts. As Young argues, 'Many trusts masquerade as broad-based entities. Trustees are accountable to no-one.'[7] So, you may find a mere shell, in reality, with the founding company doing as they wish with these trusts. It is important therefore that the trusts are established with integrity, ensuring that trustees are sufficiently strong and independent to manage both the investments and the social programmes funded from the investments.

Here, I want to signal a particularly worrisome category of trusts, the community investment trusts, popular in the mining sector and usually found in more remote rural areas. They are potentially BEE's powder keg, and I therefore devote an entire chapter to them later on.

Retail vehicles
Among listed companies, there is an increasing attraction for shareholding by the black public in what are called retail schemes. These tend to be structured in all manner of ways, but the overall approach is to offer either all black South Africans or a defined section of the population (black women or shebeen owners, for example) the opportunity to acquire a maximum number of shares individually at a discounted price. The buyer may or may not be required to put down a deposit (usually

never more than 10% of the value of their acquisition); and they will be required to hold their shares for a defined period.

The acquisition is funded by debt, held in the scheme. The loan facility is provided either by the company selling the equity or a financial institution. The buying public is not liable. The financial risk is small – potentially the loss of the deposit, if ever paid. But there is the risk of failed expectations, which comes with poor share price performance that could leave the buyer with little to no value at the end of the scheme's life.

The latest market crisis has provided a crystal-clear picture of the inherent risks. Sasol, for example, sold shareholding to the black public at the pinnacle of the stock exchange. The discount offered therefore became irrelevant as prices soon plummeted some 25% below the price paid. Still, in early 2010, the price was not much better. But markets as we know go up and down. The Sasol shareholders still have time to wait before they may cash in. The media group Naspers, however, was not so lucky; but it decided to restructure one of its schemes and extend the holding period a further two years to allow value to pick up – in this way sidestepping the risks at present.

Employee ownership
There is hardly a BEE transaction without employees receiving some shareholding, in what are called employee share ownership programmes (Esops). But the retail sector has differentiated itself, with some major retailers favouring their employees entirely. Retailers are regarded as the laggards in BEE ownership, probably because there is little threat to their businesses if they don't follow that route – the ordinary consumer will not withdraw custom because their favoured supermarket or clothing retailer has no BEE shareholding. But it is good for major listed companies to get onside. So we have seen Woolworths place 10% in an Esop for all staff, except management, while Edcon has provided just under 10%, effectively for black staff only.

Perhaps the most successful employee ownership initiative is John Lewis in the UK. The staff owns the company, with the evolution of unique and extensive governance structures. There is no sign of anything like this in South Africa, but the John Lewis model certainly testifies to the commercial value of having a committed staff, particularly when your customers are the general public.

Reasonable performance so far

On the whole, retail schemes and Esops launched in the early years of the millennium when prices were still subdued have done well. The transactions of the big four banks – all done in 2004/5 – have been good for everyone: broad-based, staff and the individually owned investment companies.

The equity interest of Standard Bank's staff had a net worth of R2.4 billion in early 2010. Shareholding was also made available to the Tutuwa Community Trust, worth R1.2 billion, and 250 small businesses selected by the bank, with an effective stake of R2.4 million each. Nedbank employees had a collective profit of some R1 billion and FirstRand employees have a potential profit of R1.8 billion. As yet, however, all are still tied in to holding their shares for a while longer.[8]

Broad-based grounds getting too crowded

The Nineties gave rise to a handful of large, well-managed broad-based investment corporations. But they have not been followed by another generation. Yes, there are many more broad-based groups around, but none have built the quality portfolios that make them leaders in the BEE domain.

Young believes the BEE field has become too competitive: 'Every man and their dog have an empowerment company.'[9] Companies therefore are feeling more confident about requiring risk contributions from BEE partners than they ever did in the past. This, of course, favours those who have been in BEE transactions long enough to have accumulated some capital to reinvest.

But it's more than that. As discussed, the Codes have encouraged a breakdown of BEE ownership to accommodate a number of BEE shareholder types, such as black women, youth, broad-based and, potentially, communities. Companies therefore frequently try to include all or most of these types of shareholders. Also, it is generally believed that the big deals have been done, and much of what is on offer today is the second helping. None of this has favoured a cohesive development of another core of substantive broad-based companies. To look again at Ditikeni: it has a good number of investments – just under twenty – but the value is low at R100 million.

It's empowerment in bits and pieces, incentivising opportunistic investment behaviour even more than ever – you've got to take what you can get. This can hardly be the required policy outcome. In the early years, before the Codes, broad-based companies managed to create a bridge between wealth redistribution and productive investment. Today, the pendulum has swung to redistribution, with the space to accumulate sufficient capital for productive purposes all but closed. Fortunately there are always exceptions, as we see in later chapters.

7

Trade unions toyi-toyi
for capital

Freedom is always and exclusively freedom for the one who
thinks differently.

– Rosa Luxemburg

If anything came as a surprise during South Africa's political transition,
it was finding militant trade unions energetically setting up investment
companies to participate in BEE transactions. Like many things in life,
this union-based capitalism started off in part through chance and in
part because of the bottom line. As apartheid gave way to democracy,
it soon became evident that international solidarity money would dry
up. BEE seemed like a good starting point to replenish the coffers. At
the same time, union membership was squeezed by retrenchments.
Extra services had to be provided to these members and their families to
secure their survival.

Chance entered in the form of a rare person in the union movement,
Bernie Fanaroff, an astrophysicist by training. I've already noted how
his crying foul over the award of cellular telephony licences opened up
access to shareholding for unions just before the democratic elections in
1994. Also by chance, Fanaroff left the union soon afterwards to become
an official in the new government, and Numsa, his metalworkers' union,
let the cellular opportunity slip. Two other unionists were far quicker
off the mark – Johnny Copelyn of the textile union Sactwu,* and Marcel
Golding of the National Union of Mineworkers (NUM). Sactwu

---

* Sactwu is the Southern African Clothing and Textile Workers Union, which is a Cosatu affiliate,
  as is the National Union of Mineworkers.

secured interests in both licences, while NUM participated in MTN, both through their newly established investment companies. They spotted the early pregnancy of BEE and made sure that not only would they be in the room at the birth but they would play a part in moulding its character in the years to come.

Both their unions had been grappling with declining sectors, ravaged by retrenchments. In the 1987 miners' strike 50 000 workers were dismissed, followed by a further 20 000 retrenchments. NUM set about establishing co-operatives to develop local industry and agriculture in the impoverished rural areas in which NUM members found themselves. Later the Mineworkers Development Agency was established to assist retrenched workers set up enterprises (a shift from the co-operatives, which had failed to perform).

Copelyn honed his business acumen in a union–owned enterprise set up in response to the 1988 retrenchments by the Frame textile group. Zenzeleni Clothing, established with R2.5 million seed capital from Frame as part of the retrenchment package, took on 300 retrenched Frame workers. They produced anti-apartheid T-shirts, but with democracy around the corner their market was short-lived. They shifted to work wear, but the enterprise was undercapitalised and needed to take a hard commercial decision; 150 jobs were scrapped.[1] This was a unique initiative that may be seen as the seed for Copelyn's later and much bigger ambition for Sactwu in the BEE arena. Ironically, however, Copelyn hasn't been able to put the history of Frame behind him. In 2009 he found himself bailing out Frame's holding company Seardel, closing down some textile divisions, and once more retrenching.

Against this background, it is perhaps not surprising that NUM and Sactwu were the first to put aside their ideological discomforts and initiate their own union investment companies – although, as Copelyn notes, 'invariably working at new frontiers is controversial.'[2] The different approaches and experiences of the two unions in their embryonic business efforts no doubt influenced the cultures of their respective investment groups, the Mineworkers Investment Company (MIC) and the Sactwu Investment Group (SIG). MIC, established in 1995, has remained firmly under the collective control of the union, whereas SIG's interests are housed in the listed Hosken Consolidated

Investments; here the union is the largest but not controlling shareholder. The MIC board only opened up to independent non-union members in recent years, but unionists past and present are still in the majority. The HCI's board does not have a Sactwu-appointed member.

Both have proved to be exceptionally beneficial for their unions, which, although not directly owning the investment companies, have ensured important added services for union members. Off a R3 million loan, MIC has leveraged a net asset value of R1.4 billion, against total assets of R10 billion[3] – a depressed figure given the market downturn. SIG* started with a R2 million loan from the union, and now has shares valued at over R4 billion based on its interest in HCI, whose market capitalisation is just short of R10 billion.[†]

Too different to co-operate

The two started out looking as if they would build a joint union investment empire under the HCI banner. In 1996 they placed their interests in the cellular provider Vodacom and radio broadcaster Highveld Stereo, then worth about R500 million, into HCI, with SIG and MIC initially having an equal interest that adjusted to 30% and 20% respectively. In four years the alliance disintegrated, with MIC selling down its stake over a period, but with most of its shareholding sold at around R2.40 in 2000. This was substantially below what the share has been trading in recent years (R70 to R80 in early 2010).[‡] But, says Clifford Elk, MIC's chief executive at the time, 'You need to recall that HCI borrowed as much as R1.5 billion against its Vodacom assets to invest in e.tv and other acquisitions.'[4]

In Elk's assessment, 'Copelyn wanted to leverage HCI off the credibility of MIC and Sactwu. The dispute however was somewhat nuanced and had a lot to do with the relative size of NUM compared to Sactwu and how values should be apportioned in transactions – in particular the Johnnic transaction, where union provident funds were required to make a financial investment. MIC believed its stake in Johnnic

---

* The Sactwu Investment Group is divided into two entities, Sactwu Investment Holdings, which has a 30% interest in HCI, and Sactwu Educational Trust with 10%.

† JSE market capitalisation in February 2010 hovered around R10 billion.

‡ The share was trading on the JSE at around R78 on 28 February 2010.

should reflect the greater value invested by the Mineworkers Provident Fund, whereas Sactwu asserted an equal partnership with MIC even though its fund contributed little if at all.'[5] Copelyn, on the other hand, says that the conflict with MIC was centred on MIC developing its own media interests in conflict with HCI while still trying to remain a joint controlling shareholder of HCI with 50% of the seats on the HCI board.

After MIC's departure from HCI, Golding stayed behind, rejected by NUM union officials. This helped cement Copelyn's reputation as a formidable deal-maker and opponent, never distracted from commercial imperatives – which others have repeatedly found to their detriment, including the BEE and the ANC heavyweight and former union colleague Cyril Ramaphosa.

MIC, on the other hand, locates itself firmly within the frame of social capital and ethical transformation, with objectives that overreach profit making. In his 2009 business review of the company, the chief executive Paul Nkuna attributes a national mandate to the company: 'MIC is in business to bankroll the long-term success of black economic empowerment so that in the long-term the process becomes irreversible.' In the same review, Kuben Pillay opens his chairman's statement with congratulations to Jacob Zuma on his election as president. Just this says enough to place the corporate cultures of MIC and HCI wide apart.

Their different cultures aside, the two companies have collected investment portfolios with marked similarities. Together they dominate the gaming industry and have significant media assets. Neither has imposed any ideological stamp on their media companies or interfered in editorial independence – hardly something one would expect from militant, socialist trade union shareholders. Perhaps much of the explanation for this lies in the rapid, but nevertheless ad hoc, development of union investment companies. In those early days of BEE, there was far more 'thinking on your feet' than considered planning.

Cosatu's discomfort

This was of concern to Cosatu, which by 2000 wanted to exercise some centralised control over union investment companies, then numbering around ten. Its strategy drew on the results of the September

Commission,* which reported: 'The separation between the unions and investment companies has been blurred. In many cases, union officials gain financially through access to cheap shares or director's fees. There is no clarity on the strategic goals of the investment funds. Decisions about investment funds have sometimes been taken in deliberate secrecy, preventing members from participating.'

The commission felt the activities of the union companies undermined union principles because they were not guided by social criteria in their investments. Their involvement in gaming is an apt example, given Cosatu's opposition to gambling and its negative impact on workers. According to the report, union companies should support a range of objectives, such as investment in job-creation projects and parenting social forms of production as part of South Africa becoming a socialist state.

Nothing came of these proposals – which was fortunate for the companies, no doubt, whose survival would have been severely tested if they had had to initiate social forms of production (whatever that means). MIC, for example, had a mandate to generate wealth for its shareholding trusts in a few short years. By 2000, it had a commitment to pay R88 million within five years, having already paid more than R30 million of that amount. There would undoubtedly have been a conflict between an objective to promote different forms of production and a requirement to pay early dividends.

Cosatu revisited union investment companies in 2005. In an internal report Naledi, its research arm, raised the problem of unions lacking the necessary 'technical capacity' and their inability to provide adequate 'oversight' over their companies. 'If Cosatu and its affiliates intend to use investment companies strategically and effectively, then capacity within the unions to oversee investment company issues must be built.'[6]

Again, nothing has come of that report. In the mean time, union investment companies have evolved, disappeared and stagnated in many different ways and for many different reasons. The most avaricious early collector of BEE investments, South African Railways and Harbour

---

* The September Commission was established by Cosatu in 1997 and chaired by the Cosatu vice-president Connie September. It was mandated to develop a set of policies for Cosatu appropriate to a democratic South Africa.

Workers Union (Sarhwu) Investments, no longer exists, while a number of others have muddled along, maintaining small portfolios with little apparent market interest in them as BEE partners. A few of these companies have acquired dubious reputations.

The attraction of union companies

It's worth taking a step back to look at the formation of these companies and what made them so attractive to white business at the time. Of all the broad-based investment groups, union companies emerged as the largest and the most successful during the first wave of BEE. They featured in at least sixty investments, shared between more than ten companies.[7]

There were a few compelling reasons for favouring union companies as shareholders. Unlike most other BEE companies, union investment arms offered the potential for real commercial value. Asset management appeared particularly attractive, given union influence over the pension and provident funds to which their members contributed. Metropolitan Life, for example, sponsored a significant initiative with the now defunct Union Alliance Holding to create a new asset manager in 1998, hoping to gain easy access to a good number of funds; Union Alliance drew together 10 Cosatu unions and two from the much smaller National Council of Trade Unions (Nactu), said to represent almost two million workers. At the end of the day, the union investment companies failed to deliver what asset managers really wanted. More often than not, union companies failed to rally their unions and their trustees on pension fund boards to support their interests.

Union investment companies also offered the potential to open up new markets. Companies in insurance and funeral cover believed that having union companies as shareholders would expand their market access. There is no evidence however that they delivered on expectations. MIC entered a different market – mine shops – by investing in the listed company Mathomo, which owned many stores on mines and at power plants. 'The logic to the investment', says Elk, 'was to leverage off the scale and footprint of the stores to bring benefits to members through improved goods and services.' MIC was an influential shareholder but essentially passive, relying on its partners to implement the vision. But experience was short, and so MIC found itself with 'ineffective partners, bad strategy and poor implementation'.[8]

All in all, the case for offering value-added services as BEE partners didn't hold. But, as Elk says, 'At least then the businesses that embraced us as shareholders and partners were forward thinkers who saw some competitive and commercial benefits by having us as shareholders, whereas today it is all about compliance.'

Established business, too, found union companies attractive for their political credibility. All but one of these companies fell under the umbrella of Cosatu and hence within the ANC alliance. Also, they could legitimately claim a defined constituency of beneficiaries – union members and their families – unlike other broad-based or representative investment entities, many of which would make spurious assertions about who and how many would benefit from their investments.

Access to finance was thought to be another advantage of union companies. There was a belief that these companies might be better equipped than others to finance their deals by leveraging their relationship with pension and provident funds. If these funds had a mandate to finance BEE transactions, the large institutions who managed them (like Sanlam and Old Mutual) would be more amenable to come forward as financiers – but yet again, a case of failed expectations. I suspect that, had union investment companies been more successful in investing their members' retirement savings in BEE transactions, there would have been more losses and tragedies for workers.

Poor governance and bad investment decisions nevertheless played their part. In one case, the pension fund of the commercial and catering trade union (Saccawu) was placed in curatorship after R100 million of wrong payments, including allegedly more than R70 million to the union's investment company.[9] I recall one BEE transaction where union officials believed their members' provident fund should provide finance to support the union company's investments. They appeared quite cavalier about the use of workers savings to finance their BEE transactions. I was not surprised to find corrupt dealings by at least one union official. Fortunately this investment company fizzled out before it had a chance to waste its members' pensions.

There was also a hope among some in the white business establishment that having unions as effective shareholders might secure labour stability

– but this was not a pervasive benefit sought from having union–related investors.

All in all, the receptiveness of white business to transacting with union investment companies came as a surprise, given the combative struggles that had marked earlier years. But white business also wanted the comfort of knowing that their investment returns would not be available to unions directly. Frankly, they didn't want to support the creation of large strike funds that could be used against them one day.

Unions, as well, tended to favour a distance between themselves and their investment arms. A large independent source of income could result in unions and their officials becoming less accountable to their membership. Most union investment companies are therefore owned by union–initiated trusts whose beneficiaries are union members and dependants, with the dividends earmarked for socio–economic programmes like educational bursaries and job creation initiatives. Kopano is one exception, as Cosatu is a direct beneficiary.

Few real successes

The benefits for union members are highly concentrated, in just two companies. Today, MIC and HCI capture more than 90% of the union companies' investment interests,[10] and they alone have reported large dividend payments to their union shareholder trusts. MIC has disbursed R368 million.* It made a significant payment to the Mineworkers Investment Trust in 2009 on the understanding there would be an effective dividend holiday for the next five years. MIC is now free to reinvest its dividends for further growth. HCI has distributed R850 million to its shareholder trusts over the years. Copelyn raises the problem of the capacity of union shareholder trusts to spend large sums of money: 'It's pointless releasing more money unless you know what you are going to do with it. How much money can be handled? Up to a point, the money is very helpful; beyond that it can be very corrupting.'[11]

MIC and HCI have a good story to tell. Each of their unions has a large bursary scheme. MIC dividends have enabled NUM's education trust to fund almost four thousand bursaries, with close to six hundred

---

* In the financial year 2008/9, MIC made a R245 million distribution to the Mineworkers Investment Trust, which fully owns the company.

graduates by the end of 2009. Development projects, along with NUM's training centre, are all funded from MIC dividends. Sactwu says it manages the country's largest trade union bursary fund, along with a sizeable HIV/Aids programme.

For the rest of the union companies, there is an evident lack of transparency about the performance of their investments and payments, if any, to their shareholder trusts. Union members will struggle to get information on their companies. It is interesting that Naledi, in its research, was denied access to documentation and had to rely on interviews instead. Most union websites make no reference to their investment companies; and some investment companies, in particular Kopano, have websites with dismal information disclosure. In reality, these companies are public, having millions of union members as effective shareholders and therefore entitled to information. It is difficult to imagine how unions can require the corporations in which they organise to disclose information when their own companies are so poor at it. Ten to fifteen years on, it is reasonable to expect much more.

Ideals give way to high returns

Union companies have also not been strong on ethical investment policies. Two of these companies control the country's largest gaming conglomerates. None of the leading ones have any restriction on investing in the 'sin' sectors like gaming, alcohol and tobacco, or in the arms industry.

While most union companies have a similar shareholder structure, there is no blueprint or uniform model. In their early years, most had a consistent wish list for their investment criteria: only invest in companies with good labour and transformation policies; be active and influential or even control shareholders; make 'strategic' investments (which tended to be ill-defined). Overall, therefore, unions justified the establishment of union investment companies on the basis of 'social capitalism'.

But ideals soon gave way to opportunistic deal making, underpinned by a single strategic objective: to realise high returns. Only MIC and HCI have acquired control over sizeable businesses that enable them to meet the union movement's objective of organisational transformation. Over the years the BEE arena has become increasingly competitive;

possibly, therefore, union companies exhibited nervousness about being seen as aggressive shareholders, too strong on transformation, and as a result locked out of deals by white business. Whatever the reason, their company blurbs offer little to differentiate them from regular business-aligned BEE shareholders. The metalworkers' Numsa Investment Company describes itself as 'a leading diversified investment house focusing on high-return and market-leading companies'. In terms of its investment criteria, it targets firms with 'strong management teams', 'strong cash flows' and 'proven track record of profit history'.

Disputes flare

There are conflicts of interest that are unique to union business. Some recent experiences show just how sharp tensions can become. A case in point is that of the chemical workers' Ceppwawu Investments (CI),[*] which was attracting media attention at the time of writing.

CI has done what some (in particular, the mineworkers) have been careful to avoid. They have used an outside management company, the Letsema group, to run their investments; they have an explicit policy to invest in the sector in which their union organises; and they seek to finance their BEE transactions using the union members' provident fund.[†]

The first conflict emerged in 2008 over an investment in the pharmaceutical company Aspen. The provident fund had financed CI's acquisition by subscribing to preference shares in a special purpose vehicle created to hold the Aspen shares. This was in 2002. Later, the Financial Services Board ruled that the fund had exceeded prudential levels for unlisted investments, and required that it relinquish its preference shares. It was then found that CI had not issued the preference shares in the first place, which led to protracted arbitration, with a settlement of just over R500 million in 2008, after subscribing for the preference shares for R108 million. At the end of the day, a very good investment – but that triggered another conflict.

---

[*] The Chemical, Energy, Paper, Printing, Wood and Allied Workers Union established Ceppwawu Investments, with shares held by the Ceppwawu Development Trust. Its first investment was in Aspen in 2002.

[†] The Chemical Industries National Provident Fund.

Letsema's management agreement made provision for Letsema to receive a 27.5% share of profits realised from any investment. No one balked until Letsema, owned by two individuals, Isaac Shongwe and Derek Thomas, claimed R45 million of a net R170 million realised from the Aspen shares. A new union leadership disputed the claim, securing a court order in late 2009 that prevented Letsema from receiving any further payments from CI while court proceedings were in process. This came after Letsema had paid out the R45 million to itself, apparently contrary to an undertaking with the union that it would not do so while in dispute. The new union officials complained that Letsema's high profit participation conflicted with the purpose and spirit of the company and its development trust shareholder.[12] Ironically, CI marketing documentation, compiled by Thomas as chief executive of CI, promotes the company on the basis that it avoids the 'criticism of enrichment'. Thomas argued that their performance fees fell within the market norm.[13] It is unclear what norm this might be; it is above the fees of asset managers, who fully manage their assets and carry high compliance costs.

HCI provides another example of individuals getting exceptionally rich from union investments. Copelyn holds 10% of HCI, valued at R870 million, while Golding holds a 7% interest. MIC has doggedly refused to allow its management team to acquire shareholding, instead favouring professional salaries and incentives. NUM officials, however, have always made known their discomfort with very high remuneration, with the majority of their members earning under R5000 a month. The income inequalities that emerge with union investment activities are a major dilemma for trade unions. How does a trade union oppose the vast discrepancies in the private sector when it has the same in its own stable?

Shareholders and work representatives

Another rocky zone is the sectors of investment. Should a union company invest in the sector in which its union is active? CI follows the principle of investing in its own backyard. MIC, on the other hand, has a shareholders' compact preventing it from investing in the sectors in which NUM organises. It has also stayed away from privatisations that were not supported by the union movement. This has cut it out

146

of a considerable amount of BEE opportunity. Initially, NUM was involved in mining only, but later it began to organise in the construction and energy sectors. So, at a time of heightened BEE transactions in mining and the promise of an almost R800 billion state infrastructure programme, MIC is losing considerable potential opportunity. Yet it has stood firm on its policy. The CI approach is premised on the assumption that the union investment company may help mediate labour or union problems in any firm it is invested in. However, its strategy could also be seen as placing undue pressure on companies to transact with it – if a company refused to include CI in a deal, this could be interpreted as potentially courting conflict with the union.

HCI has steered in and out rather than clear of the textile sector. It had an interest in the clothing conglomerate Seardel until 2006, which it resumed again in 2008. Seardel was in trouble; the banks wanted a rights issue to correct the high levels of debt; and HCI underwrote with R200 million, giving it control of the group with a 70% interest. The union hoped that this would forestall retrenchments. HCI, however, found itself in a tricky position: a restructure plan did not include the KwaZulu-based Frame textile plant* – everything else, said Copelyn, could be turned around except that. For a while, though, he stepped back and let Ebrahim Patel do the running. The former Sactwu general secretary put his new position as minister of Economic Development to quick use by trying to mobilise state resources to save Frame. He didn't succeed, and HCI proceeded to close down a number of heavily loss-making Frame divisions.

When questioned in the media about the public flak, Copelyn responded: 'This is a real sore area for me. I've spent more than thirty years of my life focusing on Frame. My entire union career was centred around getting involved with the Frame workers – to be the guy to pull the plug on the thing has been the most horrific decision I've ever had to take. So public flak is a minor piece of my troubles.'[14]

Cosatu's Kopano also found itself in choppy waters for having an interest in a fishing company said to operate disreputably. In 2009, the federation's fishing desk picked a dispute with the Department of Marine and Coastal Management concerning the appointment of a mediation firm – one among them, argued Cosatu's fishing desk, is

---

* Frame Vertical Pipeline was closed in 2009, causing the retrenchment of 1200 employees.

invested in a fishing company and hence conflicted. After a deluge of protest letters, emails and press statements, word came down from Cosatu's headquarters, effectively saying 'Lay off'. The reason: Kopano also has a shareholding in this company. The firing line changed, with the sights turned to the head of the fishing desk, who became a casualty of this dispute.*

From the start, such conflicts have been evident, like an active volcano always threatening to erupt. Back in 1997, for example, Sarhwu took the startling decision to withdraw from the restructuring committee of the troubled airline Sun Air, which had been earmarked for privatisation. It did this, favouring its investment company's position as a member of the Virgin consortium, which was one of the bidders in the airline privatisation. Virgin subsequently withdrew from the bid and the workers were left unrepresented.[15] All this took place despite Cosatu opposition to privatisation.

Today union investment companies, as a category of potential BEE partners, have dropped down the list, replaced by employee share ownership schemes. With the exception of MIC and HCI, the lacklustre performance of union companies, with their failure to deliver on expectations, brings us back to a common preference I have found in white business: if there is no obvious commercial benefit offered by the usual BEE investors, then it's better to deal with employees or good causes with proven track records – of which there are many.

Carving out a vision for union investment companies, Copelyn pointed to unions in other countries having 'co-operated with, and even initiated, the development of financial institutions that focus on the need of working people rather than corporate accounts. These often lead to better lending rates for workers and invariably make loans to workers easier to obtain.'

To date, however, this is a vision that unions have yet to pick up on. Yet there are others worldwide – private individuals and companies – who are increasingly stepping into an area of social business with a profit motive. I look at this in more detail later; suffice it to ask here whether the unions and their investment companies will to some extent reinvent themselves and join this new business space.

---

* Gary Simpson was the head of Cosatu's fishing desk, based in Cape Town.

8

BEE's powder keg

People are discontented, tempers are short. There is sharp
talk. We should dance tonight.
– G/wi San, in Lewis-Williams & Pearce, *San spirituality*

Two far-flung communities on opposite sides of South Africa have
set their hopes for survival below the sands. In the east, a growing
sprawl of rural homes testifies to a dream that a platinum mining venture
will rescue the inhabitants from poverty. Another community, settled in
a dramatic and barren landscape in the northwest, clings to the hope the
desert will one day pour forth the bounty of diamonds it yielded in the
past.

I encountered the first community while advising another mine in
their area. In order to write openly and avoid further entanglement
between the two protagonists, I have called the community 'Tshepiso'
and the company 'Karabo Mines'.

The second community, in the Richtersveld, caught my attention after
a 10-year land claim dispute with government where the Constitutional
Court eventually ruled in favour of the claimants. The reason for
government's relentless resistance is the state-owned diamond mine,
Alexkor. After eighty years of mining, Alexkor is now a shadow of its
former self; despite this,[*] the government was in fear of an inordinately
large compensation claim.

For different reasons, both communities show just how difficult
it is to redistribute some of the country's wealth using the current
framework of corporate shareholding. They raise an alert as to whether
we should be trying to correct injustice and economic deprivation
through investments that are unlikely to deliver returns for years. The

---

[*] Although never publicly admitted.

149

Richtersveld also shows that the government appears no better equipped than the private sector in managing complex community dynamics and economic claims.

When I started advising in BEE transactions, community and other forms of broad-based ownership seemed compelling. If we had to redistribute via shareholding, then better to a wide number of people who are most in need. Black business-orientated investors did themselves no favours with their opportunistic and nonproductive behaviour – there seemed little to justify placing such groups at the head of the redistribution queue.

Experience has exposed my naivety. Some models of broad-based investment have emerged successful; others have not and may return to haunt both government and business. In my view, community shareholdings in the mining industry are of particular concern. Their individual and peculiar weaknesses may accumulate into a future political powder keg. By walking through the experience of these two communities, I hope to show the texture of these complex investment experiments to redress the economic marginalisation of the majority of black South Africans.

The 'Tshepiso' experience

Starting a new mine is inevitably an intricate task. The Tshepiso committee of traditional chiefs, mine staff, municipal officials, Church, civic and youth leaders crammed into hot, stuffy halls and met regularly to discuss the myriad pressing issues that emerge in new mining operations. Land compensation, new water reticulation systems, the removal and rebuilding of schools and the relocation of grazing land took up a large amount of committee time. Less immediate, but no less engaging, was the promised shareholding in the mine. It captured everyone's dream of a better future – multimillion-rand ownership in the mine was understandably a more attractive prospect than the few thousand rand offered as land compensation.

Shareholding was endlessly discussed: the question of equity and its associated risks; share ownership; the value of the shareholding; share payment; and when and how much money may be expected over the decades. Entitlement to benefits was the key issue. The shares were to be placed in trust for the collective benefit of the surrounding community as first priority and after that for others within the provincial boundary. Investment returns and any other income from the trust would fund socio-economic projects. Traditional leaders, however, believed their standing deserved a proportionately higher recognition than any other within the community. Among them, Kgosi Isaac,* sitting silent in the meetings, believed his entitlement to be the greatest.

In the months that followed, Isaac stirred and lobbied outside the confines of the halls to advance his position. He sought political and legal leverage, engaging the support of personalities who eagerly wrote to the mining company demanding endless explanations. Amidst this flurry of communication, Isaac remained quiet. The meetings progressed and the committee continued its business. When the trust was formed, committee members and advisers trundled the paths of dusty villages to ensure that as many people as possible had the chance to nominate their choice of trustees. Trustee training was provided and complex transactional agreements were drafted.

Part way through the process, my company was engaged to advise the mining house. The heated, labyrinthine manoeuvring involved in the transaction became too much for them to handle on their own. In the thick of community interactions, they also kept inadvertently stepping on the toes of local and provincial politicians and the irascible Jacinto Rocha of the Department of Mineral Resources too. The politicians took issue with community shareholding when we met.

Why are you giving shares to the community?

Well, it will be beneficial for them, we responded. *The returns from the investment will fund development and help alleviate poverty.*

But government deals with poverty, they insisted. Local business should be supported.

The company's transactional team thought it had been doing the right thing and would secure political accolades. How wrong we had been. We had failed to calculate how much we were interfering with the lines of patronage and political control.

The company, white miners on the wrong side of the political fence, was impotent against the muscle-flexing of the new black governing elite.

---

* Not his real name.

The community shareholding was halved and provision was made for a business consortium to get the other half. In addition, the consortium brought together large numbers of people and thus also qualified as broad-based empowerment. The trust and the consortium each received a 7.5% shareholding worth just under R150 million.

There was a third black investor group, disliked by the local community – the so-called 'strategic' investor, a company of the new political elite, based in Johannesburg. Identified as the value-adding partner, its presence was justified on the basis it would bring in high-level black business participation and was committed to building a black mining company. Despite these credentials, the Tshepiso people viewed it as an outsider with no legitimate claim on the mineral resources.

At the time of this transaction, there had been enough bad experience of community investments to signal caution. At one end of the trouble zone are the community disputes such investment trusts can trigger with the creation of new power centres and trustees guarding their positions for personal interest and gain. At the other end are poorly structured investments, where companies use superior resources and knowledge to give less than they claim to the community concerned.

We therefore thought it prudent to be extremely mindful of the trust's governance. Our approach to governance was two-pronged. As an immediate move, Karabo would be represented on the trust with some strong veto rights (akin to minority shareholder rights) for as long as the trust was indebted for the acquisition of the shares – the company had guaranteed the previously raised bank loan. Most of the vetoes covered budgeting and certain expenditures, with the intention of initiating a system of sound financial governance.

According to financial projections at the time, the loan repayment would be due in about seven years. Karabo had also undertaken to make an annual contribution to the trust from its corporate social investment funds. This would enable the trust to become active immediately and develop expertise in managing socio-economic projects. We thought it unreasonable to establish a trust and keep it dormant until the loan had been serviced. We hoped that the experience built up in handling the CSI sums would serve the trust well when it eventually received the much larger dividend payments to expend on projects.

The second provision for governance related to the period after the debt had been cleared. At that time the trust would receive substantial dividend payments and be entitled to sell up to half its shareholding in the mine. This would allow the trust to diversify its investment risk, while retaining a connection and commitment to the mine for the rest of its life. Any capital realised from the sale of shares could not be redistributed, either directly to the community or to projects. Instead it would be reinvested, with the returns used to finance community needs. In this way we hoped that the community would reap the benefits of the Karabo investment way beyond the life of the mine. Any sale or reinvestment of shares had to be referred to professional advisers.

When the transaction eventually concluded, we felt we had done a reasonably good job. The community interactions took a few years and were difficult but the committee and trustees had been well briefed on the meaning and implications of shareholding. Trustee selection had been conducted on an appropriate democratic basis with trustees receiving training in all matters relating to the management of a trust. At the time they claimed to be empowered by all the information and knowledge gained. The trust and the business consortium shared professional advisers, independently selected by the business consortium when it was bidding for the shareholding, while the strategic investor had its own advisory team.

However, our back-patting was short-lived as the job well done soon began to unravel.* Disputes flared. The traditional leaders agitated for greater shareholding and more employment of people from their farms. Community distrust of Karabo's motives fuelled a push to remove the company's veto powers in the trust deed. As had happened before when political pressure mounted, Karabo found it difficult to fend off the community barrage and conceded. When the shareholding was later raised to 9% for each of the three investor groups, the traditional leaders were allocated 1.5% of the trust's total shareholding. The mine stepped back from its veto rights, and agreed it would always employ an equal number of people from each of the farms.

Relations nevertheless remained bedevilled by conflict. The mine

---

* At this point, I was no longer involved – as the critics say, consultants are never around to sort out the mess they help create.

manager clashed with some among the Tshepiso committee, which escalated into demands for his removal, and death threats. In line with preferential procurement policies to deal as much as possible with local business, the security contract had been awarded to a local firm whose employees came from Tshepiso. Could the security officers be trusted to protect the mine manager? Uncertain, Karabo brought in external security guards. The trade unions became enmeshed with community dissatisfaction, resulting in annual strikes. And so it went on, one problem after another.

The stirring had many sources. Obviously, views differ depending on who you talk to. Here, I avoid getting embroiled in the parochial dynamics and focus on the broader, national significance. A key problem lies in the manner in which BEE ownership is transferred. As we have seen in Chapter 1, the sale of shares financed through debt is, on the whole, inherently unsustainable. It is a curious form of redistribution – in all probability you will end up with less than what you started with; you will not receive any economic benefit in the interim while debt is being serviced; and you will have to wait years before you receive cash in hand – which, in mining, may be ten years or more.

In a community like Tshepiso, daily needs are immediate – there must be food on the table, clothing for the children, school fees and health care. Waiting another decade for a company to deliver what you regard as your just return after a long history of political and economic deprivation doesn't seem right; an inherently unstable underlay to such community involvement is therefore inevitable.

Futhermore, communities do not have the resources or resilience to withstand the impact of market volatility. Karabo had just started to turn the corner when the markets crashed in 2008, and losses have once again escalated. It could take another ten years for Karabo's BEE investors to service their debt. All the community's hopes and expectations are invested in this one mine. This is not the community's idea of what ownership should be. It was misguided of us to think that discussions and training on shareholding and trusts in the run-up to the completion of the transaction would be adequate. At that stage, the content of the training was abstract and not fully comprehended.

The current default position is one of distrust. Karabo may have introduced black shareholders and managers but it still *feels* like a white company with a racial divide that has to be constantly negotiated. The final outcome is a sense of alienation between corporate and community interests that cuts deeper than race or who owns the economic assets.

Another case, attracting much press coverage, is the Modikwa mine of Anglo Platinum, 50% of which is owned by Patrice Motsepe's African Rainbow Minerals. The company tripped up over fractious community issues that led to violence, destruction of mine property and an investigation by the South African Human Rights Commission (HRC). It was a protracted and messy affair that prompted unexpected responses. The vocal human rights activist Rhoda Kadalie found herself inadvertently in defence of Anglo as a result of what she believed to be an unprofessional intervention by the HRC.

The HRC reported on the discontent of a small number among the community (fewer than a hundred households) who had refused to relocate as a result of the mine development, without mention of the 1600 households who were moved successfully. Anglo's relocation costs (including new homes, compensation, farm land, schools, clinics) amounted to R1 billion by 2008. 'Why would the commission fail to report these benefits?' asked Kadalie. 'It would have been heretical for the commission to report that Angloplat was actually helping people in poor rural communities progressively realise their constitutional rights to access housing, land, water, education and basic services at a scale and rate that exceeds the government's own investments.'[1]

History, emotions, different economic expectations and needs combine to make it nigh impossible to predict or manage the numerous consequences that wash off the back of such BEE transactions. Karabo and Anglo Platinum struggled to establish reasonable relations – and have yet to succeed, even with significant resources. Without doubt many mining companies have brought insufficient commitment and resources to finding equitable solutions. It is likely many operations are overvalued, with debt raised on onerous terms, and communities signing agreements without advice or understanding.

My advice to my corporate clients is always to do a fair deal – it is less likely to come back and bite. For many, however, this doesn't come naturally. In one case I found myself uncomfortably challenging the corporate morality of my client. We were dealing with transactional agreements and provisions for forced sale of shares. If the community investment trust defaulted, they could be forced to sell with a penalty imposed. I pointed out that might be acceptable if the trust was at fault but what if a default emerged because government changed the rules by, for example, disallowing such a trust to qualify as a BEE entity? The company's business would be placed at risk for no longer having a BEE shareholder and would therefore require the shares of the trust to go to another BEE investor. As a result, the trust could be forced to sell at a time when there could be a shortfall between the outstanding loan and the share price. Would it be fair to impose a penalty and make the trust liable for meeting the shortfall, putting what other assets it might have at risk? Unsurprisingly, the company didn't want to be liable for picking up the tab, but after some hard talking they agreed that the community trust should not be unreasonably exposed to risk.

Risk exposure is high for mining communities. As with Kabalo, communities tend to be offered shareholding in the mining operations in their area. They do not have a portfolio of BEE investments that would enable them to spread their risks – the reason we made provision for the Tshepiso Trust to be able to sell some of Karabo's shares for reinvestment in other financial assets. If you add to this the inherent difficulties in debt financing and the highly probable outcome that community investment trusts will end up with less than their initial investment, these community investment trusts could become BEE's powder keg.

The Richtersveld experience

Moving on to the other side of the country, the Richtersveld is a vast area of desolate Martian beauty, whose original habitants were the Khoekhoen and some San people from as early as AD 700. About 3500 people occupy around half a million hectares, with four villages dispersed across the landscape. The Richtersveld is part of Little Namaqualand, the home of the Nama people (the core population), the Basters (people of mixed descent), a small Xhosa population who came for the mining, and a few whites.

In the late Nineties the Richtersveld community put in a claim for a narrow strip of land that runs along the Atlantic west coast, from the Gariep (formerly Orange) River that divides South Africa from Namibia to just beyond Port Nolloth in the south. Some 85 000 hectares were in dispute, owned by the state-owned diamond company Alexkor Ltd.

The claim is particularly interesting as it included every resident in the area, and not just the indigenous people – only white contract mineworkers were excluded. Yet government tried to use this non-ethnic approach as part of its argument to counter the claim. For, how could the Basters, a white trader and the recently settled Xhosa be legitimately included in a dispossession case?

In the early nineteenth century the Basters came to the Richtersveld, intermarrying with the Nama. They were followed much later, in 1949, by the 'Bosluis Basters', who, on being squeezed out of their land in Bushmanland, trekked some 300 kilometres to settle around the southern villages of Lekkersing and Eksteenfontein. Floors Strauss, one of the leaders of the land claim, was a small boy during the arduous journey of people, wagons and livestock. 'The Richtersveld became our Canaan; Bushmanland was Egypt.' This explains why they turned their back on a restitution claim on their former land. 'People felt that that had been a bad time [in Bushmanland], with bad memories. People believe that God is always with us in what is done here in the Richtersveld.'[2]

For everyone to be included in the claim, proof was needed that not just the Nama but all the Richtersveld people constituted a community. They gathered evidence – oral as well as documentation – that immigrants like the Basters 'had to conform to its [the Nama's] rules'. Even the later immigrants, the Bosluis Basters and the Xhosa, while not as integrated as the Basters, had obtained 'citizenship' of Richtersveld, which entitled them to full access to pastures, and had subjected themselves to certain Nama rules.[3] A neighbouring village, Steinkopf, was excluded as the Richtersveld Nama disputed their claims to be true Nama, 'as they [Steinkopf people] mainly speak Afrikaans and allegedly did not retain Nama traditions'.[4]

The dogged resistance of the government against the Richtersveld community stood in sharp contrast to the commitment of the ANC to support dispossessed communities through the Restitution of Land Rights Act. Quite remarkably, it argued that the Nama had not been dispossessed as a result of racial discrimination – a requirement for land to be returned to its original owners. The scales weighed heavily against the community and its small team of advisers, the Legal Resources Centre (LRC), as the state mobilised large teams of legal heavyweights in its court challenges.

In the first round, in the Land Claims Court, the community lost. In the second round, in the Supreme Court of Appeal, they won. But then government and Alexkor took the case to the Constitutional Court. It did not rule in their favour, but instead affirmed not just the community's claim to the land but also to the mineral resources, which were, by then, seriously depleted.

The problems of the Richtersveld people seem always traceable back to money; whether it was in the mid-1920s, when diamonds were discovered and they were progressively denied access to their land, or in current times, when government faced the prospect of a very large compensation claim for diamonds extracted in the Alexander Bay area – although some in the Richtersveld suspect government resistance was to do with the fact that 'we are not really black'. The irony did not escape one interviewee: 'We were not white enough under apartheid, and we are not black enough now.' Money also appears to be the reason behind fresh divisions that emerged in the community after signing the deed of settlement with government.

After the Constitutional Court ruling, government and the community began negotiations to agree a settlement. There were suggestions the diamonds extracted over the past eighty years might be valued as high as R10 billion. The Richtersveld community was claiming nowhere near as much. They put R1.5 billion on the table for minerals extracted and about R1 billion for land rehabilitation, along with R10 million for hardship suffered.

In the end, a very different settlement was negotiated, which added up to a total cash commitment by government of R485 million, along with some small change costs. The settlement amounted to a complex transaction that had the Richtersveld community crying foul before the new dispensation had left the starting block. But this got lost amidst the fanfare of the announcement by the minister responsible, Alec Erwin.*

---

* Alec Erwin was minister of Public Enterprises until the removal of Thabo Mbeki as president.

Time and again I was told how Erwin had lured the community representatives, the CPA,* away from their legal representatives to reach agreement. As time passed, the CPA would sign off on parts of the settlement and return to their legal advisers, who would advise against what had just been agreed. Eventually the time came to present the proposed settlement to a gathering of the community. The LRC prepared an analysis of the agreement. However, this is where things get murky. I was told the CPA presented the government's summary and not the LRC analysis. The CPA claims the community voted in favour of the settlement while others maintain too many had walked out for the vote to be representative.

When I visited a year later, aggrieved community members were still expressing bitterness. 'I was very hurt when I saw that they had signed. The people who signed weren't involved from the beginning and they didn't refer to the community,' complained an elder of Kuboes village, Maria Farmer. Erwin, people say, had appealed to their ANC comradeship, arguing that if they waited for the approval of their lawyers they would wait for many more years. I did wonder if government's stated position – that marginalised communities should always have the benefit of independent professional advice – applied only to the private sector.

The signing of the agreement was the first mistake. It drove an early wedge into the community's hitherto united face. 'A table has four legs and if one leg is not good, then the whole table is a problem. By signing that agreement, we feel that one of the legs is not healthy,' said an activist in the land claim, Minah Adams. But the CPA chairman Willem Diergaardt countered, 'We couldn't fight forever and forever.'

Inevitably, CPA members attracted suspicion. As latecomers to the land claim struggle, community members ruminated on the CPA's intentions: were they in it for their own gain? Why had the stalwarts withdrawn from the CPA? Strauss commented on his choice to stand down: 'It is very dangerous for one person to always drive things. We had the land, we were strong and I thought that the next step would be easy.'

Once the wedge had been lodged, other differences followed. The

---

* The CPA is the Communal Property Association, a legally constituted body that managed the land claim and is responsible today for the implementation of the settlement agreement.

inclusion of Basters (still prominent in the CPA) and Xhosa was thrown into question. 'Their ancestors were not part of the pain and suffering,' said Farmer, who smiled because her late husband was a Baster. Diergaardt felt stung by the criticisms: 'It's harder now. We fought against government with one voice, but to fight now against your own people ...'

There is a pattern here – evident across the country and one that has cascaded down from national politics. New disputes and new interests surface as soon as money and power become tangible. Once this happens, the institutional strengths and the protections (whether legal or otherwise) to secure community interests are severely tested. Most of current-day community initiatives are struggling to stand up to the test – although I discuss an exception, the Royal Bafokeng and its highly successful investment company, in the next chapter.

The success of the land claim hinges on the settlement agreement. There were a number of components to this agreement. These included the mining operations and how they should progress, along with the transfer of the surface mining rights from Alexkor to the community; the transfer of Alexkor's mariculture and agriculture operations; reparation payments; and institutional arrangements.

In terms of the agreement, future mining is to be managed under an unincorporated joint venture, the pooling and sharing joint venture (PSJV), with Alexkor having a 51% interest and the community 49%. The surface mineral rights will be pooled with the marine rights of Alexkor, and exploited under the PSJV. At the time of writing, this had not yet been concluded.

The 2007 deed of settlement is what might be called a 'keep-your-fingers-crossed' agreement, as the risks associated with this settlement are not adequately addressed. No one can say with any certainty whether there is a commercial case for further mining. This means the Richtersveld community's claim on former benefits from mining has been traded for unknown and uncertain future benefits.

The advocate Geoff Budlender, who assisted the LRC, argued the risks were even further escalated by linking the fortunes of the Richtersveld community to Alexkor, notorious for its poor performance. Budlender says that Erwin, by then committed to the revival of state-owned enterprises in contrast to a previous policy of selective privatisation, insisted that Alexkor be part of the settlement. The community had wanted the right to choose its mining partner and discussions had taken place with other mining companies. Budlender challenged Erwin, 'Would you put your pension in Alexkor?'[5] Unlikely.

Budlender felt the reparations the community was entitled to were being used to capitalise Alexkor's failed operations. Given the latter's control of the PSJV, it could finance marine operations at the expense of surface exploration. And, having done this, it has the right to offer its shares to the Richtersveld community and exit the joint venture in five years. The community has the right to call in Alexkor's share of the PSJV before that, but onerous conditions should be met.

The attachment to equity ownership as a key source of empowerment has resulted in the failure to uphold one key fact: the potential to empower is only as good as the asset. In mining, the availability of reserves is crucial to the success of any mining company. But a big question mark hangs over the value of the reserve to which the Richtersveld community are entitled. There is no recent exploration information on how much value lies below the surface and much is believed to be depleted. Ten years before the settlement, Alexkor recommended that government immediately invest around R250 million in an exploration programme.[6] In the Richtersveld settlement, however, government has offered the PSJV R200 million to recapitalise mining operations, including exploration. It is safe to assume that more millions are required to restart surface mining. Government is under no obligation to top up, even though the agreement makes provision for a government guarantee under certain circumstances.

It is impossible to value any mining operation with an unknown reserve base. In the 2008/9 financial year Alexkor reported an operating loss of almost R78 million, against a slight profit of just under R6 million the previous year, much of the loss attributed to the economic downturn and volatile diamond prices. But, as the figures show, a turnaround does not promise even adequate returns.

In reality, Alexkor is not a mining company; it manages other mining companies that are contracted to it and are responsible for mining the marine resource, which is becoming increasingly difficult to exploit. I spoke to miners who blame climate change; certainly the increasingly poor sea conditions along the West Coast have reduced the number of days for diving. Shortly before I arrived, parts of the coast had been hit by what the community termed a 'tsunami' – fishing boats in Port Nolloth were wrenched from their moorings and dumped on the rocky beach. Locals suspect the ocean bed has been disturbed by years of marine extraction and blame the mining companies.

Apart from mining, there are other uncertainties. Alexkor's so-called non-core farming activities have been transferred to the Richtersveld community. These had formed part of Alexkor's social responsibility. In the past, the mines offered a market. But today, with vastly scaled-down operations all along the coast, these businesses now find themselves too far from potential markets. Alexkor reported to parliament that of the four farms, two are closed (dairy and citrus) and two were doing well (oysters and ostrich).

Reparation payments amounted to R190 million, to be paid into an investment holding company owned by the community trust. The capital is to be grown and preserved, with the community benefiting from the returns. Some of this capital, however, may be invested in a development company earmarked to hold all the economic interests of the community, including the mining and the farms. I worry that the capital will be eaten away if it's invested in either the PSJV's mining operations or the farms.

Government and officialdom often have little appreciation of commercial risk. The Richtersveld is not an isolated incident. In northern KwaZulu-Natal I came across a successful community claim for land bearing a state-owned forest and pulp and paper plant. Community members told me government intended to transfer ownership to them. They were confused and suspicious, but the idea of owning a factory was appealing.

I spoke to the government official responsible. He confirmed the intention to transfer ownership as well as the difficulty of dealing with the intrigues and differences between the various community groups earmarked as beneficiaries.

Is the plant making a profit?

Oh no, he said, *it was never intended as a commercial venture but to create jobs.*

Why give people a loss-maker?
We appointed consultants, and they have devised a turnaround strategy.
Oh dear.

Complexity in redistribution

The circumstances of Karabo and Richtersveld are very different. Ritchersveld is a clear case of restitution in which the ownership of mineral rights was restored to the community. The right to compensatory payment was made on the basis of past wrongs, but the proceeds were then earmarked for future benefit through an investment in a mine. The Tshepiso community never owned the mineral rights beneath their land, but they envisage themselves as the rightful owners – thinking little of the legal status of the state as the custodian of the country's mineral resources. They too therefore believe that they have an entitlement to the future benefits related to the extraction of 'their' mineral resources.

It is not my intent here to debate the rights and wrongs of their respective entitlements. I start from the premise that there has been and remains strong pressure for the redistribution of economic assets across a broad base of people. To date, the principal vehicle by which this is achieved in the private sector is the transfer of equity ownership. I want to explore the appropriateness of this for poor people; my accounts of the Tshepiso and Richtersveld cases go some way to doing so.

I wish to go further and explore a framework in which we may better consider economic redistribution. I don't envisage the unwinding of equity ownership as an option. Take the mining sector: scores and scores of community investment trusts now hold different levels of BEE shareholding in mining companies for communities dispersed far and wide. No matter how imperfect their investment trusts, they are unlikely to abandon them – a whole new constellation of vested interests has already coalesced. But there may be opportunities to restructure what has been done and put alternatives in place that better meet people's redistribution needs.

Lessons of Eastern Europe

The former communist countries of the Soviet Union and Central and Eastern Europe provide an unprecedented case of economic transformation in terms of breadth and speed. Countries shifted from one economic system to another in ten to fifteen years. South Africa is not seeking to go this far. Nevertheless, the complexities of change are no less. Like the former socialist states, we need to include the vast bulk of the population in a functional and formal market economy. What lessons can we learn?

Transformation in former communist countries was characterised by privatisation, with each country emphasising different objectives. The most prevalent was increased efficiency of enterprises. But two lesser objectives are important to us: creating political support for the market economy to ensure a barrier against returning to communism; and achieving a fairer distribution of assets.[7] From the South African perspective we too seek a barrier against reverting to political instability stirred by disaffected and marginalised citizens. It is important that black South Africans believe the economy works for them. Economic inclusiveness is crucial and, given our history, this must translate into a more equitable distribution of economic assets.

As for the other objective, the voucher system was a key tool for a fair distribution of assets, favoured in Russia and the Czech Republic, for example. In Russia, however, there was preferential access for those termed 'insiders', notably work collectives of managers and employees and members of the former *nomenklatura* – the former party functionaries who controlled the government, banks and industry. The programme in the Czech Republic offered equal access vouchers, which people bought for nominal sums. They then traded these vouchers for direct shareholding in enterprises or indirect shareholding by using the vouchers to buy into investment funds. This gave rise to sizeable institutional shareholding in the economy; but, without an established regulatory environment, many of these funds became the source of much abuse. There is a large body of research that finds the Russian programme unsuccessful, in part because of the preferential access, against the equal access vouchers of the Czech Republic, said by some to have been a source of economic growth in that country.[8]

Preferential access
The issue of access is significant for BEE policy. Our approach is one of

preferential access, whether government or companies are responsible for the distribution of assets. Companies are entitled to select their BEE partners. It shouldn't be any other way; forcing unwanted shareholders onto companies creates begrudging relationships and is bound to backfire. That said, access is skewed, governed in the main by networks (political ones are most helpful), any established relationships a BEE group may have in business, and of course luck. Poor communities and individuals tend to be short on all of these.

Government also trades access on a preferential basis, which inevitably translates into political patronage. The worst offender at national level that I have found is the Department of Mineral Resources. They err in two ways. Mining companies applying for conversion of older-order to new-order mining rights find they are 'told' which BEE parties they should transact with. In the case of new exploration and mining rights, evidence points to officials dispensing these licences on a highly selective basis, with no transparency to hold them to account. The only parties I have *never* found to receive preferential access are mining communities – the only grouping that *should* be entitled to preference.

That said, they tend to be party to BEE transactions simply because mining companies cannot ignore them. But in the absence of a framework to govern community shareholding, the terms of the relationship tend to be determined by the companies themselves. I would more than hazard a guess that most companies are ill equipped to manage the complexities inherent in such relationships and disinclined to negotiate fair deals. Simply defining a mining community is a fraught process. Where do you draw the boundary? Almost inevitably, there is an arbitrary element in such exercises.

Arbitrary redistribution

To return to the lessons of the former communist countries. In some programmes, access to assets was arbitrary. This was evident in management–employee buyouts, in contrast to the voucher system – 'a worker loses or gains depending on whether he happens to be in a "good" or a "bad" firm.'[9] Equally, in South Africa, there is arbitrariness in the distribution of shareholding that may be unintentionally exacerbated by policy.

After crafting the new legislative framework for the mining industry, the minister responsible at the time, Phumzile Mlambo-Ngcuka, wrote: 'As a nation, we need to be careful of gate keeping. Government has an obligation to a broad-based constituency, and we have to service every one of our people. For assets that are state-owned, and in transactions facilitated by public policy, broad-based empowerment is a must.'[10] A year later she picked up on this theme again: 'Even if you have six mines, we want you to have six partners.'[11]

Sound intentions, it would seem. However, the consequences of promoting large numbers of new entrants are worrying. Firstly, the arbitrary nature of the deal means some get good assets, others don't; you live above platinum, I live above chrome. Hence you do a lot better than me, which makes me feel aggrieved. How are such inequalities mediated?

Secondly, the wide dispersion of shareholding, with individuals or groups unlikely to hold more than one investment, has the unwanted consequence of increasing investment risk. There is no or limited opportunity to spread risk, either by having a portfolio of investments or holding an interest in a collective investment vehicle like a mining fund. This thought from one of the US's investment luminaries is worth bearing in mind: 'Your ability to predict next year's investment winner is no better than your ability to predict next week's lottery winner. A diversified portfolio of many investments might make you a loser during a year or even a decade, but a concentrated portfolio of few investments might ruin you forever.'

Paying for redistribution

There is a very important difference between the redistribution efforts of ex-communist countries and those in South Africa – the matter of price and payment. Ordinarily, citizens in the former acquired equity without payment or for nominal amounts. In South Africa, redistribution is effected through the sale of equity at market price, with some financial facilitation. The problem is that the bulk of BEE was transacted between 2004 and 2008, when market prices were very high. Further stress, of course, is added by the fact that debt has had to be raised to pay for these acquisitions. As we have seen in Chapter 1, it is difficult to sustain such equity ownership, bringing into question the use of BEE ownership as a means for redistribution – and particularly so for impoverished communities.

In mining, however, there is some free distribution of assets, but of the wrong kind. The opaque dispensation of exploration and mining rights to black individuals and entities selected by government officials is dubious and does not qualify as an equitable distribution of economic assets. Recipients of largesse invariably engage in rent-seeking, trading their rights to the highest bidder. Herein lies a cost to the economy that is not ameliorated by potential benefits from redistribution.

Redistribution needs good governance

Institutional capacity and governance are additional issues that are important in shaping a workable framework for redistribution. BEE policy puts much of the responsibility for equity transfers on the private sector. It certainly has the institutional capacity for this, but this is not to imply it has the willingness to negotiate in good faith. The power balance is hugely misaligned, with communities lacking the knowledge, expertise and resources to match their corporate counterparts. Further, communities will more often than not lack stable governance structures through which to manage such negotiations and later the investments. The potential for BEE shareholding to stir conflict and factionalism is high. 'Each community for their own' is the current motto that underpins these transactions, leaving communities vulnerable to poorly structured transactions.

An agreed framework that defines the relationships and interests between mining companies and their communities has yet to emerge. Those that do exist elsewhere have tended to evolve over many years. Canada, for instance, has developed impact and benefit agreements over some 25 years. They follow a standard format drafted in contractual language, and in many respects are analogous to commercial contracts.[12] Over time, as indigenous communities have become more experienced in negotiating these agreements, the socio-economic provisions have become more explicit and detailed and state involvement has receded.

In a nutshell, BEE ownership policy seeks to redistribute economic assets to those who don't have the resources to pay, but who must pay if they want to participate. Access therefore is not mediated on an equitable basis and is arbitrary. And where assets may be free – as in a state-awarded mining right – the process is no more equitable or less arbitrary. Payment of income earned or wealth accumulated is deferred for years. None of this adds up to a workable solution for wealth redistribution.

Who in business is responsible?

To move from the beneficiaries of redistribution to those who are expected to make their assets available: businesses. The obligation to redistribute may be a difficult call to make for a number of reasons. If BEE ownership does not also bring the promise of productive BEE participation – which invariably it doesn't – then it becomes compensatory in intent. This raises the question of who is responsible; for a start, surely not a foreign investor (which current policy requires)? So, how do we manage redistribution within the context of globalisation? We don't have the leverage China has to impose stringent conditions on foreign investors. You could go a step further and ask whether new economic value, created after the democratic elections in 1994, should be captured for compensatory reasons. This in turn raises the issue of timing. Any compensation process requires speedy resolution; it should not be carried out over extended periods of fifteen or twenty years or more. None of this has been adequately thought through and debated.

The more I have worked in the area of BEE ownership and researched for this book, the more I return to the view that shareholding is not an appropriate tool by which to redistribute the country's economic assets – recall Mamphela Ramphele, who criticises a compensatory approach and sees it a risk to transformation.

That's not to say that equity could not have been a source of compensation. Look again at the transactional costs of BEE. Take the equity deals of the big four banks: the sale of 10% equity cost them somewhere between 2% and 3.5% of their market capitalisation. The banks, therefore, could have given away around 3% without being any worse off than if they'd sold 10%. Three percent of the market capitalisation of the JSE would have provided a sizeable and valuable share portfolio that could have been structured as a unit trust for the benefit of black South Africans or a fund whose returns might be invested for the collective benefit of South Africans.

But we didn't follow this path and we need to deal with what we have created. It is important therefore to extract the best of BEE performance and use this as a basis for review and change. This brings me to the category of broad-based entities, the early generation of professionally run companies identified in Chapter 2 that have invested in growth, while their shareholder base ensures a measure of wealth redistribution.

9

The best of BEE

I discussed how leading broad-based companies offered better value to the economy than any other. Those larger and more established are ahead of everyone – as far as productive investment goes, in exercising control over sizeable businesses, and even when it comes to starting up their own new enterprises. I also found several such companies have been prominent in major BEE transactions, putting them at risk of falling into the 'usual suspects' folder with the derogatory 'enrichment' label.

Yet, I am bound to declare, South Africa needs more companies from this category. This aligns with the results of Scott Shane's[*] research: it is not start-ups but the more established firms who have made it to the next level, that are good for growth. It would seem we now have a small core of medium-sized BEE companies that do in fact offer a glimpse of the kind of restructured corporate sector that was first envisaged with BEE. But if they are to have impact on the economy they need space to grow – without detractors holding them back for already having taken too much from the BEE plate.[†]

The companies concerned are all professionally managed, with development and education trusts as direct shareholders, sometimes having staff and institutional shareholding. I'll refer to them as 'social corporations' (profit-making, with social objectives as well) to distinguish them from the 'social businesses' (not-for-profit) promoted by the Nobel laureate Muhammad Yunus. They vary in their character and corporate cultures, but there are some shared features that contribute to their success.

Here I deal with the most prominent – and wish the list was longer. In net asset value terms the top three are: Royal Bafokeng Holdings

---

[*] An international expert into entrepreneurship, whom I return to later.

[†] There are policy implications here, discussed in Part 3.

(RBH), by far the largest black-owned company in South Africa; HCI; and Kagiso Trust Investments (KTI). In addition there are MIC and Thebe Investment Corporation. The only well-established broad-based women's group, Women's Development Business Investment Holdings, is strictly an investment holding company with no controlling interests. However, via its trust shareholding, it supports micro-financing and other business initiatives within the WDB family that are critical for marginalised rural economies.

I have dealt closely with most of the above companies for years, initially in research and later in transactions. They have several characteristics in common. All have had their fair share of knocks in the market place, some emerging with bigger scars than others; all have experienced a sequence of learning curves as they matured and institutionalised; all increasingly display the signs of good corporate governance associated with large corporations.

I begin with a brief overview of the companies concerned – except for HCI and MIC, which have already been covered.

Royal Bafokeng Holdings

It is interesting that the largest BEE company in South Africa is the one that never established itself as such.* Nor does it have the cloak of political correctness that helped kick-start the others discussed here. The Bafokeng people had a clear advantage – ownership of a highly valued asset, one of the world's largest reserves of platinum group metals – achieved not simply by an assertion of their rights but through a determination to act on them.

In the 1800s the Transvaal Republic expropriated their land. At the time it covered some two thousand square kilometres northwest of Johannesburg, hemmed in by Rustenburg to the south and the Pilanesberg mountains to the north. Using sympathetic Lutheran missionaries to hold title on their behalf, they bought back the land in the late nineteenth century. They raised the money by sending their men to work on Kimberley's diamond mines, by selling cattle and through

---

* Niall Carroll, chief executive of Royal Bafokeng Holdings, and the administration executives Thabo Mokgatlha and Bruno Seabelo, as well as the American researcher Sue Cook were interviewed for this chapter by the author in 2009.

communal subscription. It's unimaginable that illicit diamonds didn't contribute towards what had belonged to the Bafokeng in the first place – if so, sweet justice, indeed!

In later years they did battle with the Bophuthatswana government, which had signed away their mineral rights to mining houses, and then again with Impala Platinum Holdings (Implats), which had been a recipient of those rights. Eventually, as the Nineties came to a close, they reached an agreement with Implats which entitled them to 22% of the company's taxable income from five Bafokeng areas on which the company mined, and a minimum 1% royalty of the gross selling price of platinum group metals or any other metals in the Bafokeng region. In addition, they got one million shares in Implats and a seat on the board. It was a good deal for them. Ironically, the man who headed the Implats negotiations, Steve Kearney, crossed the table shortly afterwards to build a new resources company for the Bafokeng, leveraging off the hundreds of millions of rand that had started to flow from the Implats royalties.

It didn't end there. New mining legislation changed the rules, and in 2006 the Bafokeng reached another agreement with Implats – to convert its future cash flows from the royalty into a 13.4% shareholding in Implats. This has made a rural community of around 300 000 people the single largest shareholder in the world's second largest platinum producer. Today, their shareholding is worth some R16 billion.[1] It is unencumbered by debt, and is producing a good dividend stream to fund future investments and community development.

In itself this is a good story, but over the past six years the Bafokeng have done even better. They have shifted from a motley collection of nonperforming assets to quality corporate investments held by the RBH, with a net value of an estimated R31 billion in 2009, against R22 billion in 2008 when the company felt the full impact of the global market crisis. Dividend income in 2008 was R1.6 billion, with cash in hand of more than R5 billion. No other BEE company in South Africa comes close to this. These numbers make RBH the wealthiest community-owned corporation on the African continent and perhaps in the world.

In those six years, after engaging a professional investment team under the former Deutsche Bank SA MD, Niall Carroll, and with the merger of all its own investments under one roof, the RBH, the company has accumulated a portfolio of 19 investments, ranging from fairly small to very large (Vodacom and Implats).

Kagiso Trust Investments

KTI also had unusual beginnings evolving from the liberation struggle. Its initiator, Eric Molobi, ran what was effectively the largest legal anti-apartheid fund in the Eighties. The European Union had been persuaded to support the victims of apartheid, which resulted in some R300 million of funding. Kagiso Trust (KT) was created as one of the conduits. After the unbanning of the ANC in 1990 and as the country edged towards democracy, Molobi saw the writing on the wall. Foreign governments would direct official donor funding to the new South African government, leaving KT with a shortfall. Yet there remained educational and development programmes that deserved support. Molobi and colleagues looked at the still unknown waters of black empowerment and decided to dip in their toes.

So it came about that KTI was launched in 1993 with KT as its sole shareholder, and with the help of loans of R26 million from KT and JPMorgan. Today KTI has a net asset value, conservatively valued at around R5 billion, and a healthy bank balance enabling it to break away from the usual BEE financing conundrum and start investing off its own balance sheet. Over the years, other shareholders have come on board; KT remains the controlling shareholder with just over 50%, joined by a staff trust and Remgro (Rembrandt group) as the largest non-BEE shareholder.

KTI is among the few BEE companies that have continued to grow a financial services offering. It has a variety of operational subsidiaries in direct competition to the financial establishment. While it holds shares in a few leading financial institutions, it has not followed the path of many of its counterparts – sinking their own operational financial interests into the large institutions after becoming the latter's BEE shareholders.

When BEE collapsed in the later Nineties, black-owned groups were criticised for not getting their hands dirty in real (rather than speculative) business. Some took this to heart and set up operations, particularly in the financial sector where they might achieve a competitive edge with government supporting them by using their services. However, as soon as the charters and Codes had established the 25% ownership benchmark, black corporate control receded. The focus shifted to getting a cut of equity in the established companies, removing the incentive to run in parallel small black-controlled financial firms. So we saw, for example, a reputable and successful black-controlled asset manager like Futuregrowth incorporated into Old Mutual – today a FTSE 100 company – after its controlling shareholder Wiphold had acquired just 1.7% equity in Old Mutual.

This is perhaps one of the clearest cases of BEE reinforcing conglomeration rather than contributing towards a less concentrated corporate structure amenable to new entrants. Molobi did not want this and hence guarded KTI's independence and right to pursue equity investments in the established financial groups while retaining their own operations. Inevitably this led to a conflict of interest. FirstRand, which really wanted KTI as its lead partner in its BEE share sale, found a novel loophole. There were two sources of conflict. First, KTI held shares in the competing financial services company, Metropolitan Group, while KTI's own shareholders had changed to include two other financial institutions – Old Mutual and Nedbank. In the first conflict, FirstRand decided to transact directly with the Trust, selling KTI just a tiny shareholding as an incentive for it to manage the KT group's interest. In the second conflict, it couldn't tolerate allowing two of its competitors receiving benefit from its BEE deal. As a result, these shareholders had to sell out to the more acceptable Remgro.

Apart from financial services, the only other large asset under KTI's control is the listed Kagiso Media. At one stage KTI had tried to dispose of it to Nail, then the largest black-controlled corporation keen to be kingpin in the media sector. I asked Molobi why, and he claimed to be tired of the political pressure that came with being a media owner. Today, KTI is probably thankful the deal never went through – for the time being, Kagiso Media is its biggest contributor of profit (almost R175 million in 2009). All in all, KTI has accumulated a sizeable portfolio, with over forty of its own companies and investments in others.

Thebe Investment Corporation

Thebe has its roots in the ANC. Its chairman, Vusi Khanyile, worked in the organisation as its deputy treasurer-general soon after its return from exile. 'I was never a political leader,' says Khanyile, who began his career with Anglo American. 'From the start, we agreed that I would be there for two years.'[2] With a background in finance, Khanyile wanted to get back into business, but with a transformation agenda. He, along with a few others within the ANC, initiated Thebe and its shareholder, the Batho Batho Trust, enlisting heavyweights like Nelson Mandela, Walter Sisulu and Beyers Naudé as early trustees.

Thebe was capitalised with R100 000 in 1993. Seventeen years later, it had an asset value in its 2008/9 financial year of just over R3 billion, with profits of R225 million. Shareholding has changed, with the Batho Batho Trust owning 52% and the rest held by staff and financial institutions.

Of all the BEE groups, Thebe has the most interesting portfolio of investments. It reflects Khanyile's earlier commitment to being in the 'middle market'. For Khanyile, the highly concentrated corporate sector in South Africa suggested that the best opportunities lay in middle-sized enterprises. This is the arena of high growth rates, and therefore, he believed, black business could do well playing in this field. Equally, however, the risks are higher than for mature companies. So, it is not surprising that hard lessons came very quickly for Thebe. Its collection of small banks that had gone into the FBC Fidelity fold collapsed amidst jitteriness about the resilience of middle-sized banks in the wake of the Asian crisis. But Khanyile has stuck with the middle and remained consistent to a vision to 'actively manage businesses' – although there have been a few deviations, such as shareholding in Vodacom and Shell, the latter arising because Thebe established Tepco, a fuel distribution chain.

Thebe has a strong niche in the tourism sector, criticised for its slow uptake of empowerment ownership. Here, it has more than fifteen business operations. Its enterprise division housing its other investments (just under twenty) has a strong focus on financial services. Thebe Capital houses investments that are strictly portfolio in nature – Vodacom and Shell, for instance. Companies have come and gone in the Thebe stable, but Khanyile may now lay claim to knowing the middle market well – this gives a unique positioning for a BEE company.

WDB Investment Holdings

The WDB group is the brainchild of Zanele Mbeki, formerly South Africa's First Lady. She started the banking arm soon after returning from exile, to provide poor rural women with access to micro loans. She admired Yunus's Grameen Bank, based in Bangladesh, and put a replica in place – but, she concedes, she miscalculated the willingness of the financial establishment to support her efforts. Like Molobi, therefore, she saw opportunity in BEE as a source of capital to fund the bank, and WDBIH was launched with the not-for-profit WDB Trust as its sole shareholder to this day.

Unlike the other social corporations, WDBIH works closely with its shareholder and is forthright in its mandate to be an active investor by participating in the board of companies in which it invests; as its head, Tanya Slabbert, points out, 'Part of our cash incentive, as professionals running Investment Holdings, is based on how we have driven transformation in our investments.'[3]

In recent times the group restructured to strengthen the links between the investment arm, micro-financing and the WDB Trust – together they employ almost three hundred people, mostly spread throughout the country dealing with micro credit in the main. As a result, you find the investment team involved in the unusual – for example, a programme to provide cheap eyeware to poor communities, by supporting social entrepreneurs in acquiring diagnostic kits, and then getting a return on every pair of glasses sold. This keeps them close to the soul of the organisation.

Their investments are diverse, with some blue chip gems. They are in resources such as the petroleum multinational subsidiary BPSA and an Anglo American coal venture; and in the country's leading services group Bidvest and the financial services groups FirstRand and Discovery Holdings.* WDBIH, however, lags behind the others in net asset value – probably a reflection of the difficulties they have found as a women's company in securing lead investor positions. Their net asset value for the financial year of 2008/9 was some R480 million – a higher figure is expected in the coming year, reflecting improved economic conditions.

---

* My company was involved in both the BPSA and Discovery transactions, enabling a good working knowledge of the group.

Success factors

It is always difficult to define winning formulas and they can never be reduced to a single element. But it seems safe to settle on a combination of factors making this handful of social corporations into examples of BEE success.

Niall Carroll believes that RBH has 'three secret weapons': good governance; delivery on its commitments; and demonstrable social returns. In his view, if broad-based companies are not institutionally strong, 'it is difficult to manage the many relationships and at the first sniff of money, everything falls apart.'

But there are other factors. Early entry was undoubtedly important for all except the Bafokeng, who had a great asset and cash flows to compensate for a later start. The importance of access to good investments and companies – in particular the highly cash-generative, to sooth debt-financing conundrums – cannot be underestimated. Neither can the importance of good management and investment teams. The following points deserve attention.

The right mix of capital and good assets

Financial constraints have always dogged BEE and even some among the best are still dependent on BEE structured debt financing. However, for all except the WDBIH, sufficient capacity has been developed to use their own balance sheets to make investments – although the extent to which they may do this differs considerably between them. This has only been possible because of the presence of quality assets in their portfolios, acquired at good prices and thus able to deliver early cash to help fund future growth.

No matter how small the sum, says JJ Njeke of KTI, it is important to contribute some of your own capital to every acquisition. The amounts may not be enough to take the sharp edge off debt financing – but, he argues, your investment choices become more considered.

We've already seen how HCI and MIC got the first bite at South Africa's biggest growth industry, cellular telephony. HCI was able to leverage off this to rescue its new venture, e.tv, which is now profitable. The end of the tale would be different if HCI had not acquired Vodacom shares.

MIC too has been willing to invest its own money in acquisitions. Perhaps pressure from its shareholder for dividends has always ensured an early cash stream, no matter how small, from its investments. Then, in 2007, things changed dramatically for the better. It became part of a massive R13 billion restructure of media and gaming assets that involved Peermont and Primedia and released a few hundred million rand into its coffers. This enabled the release of a large dividend payment of R245 million to its shareholder, leaving a tidy sum to dedicate to the growth of MIC. However, when global markets turned bad, Primedia had to restructure its financial arrangements; this necessitated further investment by MIC but also a larger shareholding, giving it operational control of one of the country's largest media groups – certainly, a new challenge for the company.

Thebe was the least fortunate of the group – its significant assets did not survive the Nineties market crash. For Khanyile, the collapse of its FBC Fidelity banking interests was painful – and it had a lot of pieces to pick up in the early millennium years. Nevertheless, by staying true to its strategy to target middle-sized companies to invest in or start up, it has built a sizeable portfolio that is a net generator of cash. Khanyile believes strongly that 'business learnings best come by getting involved in smaller companies. It was the success of Tepco that got us into Shell.'

For WDBIH, the increase in its investment has been slower than the rest, but even as a junior partner it acquired several good assets early on and has continued to do so, with the difference being that today it is often the lead BEE partner in its acquisitions. Importantly, by early 2010, the company had one fully paid-up investment – 18%, as the only BEE shareholder, in the listed information technology company Paracon. This will support an escalation in its cash flows.

Leadership and professionalism matter
The Bafokeng experience shows that good assets or money alone are not enough. From 1999, they received substantial royalty payments from Implats: R222 million in 1999, R306 million in 2000, reaching a record R1.24 billion in 2007. This pulled the Bafokeng from the brink of bankruptcy. Even so, early investments, mainly into small, rather tacky businesses drained the Bafokeng's wealth. The shift came when

Kgosi Leruo Molotlegi assumed leadership. He appointed leading investment bankers to build a new portfolio of assets under a new company, Royal Bafokeng Finance, and a new investment team headed by Carroll. Its mining interests however were kept in a separate company until all enterprises were gathered under one umbrella, Royal Bafokeng Holdings, in 2006.

'We started with no money,' says Carroll. But the Bafokeng themselves had a bank balance that could support acquisitions of BEE shareholding on offer by South African corporations without the long delays associated with BEE financing. As good investment bankers, Carroll and his team would then restructure the financing of their transactions at their leisure, on more favourable terms than usually available to BEE companies, and shortly afterwards return any capital owed back to the Bafokeng.

In just six years, Carroll and his team have built a portfolio of 19 investments, while managing the cash, sports and enterprise development interests of the Bafokeng. They have a controlling interest in five companies. But, says Carroll, 'whether we have 100% or 10%, we like to have the same relationship with the management. They run the business. We don't want to run the business. I would much rather have a light and consistent touch than an omniscient presence just because we have more than 50%.'

KTI also demonstrated early on that a professional team could use ownership, with control, to transform the internal character and performance of an investment. They did so with a radio station acquired in 1996. At the time, the ANC government revitalised the broadcasting industry, privatising and issuing new licences. At the time no one really understood the market potential. Fortunately, it has turned out well – although far less phenomenal than cellphones. Kagiso Media secured East Coast Radio – a pedestrian station with a white listenership, an all-white male management team and one lone black voice on air. Three years later, half the staff were black, management changed to include women and blacks, and of course there was more than one black voice on air. But most striking was the change in the racial profile and number of listeners. Listeners increased by more than 50% in just three years. Listenership became equally divided between black African, white and Indian – most unusual in a still racially divided society.[4] Here was transformation at work and working, with new black owners making a company reflect the new South Africa and being more profitable as a result.

Institutional in character

The companies reviewed here stand apart from most BEE investment entities because of their institutional character. In part, this comes from having shareholders who are not personalities – a strong feature of BEE companies. If you think about Mvelaphanda and Shanduka, you will invariably think about Tokyo Sexwale and Cyril Ramaphosa. This raises the question of the institutional staying power of such companies if and when the personalities go – will the selling point go along with them?

The make-up of a shareholder is not the only contributor to the institutional gravitas of social corporations. Equally important has been a leadership with a long-term view. On the whole, their executives have sidestepped the 'get rich quick' that has characterised so much of BEE – although I don't want to suggest that some among them have not got extremely rich. Johnny Copelyn and Marcel Golding, of HCI, head the queue but most of the executives in these corporations either have shareholding or wealth-sharing arrangements. The differentiator, however, is the commitment to building businesses as opposed to getting whatever slice of the corporate cake is available to bankroll excessive lifestyles.

The leadership has also had to be adept at balancing the immediate cash needs of their shareholders with the requirement to reinvest their capital in the hope that they will deliver an annuity-like stream of income to their shareholders for many years to come. It is probably safe to say that most broad-based companies failed to manage this tension; perhaps a source of their failure to grow.

True to their ideals

The values and characters of the chief executives have had an indelible impact on the nature of these corporations. Thebe, for example, reflects the early ideals of Khanyile. When he conceptualised Thebe, he believed in black business having its own independent expression in the economy.

Given black business exclusion from the economic mainstream under apartheid, he felt that this could only realistically take place in 'the middle market'. Today, Thebe explicitly asserts itself as an 'African company' – that identity is extremely important to it, but Khanyile insists on its nonracial expression. All racial groups work in the company and participate in the staff share scheme.

'Our appeal to the market is better if we are nonracial,' says Khanyile, reminding me of the experiences of Anton Rupert in his early business ventures, particularly his first in dry-cleaning, where he eschewed everything English. Its brochure declared: 'Always support the True Afrikaans CHEMIESE REINIGERS (like you, we prefer this name to the erroneous, anglicised word: Dry-cleaners).'[5] The business did not flourish, but Rupert faltered one more time before realising the problem of placing artificial boundaries around one's market.

He also resisted executive shareholder participation – at first. 'It's because of who I am as a person,' answers Khanyile. 'We discussed at our first board meeting whether the directors shouldn't invest their money alongside the trust. Some argued that poor decisions should affect the pockets of the decision-making executives as well. I said no, I wanted to attract the person who said, "when the community does well, I feel rewarded". That's idealism – and a couple of people left as a result. It can't work always.' Today, management and staff have shareholding.

Both Molobi and Khanyile were well placed to trade their political credibility but avoided doing so. I recall a sizeable deal I was advising on, with KTI at the top of the list as the preferred partner. Not long into the meeting, Molobi made sure that everyone understood very clearly that KTI did not peddle its political credibility. 'We cannot promise to open political doors for you.' For Molobi, this was a way of sifting out the good from the bad partners – if a company just wanted a black shareholder for their political access, then Molobi didn't want them.

Profit versus social aims

Equally, his successor JJ Njeke grew up in KTI and reflects the same low-key, values-based approach to business. 'We value our association with Kagiso Trust, and so we bought into a dream. I remember years ago, we were approached by the Krok brothers, but we decided there was no way we could do business them, given their history of being involved in skin lightening products.'[6]

'Eric Molobi always called us "capitalists with a conscience", creating something that will be there for generations.' This also meant that they would not invest in businesses that could be harmful to people and the environment – gambling, alcohol and armaments being their main exclusions.

More than any of the others, HCI seems like any other company but without the usual BEE features. You could say that it has crossed the divide and normalised. Isn't that just what empowerment policy wants – black companies operating like any other, owning and growing their fair share of the country's corporate assets? Yet its critics say it is too capitalist – a step too far for a union-initiated company! Copelyn and Golding have therefore been caricatured as 'cowboy capitalists'. That's undeserved, argues Copelyn. HCI has distributed more than R850 million to its union shareholder trusts, while its corporate social investment, via the HCI Foundation, exceeds both national and international norms – 5%, as against the usual 1% to 2%. Copelyn and Golding donated almost 4% of their HCI shares to the Foundation, which has augmented its capital base of 5% of HCI's market capitalisation – that's a whopping R500 million or thereabouts, and very large by South African standards. So Copelyn unremorsefully (and with a touch of humour) ended his letter responding to a particularly harsh media report with 'cowboys don't cry'.

Interestingly, KTI and WDBIH – whose reputation for conscience and high values is regarded as the strongest in business – have been the most restrained in their dividend payments. Since its inception, KTI has disbursed some R60 million to its Trust, KT (excluding additional CSI contributions), while the WDB Trust has received R70 million. This contrasts with Thebe's R230 million and MIC's R368 million. However, given its much lower net asset value compared to its larger counterparts, the WDB contribution is significant.

The lower dividend payments by KTI and WDB may be a matter of poor luck – they didn't get fantastic assets like cellular telephony or platinum. Or maybe there has been some trade-off between commercial and social imperatives. It's difficult to say, or to judge who is more right or wrong. How the dividends are spent by the shareholders does, however, provide a basis for judgement. In other words, are the shareholders of broad-based investment entities credible? And are they spending their dividends efficiently and with integrity? Also, is there adequate governance and sufficient information available to assess the strength of accountability throughout the chain of these broad-based groupings?

These are the important questions that need to be answered positively for social corporations to offer a more socially attuned model of capitalism than what has been revealed in the global financial crisis. Our group here doesn't offer as clear a picture as we would like. There is some blurring at the edges when it comes to information disclosure.

Corporate governance

Whoever their shareholder, social corporations – and in fact, most broad-based entities – have set themselves up as representatives of various constituencies that include a fair number of people, although no minimum threshold has ever been stipulated. They get into deals on that basis – 'our shareholders are effectively poor women in Limpopo and if you make us your partners those poor women will receive the financial benefit from this shareholding.' These women – or any other such beneficiary – have an implicit right to know what they are due. As such, broad-based investors are effectively public companies, whether legally or not.

If you accept that, then it seems reasonable to require of social corporations an added responsibility to disclose information publicly about their business, financial performance and payments to shareholders and executives in particular, given the increasing sensitivity around this issue. Information disclosure is the best way to keep everyone honest and is good for business performance – so it is an extra cost worth having.

HCI, as a listed company, provides the disclosures required by JSE regulations. There is concern, though, over the absence of publicly available information about its principal shareholders, the two Sactwu union trusts. Sactwu says it runs the largest bursary fund within the union movement, but we have to take its word: no details of either this fund or the activities of the Sactwu Investment Trust are readily available.

On disclosure of company information, KTI does walk the extra mile. It provides an extraordinarily detailed annual report – better than many listed companies. But it misses out an important detail – how much it has paid in dividends to Kagiso Trust over the years. The Trust has a long way to go as far as information disclosure is concerned. Their web site provides no hard information except to say that it has funded projects of up to R1.2 billion in its 25-year history. I have no reason to believe that the Trust would not provide information if I asked, but surely it should be accessible to the public?

Thebe discloses headline financial results, as well as distributions to the Batho Batho Trust. But the Trust itself is opaque. Khanyile argues that there is a case for being a quiet giver, but that does not help to allay suspicions around Thebe being too close to the ANC.

WDBIH falters on providing detailed company information, but generously elaborates on its social activities. Its web site provides a ticker of the number of people who have received micro-credit – just short of 50 000 by early 2010.

All in all, our group of social corporations and their trust shareholder have improvements to make in information disclosure, but they remain far ahead of others. As yet, I haven't touched on the Bafokeng, only because I want to give extra space to them. There is a unique quality to the way they manage their affairs and they may be an important guide to other mining and rural communities who are gaining access to shareholding. As we've seen earlier, there are many complexities to community ownership. The Bafokeng model may not be replicable, but perhaps rural communities can draw on their experiences as more appropriate to their context. So I would like to consider whether the Bafokeng model is useful for other rurally based mining communities.

A special case

A tribal authority with an established royal house is the type of shareholder you would least expect to provide extensive disclosure of information. Yet, in 2009, Kgosi (King) Leruo Molotlegi initiated a report for 2008 that provides the kind of details about finances, community statistics and projects that we would all like to see local government providing.

All public activities are housed under what is referred to as the RBN

(Royal Bafokeng Nation) administration. The governance is impressive and unique. Twice a year, residents from the Bafokeng's 29 villages gather to listen, question and comment about the activities of the Royal Bafokeng. The responsible executives and managers – Carroll, for instance – all have to present a full report on their finances and activities. The experience prompted the leading journalist Jabulani Sikhakhane to exclaim at a ward councillor bringing municipal managers to a constituency meeting. 'Unimaginable! I am sure that if one scratched the surface of the Bafokeng structures of democracy, one would find many faults. But whatever its imperfections, what I observed on Saturday was much better than what we have had under successive ANC governments since 1994.'[8]

The more than 100-page report gives all sorts of interesting and important statistics like:

- mortality statistics and the major causes of death
- numbers and location of orphaned and vulnerable children, and the disabled
- luncheon clubs for the aged and the distribution of pension pay points
- numbers and types of crime; arrests and incidents per village; what generates crime (whether drug- or gang-related, for example)
- infrastructure projects, including when contracts have been awarded and the apportionment of tenders to local contractors.

The RBN administration is in reality a municipality – and for that, it is appealing to the South African government to allow it the same tax dispensation as any local governments.

Importantly, the RBN's balance sheet and income statement are there for all to see, although a case may be made for greater detail. Here you find the value of the assets – R25 billion in 2008 – and the bank balance of R5.5 billion. The investments of the holding company are by far the largest assets of the community, which received investment income and interest of more than R4 billion. After meeting all expenses, the RBN made a profit of R4.5 billion – cite that to the US or UK governments!

On my visit to Phokeng, executives in the Bafokeng administration pointed to the 'collective independence' of the Bafokeng, which they felt was both a positive and a negative. The collective style has evolved from a history of cohesiveness and discipline, marked in particular by the tribe's joint effort to buy back their land. But their independence also means that they 'end up paying for everything' and they are uncertain how sustainable this is. Their self-reliance creates a not unexpected tension with local ANC politicians, who get worried that any delivery is attributed to the Bafokeng and not themselves.

The RBN administration plan their budget according to a formula that ensures the sustainability of their programmes. They maintain a cash reserve sufficient to cover three years of expenditure. This, they believe, is enough time to liquidate any investments to finance community needs should this ever be necessary. 'In 1999 we ran out of money. We had to borrow money. We're not going there again and we do not forget that. These are lessons we can teach others,' says one executive. 'In ten years we have completely transformed our financial position and professionalised enormously.'

The leadership of Leruo Molotlegi is key to the current success of the Bafokeng. Like South Africa Inc, Molotlegi is shifting the tribal identity of the Bafokeng to that of Bafokeng Inc; as one executive told me, 'He sees himself as a CEO more than a *kgosi*. He is trying to move the community towards a different idiom: you've got to be educated, be an entrepreneur, so that you don't need me. He is comfortable working himself out of a job.' And so he has created institutional practices of good governance and information disclosure that reflect corporate behaviour rather than tribal practices. It is not surprising therefore that they refer to profits and losses in their accounts, and not, as governments do, to surpluses and deficits.

Sikhakhane draws attention to Molotlegi's philosophy of governance: free elections don't guarantee that a person in public office will govern with integrity, compassion or with the best interests of his constituents at heart. For Molotlegi, 'Accountability in office is the only way to really measure, monitor, and promote these things.'

None of this should suggest, however, that the Bafokeng are not also a melting pot of South Africa. There are tensions between young and old, black and white, Bafokeng and non-Bafokeng. Almost inevitably, the wealth that vests in RBH feeds rumours and speculation, particularly as most lack financial literacy.

But, like Sikhakhane, I reckon the management of RBN affairs is good enough and most certainly better than much of what we see elsewhere. They have a strong sense of communal cohesion and independence, the right leader at the right time, and some great assets to generate good income. I have serious doubts as to whether other rural communities that are now being given shareholding in the mines in their areas can emulate the Bafokeng. But they look to the Bafokeng for guidance and advice. Perhaps therefore the Bafokeng can help steer these communities away from becoming BEE's powder keg.

Part 3

Where to from here?

Part 3
Where to from here?

If parts of BEE are not working and are having
unintended consequences, let's not be religious about it;
change it.

– Trevor Manuel

If you are not prepared to be wrong, you will never come
up with anything original.

– Ken Robinson

This section is about changing the way we think about empowerment
– in part, exploring how we might bridge the many fault lines in
current policy but, more importantly, marking out new paths in a world
that is fast-changing and unpredictable. It is about being enthusiastic,
creative and hopeful – edging open doors to new ideas and debates and
not offering blueprints.

It is difficult to interpret the receptiveness there may be to
rethinking BEE policy and the Codes in particular. I have trawled media
commentaries and found suggestions that hint at a turning point in BEE
and even stronger voices that call for its termination in favour of other
priorities like education and jobs. But equally, there are demands for
stronger enforcement of what we already have.

For the moment, too, government is preoccupied with bigger
concerns – delivery of basic services to black communities that vent
their anger in street protests; increasing unemployment that is already
unacceptably high; deteriorating education results; managerial strain

within the government and leading state-owned corporations that have unprecedented infrastructure investments to make ... the list goes on. BEE therefore is not among the top priorities. The government may also believe that this is one area where it can take a back seat, relying on the private sector to drive implementation.

As always, there are trade-offs. Chapter 10 shows that BEE transactions to date have absorbed far more capital than has been invested in low-income housing and land redistribution. And BEE ownership that still needs to be completed may require similar amounts of finance again. Yet resources are limited – the more money we use to finance ownership, the less there is for housing, or building more sewerage plants, or powering up the economy. In this tight allocation of capital, interest rates will go up. The best way of making choices about BEE is to bring it into the macroeconomic frame and debate the racial imbalances in wealth and economic participation in an integrated way.

Also, we need to be consistent about our measurements. The Codes, for example, state that only those economic benefits of shareholding that can be traced back to black individuals may be counted. Such economic benefits flow to black individuals via two routes – direct shareholding, which is what BEE transactional activity is about, and indirect shareholding, which is individual savings usually invested in funds for pensions, unit trusts and life assurance. These individual savings constitute more than half of the JSE's market capitalisation, and yet they are grudgingly recognised in the Codes, with a limitation placed on how much may be counted. But there is considerable black wealth captured here, and there is no justification for not fully measuring such economic benefits. Unfortunately, however, controversy has encircled this issue and resulted in a racially polarised debate.

Understanding the trade-offs in allocating capital is one side of the coin; the other is the efficient use of capital. A central theme of this book is just how unproductive BEE investments have typically been. There are exceptions that provide pointers to new ways of promoting black control and influence within the corporate sector. But they are too few to remove the core problem of the inefficient – and often inequitable – use of our capital resources. Here, much more than just tampering with the Codes is needed. But tampering may be the most we can hope for in the coming years. Thus, a good bit of Chapter 10 looks at how the Codes may be modified to ensure better empowerment results. These are ideas only, and likely to be of interest mainly for readers who are immersed in dealing with BEE ownership and the Codes.

My thinking is underpinned by a number of principles. First, allow for greater flexibility and choices and thus open up space for innovation in transformation. Second, be sensible and realistic. For example, many businesses are not well suited to having third-party shareholders; so don't force this on them, offer alternatives. Third, reward the black businesses who are productive and who really do exercise control or influence in their investments.

Chapter 11 is exploratory, teasing out ideas that may be important for repositioning BEE and economic transformation in South Africa. I look at the new economic thinking that is taking place globally in an effort to better understand the changing and increasingly unpredictable environment that we all find ourselves in. The implications for South Africa are many. An important challenge lies in being responsive to change; policies need to be flexible and policy makers need to be nimble-footed and open-minded. None of these are characteristic of present BEE policy or the bureaucracy. Different economic measurements and information are needed – traditional measures of economic wellbeing are no longer adequate. Bhutan's concept of Gross National Happiness and the economics of happiness have captured much more attention than ever before.

Transformation, I argue, is not something that can be achieved by obeying a set of rules. It requires special effort – an explicit commitment within society – underpinned by sound values and ethics. There are many worthy voices in South Africa today calling for a different ethos, one not premised on materialism. But good leadership is crucial to ensure that this vision is given concrete expression. Despite Jacob Zuma's claim to want to initiate a dialogue on a moral code, the current political leadership seems adrift.

I journey through Vietnam's remarkably successful reforms for insights into what might help revitalise transformation in South Africa, but mindful that flipping lessons from one country to another has its shortcomings. After trying out social engineering, the Vietnamese have adopted a gradualist approach – small steps that allow what they call 'learning by doing'. Their objectives are uncluttered, they admire flexibility and pragmatism. Their practical skills, acquired over generations, are finding new channels of expression and this shows in the country's economic performance. This vital ingredient goes unrecognised in BEE policy – yet surely it should feature in a reconfigured empowerment framework.

South Africa's missing middle gets special attention. As we do personally, economies do better if they breathe deeply from the middle. I look at the importance of medium-sized enterprises for growth and innovation, and their potential to offer black entrepreneurs good investment opportunities. But they need policy attention – and policy needs to favour those black business people who are keen to build real businesses. Traditionally, the middle class is the source of entrepreneurs and therefore the black middle class needs increasingly to become the feeder for productive black investors. But there are impediments to the middle classes growing at a strong enough pace. Among them are education failures that connect with the unintended consequences of employment equity. This is politically sensitive territory, but too important to sidestep.

Finally, I consider an area that is largely missing from the transformation map in South Africa, yet expanding internationally. This is the area of sustainable or responsible investment. There are many facets to it. A particularly interesting offshoot is what is referred to as impact investment, which is investment in funds and enterprises that seek to have social and environmental impact as well as a financial return. South Africa needs to extend its transformation horizons by incorporating this area of investment in the BEE framework and getting creative.

10

Bridging the
fault lines

... almost two years after the beginning of the recession,
too little has been done to reform financial regulation.
Something will be done – but it almost surely will be less
than what is needed: perhaps enough to help us muddle
through, but not enough to prevent another crisis.

– Joseph Stiglitz

Realistically, the government is unlikely to step back from current
BEE policy – at least in the foreseeable future. Too much is vested
in it to be easily reversed. But there is space to reshape the Codes and
possibly bridge the many fault lines. This chapter teases out what may
be possible, but mindful that remedial measures may allow us just to
muddle through and no more.

Let's recap on the key constraints and unwanted consequences of the
Codes before exploring how empowerment could be better done. We have
already seen, time and again, how the Codes encourage redistributive
rather than productive ownership. Where productive investment has
occurred, it has been more by chance than design – policy itself has not
provided the necessary lever.

The redistributive character of BEE ownership has had a number
of knock-on effects. As highlighted in Chapter 8, the benefits have not
been distributed equitably: some people have been able to access BEE
deals, others haven't; some have secured good assets, others haven't. The
sustainability of shareholding is extremely difficult, due to debt financing.
Deals have been transacted using vast quantities of the country's limited

capital resource, knowing that finally some of that shareholding will have to be sold to pay off the loans used to acquire it in the first place. A puzzled 'Why are we doing this?' is in order – particularly when we consider the costs involved.

BEE ownership is also a protracted process of redistribution. The Codes say that BEE shareholding should be fixed for a long period of time, with virtually all companies obliged equally to sell a certain amount of their equity. One of the consequences is to restrict BEE investors from trading their shares. Given the meltdown in global markets, efforts to predetermine corporate structures are a bizarre expectation – anyone in the room who knows what the world will be like in five years' time, please put up your hand. Policy gurus worldwide grapple with how to plan amidst unpredictability, but they are clear on one thing, flexibility is crucial.

Perhaps most worrying is the corrupting influence of BEE ownership. It is so easy to extract wealth without being productive when a policy legitimises the process and abdicates one from responsibility to do things better and differently. And as this rent-seeking conduct escalates – particularly among the political elite and often in the guise of opening up opportunity to new entrants – BEE corporations that have built real businesses are at risk of being sidelined as the 'usual suspects' instead of being promoted as role models.

Some companies are well suited to having outside shareholders, others aren't. Yet we make no allowance for that and are surprised when firms get up to all sorts of shenanigans to limit the influence of black shareholders and benefits that are due to them. We want foreign investors who are directly involved in building businesses and not just trading in JSE equities. These investors may have had no connection with apartheid South Africa and yet the Codes expect them to assume responsibility and additional costs to repair the damage.

I doubt we will ever be able to resolve these issues within the confines of the Codes, but perhaps we can tidy up the rough edges with some policy adjustments. To open up debate and to show that there is room for manoeuvre, the rest of this chapter proposes ideas on how the Codes may be modified. My intention is to give a flavour of what could be done, rather than provide a comprehensive list of alternatives or modifications. Workable solutions will only emerge from engagement between those most centrally affected.

As a starting point, I suggest that we stop the redistributive component of BEE, and instead try to ensure that benefits filter as widely as possible. After that we need to focus attention on creating the right kind of environment for a productive black business class. This is a long-term endeavour. It cannot be achieved by ticking boxes, as Nick van Rensburg, a leading expert in business development, says,[1] but perhaps some revision of the Codes may improve possibilities.

Adjusting the Codes

My ideas on remoulding the Codes are based on these principles:

- Wind down and stop BEE ownership as currently envisaged in the Codes. Anyone who has not completed their BEE ownership obligations should do so. After that, when black shareholding unwinds, allow it to, without further obligations on companies to find other black shareholders. It is important to bring to a close the redistributive and rent-seeking character of BEE ownership and instead find other ways to promote black investment on a different basis.
- Even in a concluding round of BEE investments, offer flexibility. There is already space for exemptions and alternatives to BEE ownership in the current Codes. Expand on these, so that those who are ill suited to having third-party shareholders can meet their obligations in other ways. The area of responsible, sustainable investment offers alternative opportunities for promoting black economic participation, as Chapter 11 shows.
- Be realistic about the capacity of small- to medium-sized companies to meet all their Code obligations. Asking a small company with a R35 million turnover to dedicate 3% of its after-tax profit to developing other enterprises is a big demand. Is it reasonable? Unlike large corporations with resources and access to government, the smaller firms will respond by avoiding compliance. This places them in a grey zone, operating at best in bad faith, or at worst illegally. If small and medium businesses are a growth engine of the economy, as policy endorses, they should not be placed in this invidious position.

Some specific suggestions follow here.

Free shareholding option
Allow companies to give away say 5% of their equity in lieu of the 25% ownership requirement.* If it can cost up to 5% of the value of a company to sell 25% of its equity, why not save the capital that would have been used in making the BEE equity acquisitions and make a free donation of perhaps 5% equity and for investment in other economically important activities like infrastructure? Unlisted companies would have the added benefit of not having to go through the costly valuations required for selling shares and for measurement in terms of the Codes. Guidelines could be provided on who or what activities could qualify for the free shares. Companies could give the shares to their staff or offer them to socially responsible funds that invest, for example, in businesses involved in servicing the poor or the low end of the market. There are all manner of good things that the returns from such shareholding could support – and if the option is there, ideas will flourish.

In mid-March 2010, the JSE's market capitalisation was R6000 billion. If listed companies have met half their BEE ownership obligation (which is 15% direct shareholding, given the provision to count up to 10% institutional ownership), then some 1.5% of equity in total could be available to be given away – that is a market value of R90 billion, which is a very big give with potentially a good social return if invested well. Even 1%, valued at R60 billion, is substantial. The costs alone of past BEE deals, if we assume an effective 10% price discount, would have amounted to the same.

Let's look at another figure. In Chapter 2 we saw that another R500 billion or so of shareholding may still have to be transferred to black hands – which assumes asset values worth R2000 billion. A free 5% would be R100 billion. These figures are just guesstimates, but they suggest that substantial amounts of money could be made available for good purpose.

---

* This is not a new idea. Many years ago the former editor of the *Financial Mail*, Stephen Mulholland, mooted a similar suggestion.

Promote productive relationships

It is important to encourage solid relationships. We should move beyond shareholding alone as the defining factor in a partnership. So, be flexible – don't force companies to have black shareholders, leave it to them to choose black shareholders if they think they will be productive partners.

Right up to the penultimate draft of the Codes there was a provision that black-controlled companies could leapfrog their BEE recognition levels if they had more than 50% black ownership. So, if such a company scored a Level 4 in terms of the Codes' scorecard, it would be ratcheted up to Level 3.* This would have given them a potential competitive edge when bidding for business. But why not introduce another form of leapfrogging? Measure more than ownership: require black shareholders to become involved in management as well. A black-owned company would then be able to select its shareholders freely, without the Codes' requirement for a specific shareholder profile with black women and broad-based ownership. The only relevant black shareholders would be those willing to become owner-managers.

Should black control be a requirement? White-owned companies may be happy to work in a real partnership with black shareholders but unwilling to relinquish control – at least in the early years of a partnership. So, allow the black ownership threshold to be below 50% but be very firm on owner-manager participation. This is a model successfully pursued by Anglo Zimele, headed by Van Rensburg, who points out: 'More than 50% BEE ownership is not always possible or sustainable. It may be better to do a deal at 26% to 49%, with BEE shareholders able to build up their shareholding over time. A fixation with BEE ownership and control at the expense of making sure that adequate skills are first obtained is a recipe for disaster. Further, trying to enforce BEE control could result in a reduction in BEE activity and deals.'[2]

Once empowered, always empowered

Remove the 'realisation' principle and the requirement of continuous measurement over the years. Be more flexible and allow BEE ownership

---

* In my interviews with those responsible for drafting the Codes, no one could give a clear reason why this provision fell away in the final version of the Codes. They seemed to think it may have been the consequence of final drafting, and thus accidental.

to be fully recognised as soon as the shares are sold. This is the controversial 'once empowered, always empowered' point that is accepted in the Financial Sector Charter but rejected by DTI. The Codes make some provision for the unwinding of ownership, but it is too complex and companies are still penalised if their black shareholders move on, even if they had a good and productive relationship and expect the same elsewhere. The FSC still provides the best guideline to date. If BEE transactions are done in good faith, let them unwind after a reasonable period without negative scorecard consequences for anyone – three years would be reasonable.

More leeway for smaller firms

Recognise that not all companies are well suited to having external shareholders – even for a share give-away to a favourite charity. Family businesses are the obvious example, as we've seen. Many small- to medium-sized companies also have shareholders with longstanding, close relationships, and they may be equally reluctant to take on outsiders. What is the point of forcing relatively small, owner-managed businesses to have outside owners? It doesn't make a lot of sense and encourages bad practices like fronting. One way of trying to manage this problem is to raise exemption levels.

Small to micro enterprises, with a turnover below R5 million, are not required to implement the Codes, while the next level of companies with less than R35 million may elect not to do ownership in favour of other components of BEE. How appropriate are these thresholds? They appear to have been politically determined. Before the Codes were finalised, there was a push within government to raise the thresholds. When I asked Polo Radebe, who headed the DTI team at the time, why they had not done so, she said that black business would never have accepted this – as it was, the current levels were difficult enough to sell.

In economic terms, the cut-offs were arbitrary. By most standards a business with R35 million or so turnover is relatively small. No data are available, but probably most businesses with closely knit shareholders that are owner-managed are found at under R100 million. Once businesses rise higher, they are likely to have an increasing need for third-party shareholders to fund their growth. From there they may graduate to becoming public companies, making them much better suited to having BEE shareholders. So, as a general rule, higher thresholds for both micro and small businesses would be more appropriate.

But sector variations may also be called for. There is no commercial reason for a business with, say, a R50 million turnover to be better placed to implement all the elements of the Codes than one with R25 million. Margins across sectors – such as profitability or returns on equity – differ enormously, which could mean that a smaller business is better positioned to implement the Codes than a larger one. To take some ratios from Stats SA: the profit to turnover ratios are low for the trade and construction sectors, with manufacturing faring better but still well below business services and forestry and fishing, for example.[3] Against these ratios, a R50-million trading operation may realise a before-tax profit of R2.5 million, while a R25-million forestry operation could achieve R8.5 million. Ask yourself, which business would you prefer to have shares in? Even if you didn't have to put down any capital upfront, just the time spent on acquiring an interest in the first trading business hardly seems worth the effort.

Ease up on foreign investors
Create an exemption for new foreign investors and simplify the ownership provisions for foreign multinationals. Currently, if multinationals have a global policy against minority shareholding in their subsidiaries, they may replace BEE ownership with what is referred to as an 'equity equivalent'. This means they may embark on other programmes of social and economic significance to South Africa. The contributions need to be 25% of the value of their South African subsidiaries, which may be spread over 10 years. Broad categories of activities are provided for in the Codes, such as enterprise development, foreign direct investment, empowerment of black rural women and youth, education and skills development, and infrastructure investment. The programmes are also expected to have a broad-based impact on black South Africans.[4] So, they may invest in a project that offers them a direct return or they may embark on training – as the US technology group Hewlett Packard has done – hoping for an indirect return (HP's focus is on enterprises that are partnered with it and individuals who may later work for the company).

It is difficult to envisage new foreign investors looking favourably on equity equivalents. They come to South Africa to invest in what they know best – their own business – and not to assume additional investment responsibilities related to redressing the economic disadvantages of black South Africans. We need to question afresh the imposition of equity-type obligations on new foreign investors. They are not responsible for the racial imbalances in wealth and therefore carry no obligation to correct them. Besides, an equity equivalent programme may be complex and very expensive – a BEE transaction may cost somewhere between 2% to 5% of the value of a 25% sale of equity, whereas the equity equivalent requires the full 25% value to be committed to other projects. Add to this the process of formulating these projects and getting government approval. This is not the way to attract foreign players.

The DTI seemed resistant to equity equivalents until moments before going to press, when Microsoft announced an equity equivalent. Until then, only one such programme had been approved in three years, that of HP. Perhaps there is a shift in approach – if so, a positive development.

The concept of equity equivalents could be more broadly applied if simplified. For example, the government could specify programmes or funds in which any company that chooses not to do BEE ownership could invest.

Like government, the South African business establishment has not been in favour of much exclusion from BEE ownership – but for different reasons. In the drafting of the Codes it argued for a level playing field – the principle being 'If I must comply, so must everyone else.' However, the sensitivities around exclusions may be less relevant in an environment of greater flexibility and more incentives to perform better. This should underpin any new approach to the Codes, rather than adopting a more punitive stance, as some have suggested.

The political analyst William Gumede has argued for BEE to be dropped as a policy; 'give companies BEE points for how much they invest in job creation, black education and housing; and for uplifting the physical and social infrastructure of townships and rural areas, and supporting the five-million entrepreneurs in the informal sector'.[5] Perhaps the ideas I have put forward go some way towards addressing his concerns – and those of many others – short of the drastic and politically unpalatable step of scrapping BEE or the Codes.

Getting a different measure of black wealth

We can measure wealth and its racial imbalances in South Africa in other ways too. Direct black shareholding has assumed a kind of proxy status for black wealth and participation in the mainstream economy. Any suggestion that there should be other gauges tends to spark political sensitivities that stultify debate. But, as dry as measurement issues are, they are crucial to understanding how we may approach black empowerment differently and what we need to prioritise. Unfortunately they are bedevilled by a lack of data, making guesstimates the basis of analysis. But let's remember, the Codes themselves were devised from guesstimates. The vital factor is good constructive vision.

If policy is guided by an incorrect or incomplete set of measures, it may appear to have failed or succeeded when it hasn't (or for reasons we can't see). This is the case with BEE – the government is shooting itself in the foot and the Codes are the smoking gun. Look at the accompanying table of the black controlling interests in JSE listed companies over the years. Less than 3% after some fifteen years of empowerment effort seems like a failure. In the past decade the market capitalisation of the JSE has increased fourfold as against the share of black control increasing only about two-and-a-half times.

Black-controlled companies as % of JSE market capitalisation and value

	Feb 1998	Nov 1998	Jan 1999	Feb 2000	Mar 2010
%	4.8	6.8	5.5	3.8	2.7
Value R billion	55	66	59	61	162
No. of companies	27	33	35	36	18

Sources: *Empowerment 2001* and *Empowerment 1999*. The March 2010 value figure is derived from my own research of listed companies that are black-controlled.

It is important to pinpoint what we are measuring – black economic benefit (or wealth) is very different from black control (or influence). The latter is usually not exercised through shareholding. Major corporations today are largely run by their managements, with shareholders having little direct influence.

Since BEE ownership is much more about the redistribution of wealth than active black participation in the corporate sector, our focus should be on measuring black shareholder wealth in its entirety – not just the shareholding that is directly held by BEE entities. More than half of the JSE's equity is held by institutions that have collected the savings of blacks and whites and invested these in listed stocks – these institutions are the pension funds, unit trusts and life assurers, for example, with financial intermediaries usually appointed to manage these investments. Most people with an equity interest in the JSE hold it via these institutional investors rather than directly.

When we factor in indirect black shareholding we get a very different picture of black shareholder wealth. The ultimate black equity interest in JSE-listed companies may potentially be 35% to 60% of the total market capitalisation of the exchange, excluding foreign equity holdings. Of course, much of the directly held shares by BEE investors are unencumbered by debt and so net wealth would be lower.

Black share of JSE corporate wealth 2008/9

	Direct BEE shareholding		Indirect black beneficial shareholding		% foreign	JSE market cap less foreign	% Black beneficial interest less foreign		% Total black beneficial interest (excl foreign)
	%	Value (R bn)	%	Value (R bn)			Direct	Indirect	
Low	10	600	15	900	30	4000	15	22.5	37.5%
High	20	1200	22.5	1350	30	4000	30	33.75	63.75%

Note: To gauge the current direct BEE shareholding in the JSE, I took the companies listed on the JSE's Top Forty index (41 companies are included!), which make up some 65% of the total market capitalisation of the JSE. I weighed up the BEE equity interests in these companies against their total market capitalisation, giving an aggregate direct BEE shareholding of marginally under 20%. I assumed that the remaining corporations had not bettered the Top Forty in terms of BEE performance and therefore set 20% as the high mark. It is also unlikely that companies will exceed 15% at the end of the day, as they may attribute 10% of the 25% to institutional investment (what the Codes refer to as mandated investments), and so I set a low mark of 10%. I assume these figure are what we might expect up to 2012.

For indirect black beneficial shareholding, my figures are based on an assessment of three studies undertaken over the years. One is 'Black ownership of the SA banking sector', a study commissioned by the South African Banking Council (renamed the Banking Association of

Let's look at some other measurements that should make us think again about our priorities. If we consider the main elements of individual wealth (direct and indirect equity ownership, land and housing), BEE corporate shareholding has taken by far the lion's share of investment capital. The disclosed value of BEE transactions up to the end of 2008 is some R500 billion, suggesting that the total value of these transactions may be in the vicinity of R550 billion to R600 billion. Government spending on welfare and affordable housing over the same period is an estimated R63 billion[*] and bank finance for mortgages for affordable housing is R53 billion[†] for 2004 to 2008 – which is the FSC period for which a target of R42 billion was set. Government spending on land restitution and redistribution up to 2008/9 was R24 billion. This means that some R600 billion of the country's capital has been invested in BEE ownership against some R140 billion in housing and land ownership.

There have been important shifts in both home and land ownership. Again, data are far too limited to get a clear picture of the results. In 2008, more than 40% of black African households owned their own homes, of which half were fully paid up. Further, black Africans owned more than 62% of all formal houses on separate stands.[6] There is no data available on the value of black home ownership, but deeds office surveys suggest that it remains significantly below that of whites.[7]

South Africa) in January 2002; the study was conducted by the BusinessMap Foundation. It found indirect black ownership in the four major banks to be between 14% and 16%, and higher when foreign shareholding in the banks was excluded (17% to 26%). The second is a report in the same year by Cazenove, a financial institution that provides shareholder analysis as part of its services – 'Black economic empowerment: Float like a butterfly or sting like a BEE', October 2002. It calculated a 22% indirect black interest for the JSE as a whole (excluding foreign interests (36% of JSE market cap at the time) and corporate cross-holdings. It assumed this figure would increase to just under 35% by 2012. The third study is by the white union Solidarity: 'The JSE and insurance ownership report', South African Transformation Monitor, March 2010, www.solidaritymedia.co.za. It found the indirect black beneficial interest to be 18.8% in 2007.

On the percentage of foreign equity, Andrew McGregor, of *Who owns whom*, reported that 33% of the 2008 JSE ownership was held by foreign investors. This figure changes all the time (it was 36% in 2002, according to Cazenove), so the relative share of corporate ownership between the respective categories changes all the time too.

* This figure is my estimate of the cumulative budget for the Department of Human Settlement, of which a high proportion, but not all, would be for the delivery of welfare and affordable housing. While data from 2002 were publicly available from the National Treasury (less information was available from Human Settlement), I had not got the additional information by the time of going to press and estimated an average annual expenditure of R3 billion.

† Unaudited figure provided by the Banking Association of South Africa.

Land reform programmes address restitution and redistribution (for the promotion of black agriculture). They have made slow progress, with less than 5% of land redistributed. However, there are no official data available on ownership covering both rural and urban areas, with a racial breakdown. According to a private survey, funded by the Development Bank of Southern Africa, in 2001 blacks owned 20% of land, whites 44%, coloureds 9%, and municipalities more than 25%.[8]

While available data are inadequate, it is not unreasonable to assume that priorities need to shift away from ownership as a source of wealth to land and housing and other economic areas. Black shareholder wealth has undoubtedly advanced more significantly than the other forms of wealth – and it will continue to grow of its own volition as black employees occupy an increasing proportion of jobs (particularly at the higher levels) and thus capture a greater share of the institutional savings that are invested on the stock exchange.

It is also important to remember that trade-offs have to be made when allocating the country's capital – it is not an unlimited resource. Alan Hirsch, responsible for economic policy in the Presidency, notes that 'the growing investment plans of the public sector and the private sector' are competing for funds.[9] This became evident in the conflicts that emerged in the FSC negotiations over how much money should be invested in housing the poor, small business development, infrastructure investment and the financing of BEE transactions. In fact, Hirsch says that the total financial commitment agreed to in the FSC for all these needs was wholly inadequate to finance just the 25% BEE ownership obligation across the private sector. So choices need to be made and new priorities set.

Shareholding as a source of corporate influence

A consistent case has been made by black business representatives against recognising institutional shareholding as a source of black ownership. It is seen as passive ownership, useless as a way to transform the corporate sector. Only direct shareholding, they argue, can create a black business

class able to exercise influence directly over the corporate world.*
This is an ideal not matched by reality. Worldwide, large corporations
are invariably not controlled by their owners. As the Nobel laureate
Joe Stiglitz writes, 'Most large firms don't have a single owner. They
have many shareholders.' The 'ultimate owners ... typically have little
control'.[10]

If we look at JSE-listed companies, the vast majority are not directly
owned by white South Africans – institutional ownership and corporate
cross-holdings dominate. Besides, we must compare apples with apples.
If we want to focus on direct black shareholding only, we need to
compare this to direct white shareholding. That said, I cannot see how
going down this road will be helpful to transformation.

Issues of control and influence need to be seen in the context of
who is managing South Africa's corporations and how institutional
investors are exercising their rights as shareholders. Racial balance in
management, particularly at the higher levels, is crucial to having a
corporate sector that the majority in society can trust and identify with.
Anyway, institutional ownership should not be written off as passive or
irrelevant to promoting black economic interests. There is enormous
transformational potential here, which is increasingly being exercised
worldwide but has lagged in South Africa – perhaps because we have
been too narrowly focused on direct shareholding. An entire new asset
class of socially related investment is evolving and South Africa needs to
look at this as a source of black empowerment. These ideas are explored
further in the final chapter ahead.

---

* Initially the DTI adhered to this argument in the drafting of the Codes and omitted indirect
  black shareholding. However, a lobby from established business led to institutional shareholding
  being included in the calculation of BEE ownership. Of the 25% BEE ownership required,
  10% may be attributed to what the Codes refer to as mandated investments. This allowance is
  relevant to listed companies only, as the equity interests of institutional investors are almost
  entirely held in listed companies.

11

Beyond BEE

I never imagined that my *Where to from here?* micro-lending program would be the basis for a nationwide 'bank for the poor' serving 2.5 million people or that it would be adapted in more than one hundred countries spanning five continents. I was only trying to relieve my guilt and satisfy my desire to be useful to a few starving human beings. But it did not stop with a few people. Those who borrowed and survived would not let it. And after a while, neither would I.

– Muhammad Yunus, *Banker to the poor*

Who would have thought that a small society amidst the secluded foothills and cliff faces of the Himalayas would acquire international acclaim for innovation in economic thinking? Yet Bhutan has. It has taken the Buddhist tenet of happiness and made it the country's measure of economic wellbeing. The model of Gross National Happiness (GNH) aims at 'synergistic and harmonious balance between material well-being and the spiritual, emotional and cultural needs of an individual and society'.[1]

As Bhutan has been evolving this normative approach to development, interest in the economics of happiness has grown – and will no doubt gain in importance after the latest global financial meltdown. The increasing modernisation and complexity of economies have shifted issues of wellbeing and sustainability into the political and economic mainstream. This was signalled by the French president Nicolas Sarkozy when he appointed an internationally acclaimed commission of experts to consider new measurements for economic performance and social progress.[2] The

Institute of New Economic Thinking is another initiative, sponsored by George Soros, to think afresh after the global crisis exposed much bankruptcy in traditional economic theory. Alongside these intellectual endeavours are new trends in socially relevant investments designed to find a balance between profit making and long-term sustainability.

For Bhutan, the GNH seeks to go beyond the conventional income-based measures of development and attempts to address the ends rather than just the means (in Buddhist teaching all actions have consequences). There are four foundation goals: sustainable and equitable socio-economic development; environmental conservation; preservation and promotion of culture; and good governance. The planners see their approach as 'intuitive economics',[3] a middle road where there is balance between sustainable growth and the pursuit of wealth. It's about Karma: what goes around comes around. It's rooted in values and is necessarily flexible to ensure the means never supersede the goals.

In the economics of happiness, there are consistent themes: relativity of circumstances, and education, health, income and certainty are important for wellbeing. Studies have found that 'some simple patterns hold: a stable marriage, good health and enough (but not too much) income are good for happiness. Unemployment, divorce and economic instability are terrible for it.'[4] In particular, uncertainty is 'one thing that people have a hard time adapting to' and those who have made the most income gains are also the most critical of their economic situation.[5]

Relative income is said to convey most (though not quite all) of material wellbeing. Obviously, a spectator who leaps up at a football game gets a much better view of the match, but only for the moment before his neighbours do the same, after which he has no better view than before.[6] This explains why the citizens of growing economies like the United States are not happier today than they were in the 1950s – relative to each other, Americans don't see themselves as better off and therefore they are no happier in absolute terms. However, in a society like South Africa with pervasive poverty, relative positioning only matters beyond a satisfactory level of income; up to that point absolute improvements in income are critical to wellbeing. One study on transitional societies also found that income inequality may be a strong source of dissatisfaction – not so evident in developed economies.[7]

Sarkozy's commission, led by two Nobel laureates, Joseph Stiglitz and Amartya Sen,* addressed the inadequacy of traditional measures, such as gross domestic product (GDP), in understanding current-day wellbeing and its maintenance for future generations – what is generally referred to as sustainability. Importantly, 'what we measure affects what we do; and if our measurements are flawed, decisions may be distorted'.[8] The risks and implications today of making the wrong decisions have perhaps never been greater, as the world faces the mega-challenge of picking up the pieces of the financial meltdown and climate change. The latter will force significant reallocation of resources amidst a complex global economy and localised poverty and devastation.

This growing emphasis on societal wellbeing offers important threads for South Africa to weave into its policies of transformation and BEE. As much of this book shows, the values and social goals that underpinned the early initiatives to create a racially inclusive economy have dissipated amidst the unintended consequences of empowerment policies in particular. The achievement of material wellbeing has come to dominate, at the expense, many feel, of all else – South Africa's own Brave New World. But more than that, policy is locked into old paradigms. BEE is informed by approaches to affirmative action first implemented half a century ago in the United States and even earlier by the British in colonised Malaya.

Other transformation initiatives reflect a similar reliance on old formulas. Land redistribution is illustrative. In 2009, the government announced a fresh effort to redistribute agricultural land to black owners by relocating white farmers to other parts of Africa.[9] This, it is hoped, will free up sufficient land to meet the 30% redistribution target, which is already way behind schedule. Liberia responded immediately: South African farmers have a reputation for managing difficult conditions and Liberia, with its failed state-owned farming programme, needs such expertise. In fact, we are not short of takers throughout Africa – in anticipation of this white migration, Angola and Uganda put aside prime agricultural land, and for some years Mozambique has attracted South African farmers who, on their side of the border, faced uncertainty as a

---

* Joseph Stiglitz and Amartya Sen are also members of the Institute of New Economic Thinking.

result of land claims.* How do we envisage coping with the implications of climate change? With agricultural yields expected to reduce by anything from 15% to 35% due to climatic impact, it hardly seems sensible sending elsewhere those farmers most capable of dealing with difficult conditions. Is there not another way of ensuring land reform without it becoming a negative sum game, as it already seems to be? By government's own admission, 90% of redistributed land is no longer agriculturally functional.[10] What other ways should we use to address the problems of black landlessness?

It is vital to step back and think about the components of a new discourse on economic transformation in South Africa. Rather than trying to provide an exhaustive list of what could be done, I focus on a few keys areas, which fall into three categories:

- *Foundation issues*: Any attempt at a thoroughgoing review of BEE and economic transformation will not leave the starting blocks without them. Here I deal with a new policy-making framework to accommodate the unpredictable environment and, as such, be responsive to change. I also consider the importance of the reinstatement of values and commitment to transformation that got lost in the number counting.
- *Transformation priorities:* What needs to be high up the priority list to ensure a growing economy that is also transformative in character? Without dismissing the need to target the poor, I restrict my focus here to the middle level of the economy – the black middle class and medium-sized enterprises. For individual health, we do well by breathing deeply from the middle – and I assume the same for societal health. An altogether bigger middle would reduce unacceptably high income inequality and provide a basis for productive BEE results. But the middle growth depends on significantly improved education performance as well as information and communication technology. Small and medium enterprises can leapfrog many of their inherent disadvantages through the internet, for example, but as yet South Africa's

---

* White farmer numbers have dropped from around 60 000 in 1994 to a current estimate of 40 000.

ICT infrastructure and costs are a drag on economic efficiency. Innovation is also fundamental to economic transformation. New ideas and research and development are needed to open up markets, products and services to those who are excluded and often seen as noncommercial.

- *Sustainable investment:* The myopic focus on BEE ownership has resulted in South Africa paying too little attention to other forms of transformative investment. Since the Eighties there has been a gradual but growing trend towards ethical and socially responsible investment mandates, which have guided institutional investors. Today there are many legs to socially relevant investment initiatives, with the environment or green issues now dominating the mix. South Africa needs to look afresh at this sector of investment and explore its relevance for BEE and sustainable growth. For example, as a new high-growth sector, mobile telephony supported the growth of some of the country's best BEE companies. The same potential lies in the green sector – but with a word of caution against opportunistic, unproductive BEE investors.

Foundations for new thinking

There are many foundation issues, a few of which have already been touched upon earlier. For example, we have seen that the ANC is highly dependent on the current rent-seeking character of BEE ownership to meet its financial needs. Without other sources of political funding, the organisation is unlikely to challenge the current formulation of BEE ownership in any way that could put at risk its financial position. This suggests that the resolution of party funding is crucial to opening up a meaningful review of BEE.

Another example is the compliance mindset encouraged by the Codes. This has tended to remove personal and organisational responsibility, whereas social and economic transformation requires just that, along with a strong underpinning of values and commitment.

Less attention has been paid to the changing understanding of economics and what this might mean for policy making and the management of transformation. Uncertainty and social context sit at the centre of much of the new thinking on economics. For some time, standard economic theory has come under growing scrutiny for relying on assumptions like 'general equilibrium' and the 'rational agent'. But with the 2008 global meltdown, it became obvious that economic theory had failed everyone, proving 'virtually useless in anticipating the crisis, analysing its development and recommending measures to deal with it,' writes John Kay, the *Financial Times* columnist and a member of the Institute of New Economic Thinking.[11] Why? Fundamentally, the theoretical reliance on 'rational expectations' is an 'implausible notion', he says, but one that has allowed universal economic theory. Drop the rational part and we are left with a description of the world that must acknowledge that 'what people do depends on their fallible beliefs and perceptions'. This introduces uncertainty and social contexts into economics and rules out the universal application of theory. In Kay's view, 'new economic thinking must necessarily be eclectic'.

Implications of uncertainty

What are the implications for South Africa? For a number of reasons, the country has many layers of uncertainty. It is a transitional economy still grappling with restructuring. This implies greater unpredictability than ordinarily found in the developed world. Millions of people coexist with uncertainty because of high unemployment and underemployment, inadequate education and the high prevalence of HIV/Aids. Then there is uncertainty among whites, still a crucial cog in the economy. The South African author Jonny Steinberg[12] finds 'a whole stratum of whites' unable to 'imagine a future' and the fact that they may grow even more prosperous does not make them any more able to do so. There will always be a sense of 'borrowed time'. Then among the black elite, there appears underlying grievance over the results of economic change, and BEE policy in particular, despite having gained the most since democracy. Their expectations are flailing and rubbing up against white uncertainty – an irritant for race relations. Public opinion surveys show diminishing confidence in a happy future for all races, deteriorating race relations and people increasingly feeling that the country is not going in the right direction.[13]

In addition, the country as a whole finds itself on an unpredictable global stage that always has the potential to bedevil national strategies. It is easy to feel out of control. Trying to transform an economy with high levels of uncertainty places a heavy load on governments. The traditional reliance on sound policies and strong institutions isn't enough. Governments need to have the capacity to be highly responsive to change. This presupposes a shift from bureaucratic styles of government to flexible, knowledge-based systems that draw on expertise and innovation, supported by strong information systems. This has enormous implications for South Africa, which has spent all its years as a young democracy implementing new policies and changing institutional structures – it has been an onerous task. Now, it needs to think afresh, with an intellectual nimbleness that will allow it to approach the new challenges with the necessary flexibility to cope with the changing environment.

Does it have this capability? There are pockets within the government that are well aware of the new demands and responding accordingly. In 2009 Trevor Manuel, for example, proposed a planning commission under his stewardship with the objective of mobilising knowledgeable, independent thinkers. 'It's not a bad idea to have outsiders around you, we need their contributions. We need more rigorous testing of ideas inside the house. There must be freedom to debate, read and inform your arguments. This gives ideas robustness,' he commented in an interview [14] – after bumping up against opposition from some within the ANC who were uncomfortable with working outside the boundary of party loyalty. Ebrahim Patel, the minister responsible for economic development, followed suit with an advisory panel that includes Stiglitz – although he has come under criticism for having too many like-minded people.

But eminent advisers cannot compensate for an ill-equipped civil service. In general, and more particularly at the lower levels of government, there are neither the right skills being set nor the necessary information for a new approach. As Neva Makgetla, an economist on Patel's panel, puts it: 'If a car stops in the middle of rush hour and the driver dashes off for petrol although the problem is obviously a flat tyre, you are probably stuck behind a government policy-maker. One of our main policy sins has been the tendency to jump to solutions for presumed problems without taking the time to assess the available evidence and consider alternatives.'[15]

Still, information from some parts of the state is better than it was. The Office of the Presidency, for example, now provides a wide-ranging set of development indicators to address the same questions being raised by the Sarkozy commission. That said, the value of information lies in its use – good analysis and ability to act on it are crucial. So we are back to people and human capital. There is a growing criticism that civil servants are not up to meeting the challenges. Many point to employment equity as a source of the problem; too much experience was lost too quickly in a bid to change the racial and ideological profile of the state. Manuel believes that the fast-tracking of black professionals, too young and inexperienced for the 'tremendous decision-making powers' they assumed, has in many instances resulted in civil servants who have become 'arrogant and not open to persuasion'.[16] Aggressive affirmative action necessarily undervalues experience, leading to reduced efficiencies. It is difficult to envisage this effort being done in any other way. But today, as the negative consequences overwhelm the early benefits of change, our situation cries out for a different approach.

In particular, opposition to the ANC's policy of 'cadre deployment' within the public sector is growing. Paul Hoffman, of the Institute for Accountability, notes that 'cadre deployment' is rife but unconstitutional: 'It appears that those [in the state] responsible for recruiting are either beholden to [ANC] cadre deployment committees or actually on them.'[17] The practice, he adds, disadvantages all suitably qualified people, black and white. Other reports suggest that the politicisation of public positions has discouraged black professionals from taking up public office, whether in a government department or in state-owned enterprises. Fundamentally, the civil service needs to be professionalised. This would go a long way to resolving some of the missing layers in the foundation needed for new thinking.

Reinstatement of values and commitment
Mamphela Ramphele talks of 'transcendence' – a shift in the frame of reference for transformation that is 'deeply spiritual' and 'forces one to be true to deep convictions'. Implicitly identifying with Bhutan,

she says, 'It is about making oneself vulnerable by abandoning known ways of seeing the world and engaging with others to explore different approaches.'[18]

Sampie Terreblanche, a leading Afrikaner academic, makes an appeal to his white compatriots, arguing that they have particular responsibilities for crafting a different future: 'Of course, it has not been easy for white South Africans (or most of them at least) to acknowledge the evils of colonialism, segregation and apartheid ... However, if whites do not critically re-evaluate their past, they cannot expect the victims of colonialism to accept them as trustworthy companions in building a common future.'[19]

Both seek a different basis for transformation. It is quite different to the approach taken in the BEE Codes – one underpinned by compliance. Instead, as William Gumede articulates, there needs to be 'a renewal in values, morals and ethics'. For him, the ANC has succeeded in 'articulating hard political values', but it has been 'unable to deal with the soft values that hold the social fabric of society together'.[20] Such 'soft' issues may be framed as cultural capital, alongside the other forms of capital that tend to receive more attention, notably economic, human and social capital.

In the past few years, the debate around transformational shortcomings has strengthened, although still largely made up of individual voices. Constituencies within civil society, such as business, and within politically aligned groupings have not engaged in a consistent, organised way, although there have been some limited initiatives.[*]

BEE is a central focus of the criticism, seen as a major culprit in constraining socio-economic transformation. It is even regarded as an obstacle to open debate. Ramphele, for instance, suggests that BEE may unintentionally create 'disincentives for critical independent voices'. She explains: 'Access to preferential procurement and other BEE benefits is often heavily influenced by public officials who might withhold approval of competitive bids for goods and services from those seen to be too critical of the powers that be.'[21] And the sharp political sensitivities associated with BEE and exploited by those with heavy vested interests

---

[*] The Dinokeng scenario, initiated by Mamphela Ramphele among others, brought together various stakeholders in 2009 to consider South Africa's economic development challenges.

have dampened critical debate – it is worth remembering how quickly white business ducked its head after Thabo Mbeki's cutting objections to corporations that cited BEE as a business risk.

BEE, many critics believe, is also undermining the ANC's longstanding policy of nonracialism and distorting black identity. Moeletsi Mbeki says it has positioned its main beneficiaries, the black elite, as 'underlings'. For him, BEE is a form of reparations that one can only justify drawing as 'a victim'.[22] Ramphele also sees the psyche of victimhood as a posture that feeds off policies of preferential treatment.[23] She refers to Frantz Fanon's exposition of the 'scarring of the black psyche' that resulted from colonial oppression. A symptom, she says, is sometimes the 'defensive romanticisation of indigenous culture. Such idealization of tradition makes it difficult to adapt to the demands of an evolving socio–economic and political environment.'[24]

Ubuntu – working with a collective interest – is one such concept that was heavily idealised in the early years of democracy. It offered the potential of a new workplace ethic that could be integrated into BEE, but it never took root. Scant attention was paid to the detail of making it adaptive to the corporate environment. Instead, the traditional corporate culture remained largely unchallenged.

The educationalist Neville Alexander believes that BEE has undercut nonracialism by perpetuating racial identities and injecting 'dangerous divisive potential' into society. For him, transformation policies need to move beyond racial labels. If properly focused on the needy, they will inevitably focus on black people. Even in employment, he argues, it is possible to have a bias towards blacks without racial profiling – for example, the state could require that new civil servants have a proficiency in one or more indigenous African language.[25]

Gumede speaks out against a 'retribalisation of South African society' – simply replacing black faces with white faces rather than developing a 'new democratic ethos'. Such concerns fit with international debates on race and how much we emphasise difference rather than commonality.

Placing the foundation

What will ensure these foundation issues can be addressed? They are big, difficult to conceptualise in practical terms. Among the magic ingredients, I suspect, is leadership as the starting point. Political leadership is particularly important to mobilise and revitalise a commitment to transformation, with space created for new ideas and innovation in a well-constructed dialogue. This was very much a feature of the early reform years after the unbanning of the ANC in 1990.

However, it is in the area of leadership that I feel least confident. The ANC is not monolithic; there are leading figures apparently mindful that the organisation has strayed from its moral compass. Kgalema Motlanthe is concerned that 'the ANC rules, not leads' – and wants to see a reassertion of national 'unity' as a central pivot of party and state policy.[26] Mathews Phosa, the ANC treasurer-general, signalled that the ANC's company Chancellor House would withdraw from transacting state business, and specifically from the controversial contract with Eskom. Unhappy, the ANC secretary-general, Gwede Mantashe, kicked back, but then the Finance minister Pravin Gordhan and another ministerial colleague, Barbara Hogan, followed through with appeals to the ANC to do the right thing. For the moment, however, their voices are like interjections – it remains to be seen whether they become groundswells within the party.

Transformation needs a special kind of commitment and persistence. The results cannot be achieved simply by applying a set of rules with which people are expected to comply. Commitment generates positive energy and innovative thinking, whereas compliance dulls it. What practically can be done? Jeffrey Sachs, the director of the Earth Institute, covers the same problematic in relation to climate change. 'Sustainability', he notes, 'has to be a choice of a global society that thinks ahead and acts in unaccustomed harmony.'[27] Governments cannot meet the global challenges alone. 'Complex social problems have multiple stakeholders who are all part of the problem and who generally must all be part of the solution. Gaining the co-operation among the disparate stakeholders is the toughest challenge of all.'[28]

Many South Africans will agree, and heave a heavy sigh. The country's transitional experience is marked by numerous stakeholder negotiations and dialogues; many can testify to how difficult co-operative problem-solving is. Yet, because of this, the country has the necessary institutional framework to manage it – although possibly in need of some renovation. Importantly, there is an increasingly favourable mood towards a recommitment to a new dialogue. The deputy chief executive of the JSE, Nicky Newton-King, says, 'It is no longer good enough for us to stand on the sidelines and look to others to construct [South Africa's] future. We have to get involved, and so act more bravely and forcefully than we have in the past.'[29] Makgetla points to the 'hard choices' that have to be made in allocating resources: a 30% land redistribution target will require R50 billion, improving municipal services in the former Bantustans needs an extra R15 billion a year, as would social grants should the level be raised to the international poverty line. For her, 'a more open national discourse' is needed for a 'more balanced outcome'.[30]

But more than that, 'unaccustomed harmony' in South Africa will require many practical partnerships that cut across the racial divide and acknowledge the importance of shared skills – the promotion of unity and nonracialism will matter enormously in providing the necessary gel. Such co-operation cannot take place in an environment where some views are regarded as more legitimate than others. The current political discourse, even within the ANC itself, is too often conducted disrespectfully, with discussion marred by political swear words.

Transformation priorities

Sachs emphasises innovation, technologies and scientific research as core responsibilities for governments and civil society to meet the challenges of sustainability.[31] These require meticulous attention to education and skills. Most worrying is that all are very weak links in South Africa. Rather than trying to answer these vast and complex problems, I shall tease out some questions that may be important for rethinking BEE and moving beyond the current policy boundaries for economic transformation. To do so, I take a detour via Vietnam.

As part of my research for this book, I visited Vietnam.* A surprising choice when researching affirmative-action policies – it is largely a homogeneous society† with a very different economy. But the two

---

* The information and quotations that follow come mainly from my visit in June 2008, when I interviewed state officials, Vietnamese think-tanks in economics and politics, small business representatives and multilateral development agencies.

† There are ethnic minorities in Vietnam that constitute 14% of the population but more than 40% of the poor, so there is some focus on special measures to address this problem.

countries have similar histories of struggle, both still grappling with how to bridge past ideological affinities while coping with the realities of managing economies in the context of globalisation. Both have prioritised economic transformation. Remarkably, in just on a decade, Vietnam has reduced poverty faster than any other country in recent history, a far cry from being the third poorest in the world in the Eighties, when more than 60% of the people lived below the poverty line, against some 15% today. This has been achieved by allowing a previously prohibited private sector to emerge under a reform policy called 'Renovation' (*Doi Moi*), designed to create a 'socialist market-orientated economy'.

Some months before my visit, a South African government delegation had been there on a fact-finding mission. It had been impressed, I was told, with Vietnam's policy towards state-owned enterprises – notably to introduce private ownership but retain state control in many instances. Around the same time, the South African department responsible for state enterprises shifted towards a similar stance. I wondered if the Vietnam visit had anything to do with this. If so, they had come away with the wrong lesson.

The important changes in Vietnam lie not in the retention of state ownership, but in the introduction of a market economy. Also key is their approach, one of gradual reform, with the emphasis on what is termed 'learning by doing' – taking the small steps that James Scott recommends instead of grand schemes aimed at social engineering. As the Hanoi government has loosened its control over economic activity, the *metis* (practical intelligence) that Scott highlights has produce some remarkable results. Rice farming is illustrative. In just three years into the reforms, Vietnam changed from being an importer to an exporter of rice. 'It's as if there is an inherent ability to trade,' a development adviser surmised. 'As soon as restrictions were lifted, people traded.'

The farmers succeeded because the state had removed itself and allowed them to apply their expertise in an 'autonomous' way, a requirement that Malcolm Gladwell in *Outliers* identifies as essential for rice farming to thrive: 'The whole process of wet rice farming is very exacting. It's a crop that doesn't do very well with something like slavery and wage labour.'[32] Further, more land is not available nor equipment affordable to offer productivity increases, and so, Gladwell points out, people had to become smarter to improve their yields – they had to be 'skills orientated'.[33]

The Vietnamese seem to have applied the same approach to becoming a modernised and competitive economy. Their strategic priorities are focused, uncluttered by too many objectives that risk distraction – as they would be in caring for a rice paddy. For example, they decided that information and communication technology (ICT) had to be high among the priorities. On the whole, they are delivering according to plan. Today 25% of the population are said to be internet users and Vietnam's ICT development has overtaken some neighbours, previously far more advanced.[34] It also prioritised the development of an ICT hardware industry through foreign investment, attracting billions of dollars in commitments.[35] Some development agencies told me that because the government tends to do what it says it will do, this has created a measure of credibility that then allows Vietnam some slack when things don't go according to plan.

There is a lexicon found across the state and development sectors that talks to the kind of people the Vietnamese are and how they approach challenges. 'Pragmatism', 'flexibility', 'independent', 'forward looking', 'good at managing instability' are some of the attributes that the Vietnamese give to themselves. People create their own storyboards about themselves that often become self-perpetuating stereotypes. However, in Vietnam, it is as if the frequent use of these words gives political permission to act accordingly, thus overwriting the ethos of control within the governing socialist party. So, when I described BEE obligations to a state-employed economist, he smiled wryly: 'Fifteen to twenty years ago, the government said to everyone, "This is what I want", and required everyone to do it. But that has changed … We followed a pragmatic approach.' A leading analyst talks of the Vietnamese 'not looking back, but forward … After domination by other powers, we didn't ask for compensation … and so we own our strategies, we own our policies.' Drawing on this sense of independence, the government managed the very politically sensitive issue of opening up to American foreign investors – they could accede to investor needs because of their pragmatism and not because they were beholden.

There are some useful pointers from the Vietnamese experience –

but I mention them mindful of the need to be cautious when flipping experiences and lessons from one country to another. The first is about being focused; transformation policy in South Africa is packed with objectives – and so priorities have got lost amidst the clutter and delivery has suffered. Unlike Vietnam, the South African government has lost much of the credibility it earned, for instance, when it stabilised the macro–economy. Another lesson lies in the importance of small steps – that, too, helps focus. There may also be value in looking at changing some of the political language in South Africa to facilitate a new dialogue and mobilise commitment to transformation.

But perhaps the most useful message from Vietnam is that *metis* really matters, as does being 'skills orientated'. We have the benefit of Gladwell popularising such issues. His account of Jewish garment makers, who had immigrated to the United States in the mid-nineteenth century, complements that of the rice farmers. Working from tiny New York apartments they made the city into the single largest clothing centre in the world. This 'did not come from nowhere ... this was their field' when they lived in Europe. They 'worked like madmen at what they knew.'[36]

Thomas Sowell,[*] an African American academic, takes the same theme to support his argument against affirmative action policies. The assumption that there may be an 'even distribution or proportional representation of groups in occupations or institutions' is, he argues, 'an intellectual construct defied by reality in society after society.'[37] He is careful to emphasise that the embedded group skills like those of Vietnam's rice farmers or Gladwell's garment makers are not 'permanent, much less hereditary'.[38] People can and do expand their horizons.

In South Africa, the BEE Codes are premised on the assumption that Sowell disputes – that there is a 'one size fits all' set of targets, with little room for flexibility and nuance. For the moment these targets are not demographically proportional for the various levels of management, but there is powerful backing for this idea. However, if we are to look beyond the current construct of BEE, there may be value in exploring the *metis* of black South Africans and seeing if policy could recognise this as an additional basis to further black empowerment by building

---

[*] It is interesting to note how little of Thomas Sowell's work is referenced in South African research on employment equity, possibly because of his conservative approach.

off people's strengths. For instance, could communication skills, evident in multilingualism, be an advantage that is used to expand investment opportunities in the ICT sector, such as call centres? Music and the film industry are other promising spheres. Naturally, in a racially charged society, this may be difficult territory to tread for fear that it implies further racial compartmentalisation of people in the economy, or may emphasise racial stereotypes.

The seemingly intractable problems of education are another reason for putting aside expectations of demographic proportionality in the workplace. Targets for certain professions – engineering is a good example – cannot possibly be met unless the universities produce more graduates. The annual output of engineering graduates is static while local demand is growing. Adding to pressure is high international demand that is pulling more engineers out of South Africa. Logically, if black graduates are insufficient for the employment equity targets that are being enforced, there will be unwanted consequences – for example, jobs may not be filled for lack of black candidates, and not for lack of candidates, resulting in false skills shortages. Alternatively, and all too often, jobs are filled by underqualified people rather than being made available to qualified white candidates.[*]

Raising any questions about employment equity stirs emotions; they are politically sensitive and so there is a tendency to tiptoe around them. The sensitivities are understandable. Black presence at the higher echelons of the private sector remains low. In 2008, less than 25% of top and senior management was black, against some 80% in government.[39] However, effective black participation in the workplace needs the

---

[*] As an example of how employment equity can go wrong, the engineer in charge of medium to high voltage work for the City of Tshwane needed more staff for his department to function properly. To shortlist applicants, he set a test to assess their suitability, and the municipality approved it. The posts were advertised, the candidates tested, and the resulting shortlist proved to be entirely white. This was unacceptable to the municipality. The posts were readvertised, directed at 'employment equity candidates'. Their scores on a simpler test ranged between 2.2% and 32.2%, figures that were then adjusted up by 10%. The engineer considered that hiring such underskilled people would put themselves and others at risk. He reported the matter to the Engineering Council of South Africa, adding, 'I wish therefore to distance myself from this process, and I wish to be exonerated of the negative impact this process might have on the performance of the Power System Control Section, the Electricity Department, the Council and the public of Tshwane in regards to safety as well as service delivery.' The municipality took umbrage and instituted disciplinary proceedings against the engineer in a whistle-blowing case *(City of Tshwane Metropolitan Municipality* v *Engineering Council of South Africa and Another* 2010 (2) SA 333 (SCA)).

difficult questions to be asked. It also needs joint responsibility between the government and the private sector.

The first port of call must be education. It is the weakest link for BEE and economic transformation. Jacob Zuma pinpoints it as priority number one, yet a sense of urgency seems lacking, leading to questions about the government's seriousness. If we compare ourselves with Vietnam, this assessment in 2006 is illuminating: 'A recent study assessed the secondary education system of Vietnam against an international benchmark. On most counts the findings were encouraging. The study found that teachers are well educated and have at least two years' training. They prepare their lessons and are assiduous in teaching the prescribed curriculum. Textbooks are mostly in adequate supply. Buildings and equipment are not characterised by lavish standards, but most schools have the basics, including libraries and a reasonable range of teaching aids. Class size is well within the acceptable range. Principals manage in a "hands-on" way, and further supervision is provided by regular formal inspection.'[40] Against all these ticks for Vietnam, place a cross for South Africa – and yet, for some years, each one of these points has been identified by educationalists, inside and outside government, as key problems to be resolved.

The training system is another grand plan that has gone horribly wrong, Everybody talks about it, but it's as if much-needed action has taken leave. Repairing big mistakes is difficult and costly – 'learning by doing' may be an important guide for future changes.

The missing middle

Mark Gevisser notes the stimulating home life that the Mbeki family and others like them had as a matter of course sixty years ago, a phenomenon for many in the generations that grew up before Bantu Education. 'When I asked him [Thabo Mbeki] about the roots of this intellectual approach, he went straight back to his parents: 'You see, we grew up with books around the house and whenever we were together with the parents … you could say anything, and it would be discussed.'[41] Govan Mbeki recalled arriving unexpectedly at the Queenstown home of Michael Moerane a few months after Thabo had moved there, aged eight, to continue his schooling in 1951: 'I came there in the early evening and found my brother-in-law sitting at the piano, and his six children plus Thabo all with an instrument of his or her own. My brother was playing, and they were accompanying, Thabo on the flute ... these sessions happened almost every night.'[42]

The erudite evening activities make Mbeki's upbringing look decidedly middle class. His upbringing was unusual but not unique: a small black middle class, with good education, had emerged despite the impediments of racial discrimination. Later, however, apartheid all but snuffed it out, and the revolutionary ideology of the ANC during some thirty years of armed struggle demeaned the black middle class, small as it was, as offering a buffer against radical change. This ideological discomfort still rankles. Mbeki's intellectualism became identified as cause for his distance from 'the people', and the emphasis of BEE on promoting middle-class interests is often the reason for criticising it. Yet, a sizeable black middle class, along with a significantly enlarged medium-sized enterprise sector, with a strong black presence, is fundamental to a transformed economy.

The current structure of the private sector is not conducive to a highly innovative and competitive economy. It's as though the economy took a deep breath, pulled in its stomach and never let it out. So, a priority is to do just that and allow a significant widening around the girth. There are a number of reasons why this will help transform the economy.

One of the consequences of sanctions was a highly concentrated corporate sector. Just before the ANC took over in 1994, the top six conglomerates controlled companies accounting for some 85% of the market capitalisation of the JSE. Today, the figure is around half that, but that is still high. Concentration means market dominance, which in turn means less competition and the exclusion of newcomers. Networks were also concentrated. A small, white, male inner circle controlled the corporate sector. That too has changed, with black entry into corporate boards, but the culture of elitism persists. The concentration of networks restricts the free flow of new ideas and information, the lifeblood of an entrepreneurial and innovative society. The middle class has also grown as black economic participation and education has improved. Living standard measures (LSM) show a marked increase in the middle range of LSM 5–7 through the 2000s – from 31% of adults in 2001, to 34%

in 2004, to 41% in 2007. Yet South Africa's income inequality remains among the highest in the world, suggesting that just not enough of the middle has filled out, with sufficient mobility from the lower income levels into the middle classes.

Research suggests that high growth may be better achieved by promoting medium-sized enterprises than small to micro enterprises and in particular the start-ups that tend to dominate among small firms. Enterprise development programmes have neglected medium enterprises. There are possibly two reasons for this. First, there is a popular view that small enterprises are good for growth and job creation. Second, most black businesses are captured at this level, whereas medium-sized enterprises are, on the whole, white-owned.

Scott Shane, responsible for pioneering research on enterprise development, points out that 'to get more economic growth by having more start-ups, new companies would need to be more productive than existing companies. But they are not ... The results show that productivity increases with firm age.' Further, 'as a whole, new firms have net job destruction after their first year' and 'jobs in new firms pay less, offer worse fringe benefits, and provide less job security than jobs in existing firms.'[43]

So, small and micro enterprises may be good to support for reasons of self-employment but not necessarily for economic growth. Given our high levels of unemployment, such support is important; without it, people would be forced to join the social grants queue. Medium-sized enterprises, on the other hand, generally have matured enough to be sustainable but not enough to have lost their youthful energy for high growth – unlike fully matured corporations. Also, BEE is barely captured here. As we've seen with mobile telephony, high growth opportunities make an enormous difference to the sustainability of black ownership. This suggests that there is a case for a rethink around revitalising policy to support medium-sized enterprises as specific economic growth and BEE priorities.

Some black entrepreneurs have grown into the medium level by dint of determination; others by partnering with experienced white entrepreneurs; and a few have emerged as offshoots of the leading BEE companies. Most will testify to a largely unsupportive environment, particularly for finance – the obvious sources, the state-owned National Empowerment Fund and the Industrial Development Corporation, are still difficult to access. An experienced organisation like Anglo Zimele can only do so much, and there are few others like it. So, it would be important to mobilise all this experience and knowledge to ensure an appropriate policy rethink. If nothing is done, the likely outcome is another round of BEE transactions (now focused on medium enterprises given that the top end has been all but done) that add no real economic value and discourage people from taking the risks of building real businesses. This won't be good for black empowerment or economic growth.

An interesting facet of a strong black middle class is its potential role in the development of medium-sized enterprises. There are plenty of studies that debunk the 'rags to riches' stories. Most entrepreneurs emerge from the middle classes, where people are prepared to take the necessary risks because they have a safety net of families and friends, and they have a basis for success through their education, expertise and networks. For South Africa to expand the layer of medium enterprises it will need many more potential entrepreneurs – that means, on the whole, educated black professionals and managers willing to leave the comfort of corporate offices and take the risks of creating and growing businesses. BEE policy has supported the growth of the black middle class, but there is also the potential for it to distort this growth. As we have seen above, employment equity targets that are not supported by the education system can lead to serious shortages of black skills. This in turn can result in hefty premiums on black salaries, which in turn may discourage black managers and professionals from leaving the comfort of their offices. So, once more, everything turns on education and training.

Sustainable investment

Income inequality is one of the main barriers to sustainable growth. A pyramid economy with most of the population at the bottom and the wealthy few at the top is eventually dragged down if mobility into the upper chambers is denied.

In 2009, South Africa was said to be 'the most unequal society in the world'.* This is unlikely to be the case if the government's social spending – heavily biased towards the poor – is factored into income calculations. Earlier studies have found that inequality measures drop quite significantly when this is done.† But even if South Africa is not among the most unequal economies, the racial element in the income divide creates the perception of unacceptable inequality. Further, the status of South Africa as a middle-income economy is deceptive. Stiglitz points out that the traditional measure of average GDP per capita 'can be going up even when most individuals in our society not only feel that they are worse off, but actually are worse off.' Better to use the measure of median income to understand wellbeing.‡ The differences between these two indicators are salutary and startling. Average GDP per capita for 2008 is almost R26 000, as against a median of just under R360.§

As discussed earlier, the economy would be invigorated by an expanded girth – this would go some way to reducing inequalities. But economic efficiency must be achieved. A BEE policy designed to promote a black middle class may only exacerbate inequality if black ownership remains unproductive and employment equity is not pursued sensibly in concert with an improved education system. Further, reliance on more social spending to shore up the income differences is not sustainable – it is already very high, with government spending 5.5% of GDP on social grants in 2008/9, up from 2.9% five years earlier. There have to be other solutions, and this brings us to a potentially large area of investment, commonly referred to as sustainable or responsible investment.

While responsible investment has been around for thirty years and more, it is has only recently moved into the mainstream, with growing amounts of private-sector investment dollars directed towards funds and companies that find business opportunities in serving the poor or satisfying environmental objectives. There are many examples of innovation. One is LeapFrog Investments, a global investment fund

---

* Donwald Pressly, 'Study finds SA now falls below Brazil', *Business Report*, 28 September 2009.

† Servaas van der Berg and Ronelle Burger, 'The stories behind the numbers: An investigation of efforts to deliver services to the South African poor', a report prepared for the World Bank, 2002, www.worldbank.org.

‡ Stiglitz, 2010, pp 284–5.

§ Development indicators 2009, the Office of the Presidency, www.thepresidency.gov.za, p 23.

founded by South Africans with an office in Johannesburg. It is dedicated to investing in businesses in Asia and Africa offering micro-insurance. In the midst of the financial crisis, it raised more money than targeted – over US$100 million to invest in companies that provide insurance to markets that have traditionally been neglected by conventional financial institutions and investors. So LeapFrog is out there to demonstrate the power of 'profit-with-purpose'.

Financial and social returns

Responsible investing is about investing for returns while simultaneously focusing on the 'impact of investments on wider society and the natural environment, both today and in the future'.* Climate change is the superstar that has thrust the issue of sustainable development into corporate boardrooms. This is no longer the domain of alternative people – the likes of the 'tree-huggers'. As LeapFrog's president and founder, Andrew Kuper, says, 'Unusual and extraordinary people often get involved in this area.' Professional skills and innovation are their important hallmarks; they come from many different backgrounds and have various political persuasions. 'Market-based solutions to mass poverty can unite and appeal to almost everyone,' he says.

LeapFrog made its first investment in South Africa in AllLife, a company providing one of the supposedly 'impossible-to-do-profitably' services, except that it is doing it profitably. This is life assurance for people with HIV. Instead of focusing on average years to death (mortality rates) irrespective of how you manage your disease, as the basis of risk assessment, AllLife developed a model based on the probability of living when the insured commit themselves to following a 'health monitoring and treatment program'. Instead of telling people that those with HIV/ Aids are likely to die within seven years or so, AllLife tells them that, if they manage their health, they are going to live for a long time, twenty years or more on current technology, and so are eminently insurable. They need not be excluded from financial services and thus the larger economy.

---

* Mainstreaming responsible investment, World Economic Forum, Geneva, 2005, p 7.

The make-up of responsible investment

There are a number of facets to responsible investment. LeapFrog falls into a relatively new capital market that some refer to as 'impact investment'. It is estimated that the total assets invested in funds (like LeapFrog) and enterprises that seek to generate social and environmental impact together with a financial return are US$50 billion in the past few years, growing at an annual average of 35%.* If just 1% of total assets managed globally are channelled into this capital market in the next decade, some R500 billion will be invested.

Responsible investment first emerged as the negative screening by institutional investors of a wide range of issues – for instance, companies involved in arms, tobacco or sweat shops would be screened out and excluded from receiving investment funds. Apartheid was one such issue in the Eighties. Large US-based funds, like the powerful Californian state pension fund CalPERS, threatened to withdraw their investments in major American multinationals if they didn't apply codes of conduct in their South Africa operations. This socially responsible investment (SRI) activity has grown at an extraordinary pace since the mid-Nineties. By the end of 2007, SRI assets were some US$2.7 trillion – 11% of all funds under management in the United States – and the number of socially and environmentally screened funds had increased to 260.†

All manner of benchmarks exist to monitor and assess SRI activity. The Global Reporting Initiative offers the most widely used sustainability reporting framework, while the UN Global Compact, launched in 2000, has become an internationally recognised platform through which investors and corporations formally commit themselves to ten principles that relate to human rights, labour, environment and anti-corruption. ‡

The responsible investment arena offers considerable business opportunity. As Muhammad Yunus, of Grameen Bank fame, says,

---

* There is an initiative called Iris (Impact Reporting and Investment Standards) that involves the Acumen Fund, the Rockefeller Foundation and B-Lab, designed to ensure that standards are established for impact investments, which is a new capital market in the socially and environmentally responsible field. See www.iris-standards.org. There is also now the Global Impact Investing Network, www.globalimpactinvestingnetwork.org.

† Robert Kropp, Many SRI funds are outperforming benchmarks in 2009, www.socialfunds.com.

‡ Details of the UN Global Compact are available on www.unglobalcompact.org.

'Competition in the marketplace of ideas almost always has a powerful positive impact.'* Yunus has thus championed the notion of 'social business' and is even involved now in setting up a 'social stock market' where companies are tracked for both financial and social returns. Surprisingly, South Africa has lagged in these areas of social business and investment when it comes to enabling policies, not for lack of innovation or interest, but what appears to be lack of interest among policy makers. BEE took the limelight at the expense of a broader framework for investment to turn around the marginalisation of the majority of the population.

Experience in South Africa

In the early Nineties there was a tentative trend towards responsible investment. On behalf of the trade unions, the Labour Research Service (LRS) spearheaded the Community Growth Fund, the first of its kind in South Africa, screening company performance in terms of labour criteria. 'Cyril Ramaphosa and Kgalema Motlanthe instantly saw the value of a collective fund, but other leaders within Cosatu were less interested,' says Gordon Young, then with the LRS. Ultimately the union focus shifted to the opportunities in the sale of corporate shareholding to BEE groups, and, as Young puts it, 'the trade union investment company model won.'

Over the past fifteen years, funds of the SRI type have come and gone, with some focused on the financing of empowerment deals rather than broader issues of social responsibility. Overall, this market has been static – but good experience has accumulated. Inexplicably, trade unions and their trustees in retirement funds have been passive in this area. They have the potential to influence the investment mandates of these funds, requiring that fund managers consider the social, labour and environmental practices of companies before investing in them. This is not something that could happen overnight, but at least a start could be made with a commitment in the right direction.

More recently the state-owned asset manager, the Public Investment Corporation, picked up on the UN Global Compact and required fund

---

* Muhammad Yunus, *Banker to the poor: Micro-lending and the battle against world poverty*, Public Affairs, 2007, p 273.

managers wanting to tender for business to register with the UN body. The PIC has also tried its hand at shareholder activism, using its influence – often as the largest single shareholder in major corporations – to ensure much stronger black representation among executives. On the whole, however, the PIC has strongly endorsed the BEE framework – insisting on compliance by asset managers keen to have a share of its vast funds or by funds or companies seeking direct funding from the PIC. One of my clients, an international company in the area of responsible investing, could not entice the PIC to invest in its fund because it did not have BEE ownership within its South African subsidiary. In 2010, however, there was a discernible shift in the PIC's thinking when it signalled the need for pragmatism and achieving social impact. My client therefore eventually got funding from the PIC without having black shareholding. Such a change of direction by the PIC could have enormous impact on responsible investment in South Africa; no other asset manager comes close to wielding the power it has, with some R800 billion worth of assets under its watchful eye. Perhaps this will stir the trade unions into being more proactive about responsible investment.

Glitch for the Financial Sector Charter
The Financial Sector Charter has a strong focus on social and economic transformation, in addition to the usual empowerment provisions. This charter made unique provision for responsible investment as part of black empowerment. The financial institutions agreed to increase access to financial services for low-income groups and to put additional funds into 'targeted investments' such as infrastructure, low-income housing, agricultural development and small- and medium-enterprises financing. Forty percent of the scorecard points were for these investments. Large sums of money were invested and the traditionally conservative financial institutions found that they could work in markets previously thought to be unviable. Financial institutions dedicated to lower-income markets are growing in scale and number.

The FSC is also differentiated by having a lower threshold for direct BEE ownership – 10% rather than the 15% required in the BEE Codes, with the balance being made up by institutional shareholders to ensure the full 25%. This is where matters have gone awry. The FSC came up for review in 2008 and needed to be converted to a sector code. However, a key constituency, a coalition of community organisations, refused to back any conversion unless a further 5% of shareholding was made available for BEE ownership. This was a turnaround on their earlier position when they joined the FSC council a few years ago. The chairman of the community coalition at the time, the South African Communist Party general secretary and now also a government minister, Blade Nzimande, commented: 'Frankly, we are less concerned about [black] shareholding than issues that affect our people such as access to banking and HIV/Aids. It's a new colour of owners without transforming practices.'*

The National Treasury backed the financial institution in their opposition to this demand, saying that the emphasis on BEE ownership detracted from 'important transformation objectives.'† It may do more than that, and leave much less money available for transformation. At the height of the dispute in 2009, the Banking Association estimated the market capitalisation of financial institutions to be R500 billion. The further sale of 5% equity therefore would be R25 billion – finance that could be used for other transformational purposes.‡ At the time of writing, this dispute had not been resolved and the only empowerment initiative to promote responsible investment is now moribund.

New dialogue for transformation
The FSC experience shows the importance of opening up a national dialogue to rethink BEE and look at transformation beyond the current BEE parameters. South Africa is well positioned to take a lead in the arena of responsible investment. It has a well-developed financial sector, able to encompass new investment instruments and with proven

---

* Blade Nzimande, minister of Higher Education and Training and general secretary of the South African Communist Party, *Business Day*, 27 May 2004.

† In a letter to *Business Day*, 6 April 2009, Ismael Momoniat, the deputy director-general of the National Treasury, referred to the ownership debate as a 'red herring' for two reasons: 'First, it takes the debate away from important transformation objectives. Second, the focus on ownership may negatively affect the stability of the banking sector, if not handled with care. The financial sector is a regulated industry, and in line with international regulatory standards, anyone owning a significant share of the bank could not do so by borrowing funds from that or another bank (which BEE shareholders have to do).'

‡ The Banking Association of South Africa have provided their calculations of market capitalisation as at July 2009.

expertise. Creative use has been made of technology to access markets previously closed to private sector investment — and considerably more could be done with further investment in the technology sector itself. South Africa has a lot to gain from creating an environment that supports responsible investment across a wide range of activities, with benefits that it could also share as a leader on the African continent. A broader and more enabling policy environment that takes the concept of empowerment out of the confines of the current BEE box will stimulate innovation and open up new areas of investment.

The BEE companies that I looked at earlier, the best of BEE, can be earmarked for special support, to expand in the areas where they are already making a difference and have gained experience. BEE ownership has worked up to a point, but it is time to move on and create new space and opportunity for economic transformation.

Appendix

Summary of the BEE Codes on ownership, management control and enterprise development

The Broad-Based Black Economic Empowerment Codes of Good Practice (the Codes) were gazetted in February 2007, following the release of a number of drafts for public comment. The Codes were a requirement of the Broad-Based BEE Act of 2003, with the Department of Trade and Industry given responsibility for implementing them. The Codes were preceded by three sector-related transformation charters: the Charter for Empowering Historically Disadvantaged South Africans in the Petroleum and Liquid Fuels Industry, 2000; the Broad-Based Socio-Economic Empowerment Charter for the Mining Industry, 2002; and the Financial Sector Charter, 2002.

The Codes will endure until amended or repealed by government. The Trade and Industry minister will, however, review them in 2013, ten years from commencement.

There are seven elements of BEE in the Codes, which together score 100. 'Qualifying small enterprises' have a scorecard with different weightings.

Element	Weighting
Ownership	20
Management control	10
Employment equity	15
Skills development	15
Preferential procurement	20
Enterprise development	15
Socio-eco development (residual)	5
Total	100

The summary below provides an overview of the requirements in the Codes, but does not detail the many formulas used to calculate points in the scorecard. The BEE Act, BEE Strategy and the Codes are available on the DTI website www.dti.gov.za.

Principles and objectives of the Codes

The two most important are:

- The fundamental principle for measurement of BEE is that 'substance takes precedence over legal form'
- Compliance scores (in terms of the scorecard) are based on performance of each of the BEE elements at the time of measurement, and as result there is continuous measurement throughout the period of the Codes.

Applicability of the Codes

The Codes are a regulatory instrument. They are not a legal obligation on the private sector, but an effective obligation on all companies operating in South Africa, with some exclusions. There is a specific obligation on all organs of the state and public bodies to apply the Codes, and hence to oblige all companies with whom they do business to implement the Codes too. Equally, companies that do business with organs of the state are expected to require firms that do business with them to implement the Codes.

The state is thus using its buying power to enforce the Codes. The mining sector, however, differs in that the government has introduced legislation that makes the Mining Charter legally enforceable.

Even not-for-profit organisations, including higher education institutions, are expected to meet BEE obligations in terms of an adjusted scorecard that does not have ownership as a requirement.

There are limited exclusions:

- Micro enterprises, which are those with an annual turnover of less than R5 million, are automatically given a Level 3 status.
- Small businesses, defined as those with an annual turnover of more than R5 million but less than R35 million, are required to implement four of the seven elements of BEE.
- A start-up business, whatever its size, is not required to apply the Codes in its first year of operation. It is automatically deemed to be Level 4 (100% recognition).
- Foreign multinationals that have a global policy of not having third-party shareholders in their subsidiaries are exempt.

The BEE Act makes provision for transformation charters that need to be developed by stakeholders in any industry or sector on the basis of consensus. Once a charter is agreed it is then published in the *Government Gazette*. The

Codes, however, overrode the significance of charters by stipulating that charters would 'not [be] binding on organs of state or public entities' until they had been converted into sector codes; the approval of the minister of Trade and Industry is required for this.

BEE recognition levels

There are eight BEE recognition levels, based on the scorecard points. For example, 100% BEE recognition is Level 4 and may be attained with points between 65 and 74 (out of the 100 in the scorecard), Level 3 is 110% recognition with points between 75 and 84, up to the highest level with 100 or more points, giving 135% recognition.

Ownership element of the Codes

Here is the scorecard for measuring BEE ownership.

Ownership indicator	Weighting points	Compliance target (shareholding)
1 Voting rights		
- Exercisable voting rights in the enterprise in the hands of black people	3	25% + 1 vote
- Exercisable voting rights in the enterprise in the hands of black women	2	10%
2 Economic interest		
- Economic interest of black people in the enterprise	4	25%
	2	10%
- Economic interest of black women in the enterprise	1	2.5%
- Economic interest of the following black natural people in the enterprise:		
• Black designated groups		
• Black participants in employee ownership schemes		
• Black beneficiaries of broad-based ownership schemes, or		
• Black participants in co-operatives		
3 Realisation points		
- Ownership fulfilment	1	See Codes for
- Net value	7	measurement formula
4 Bonus points		
- Involvement in the ownership of the enterprise of black new entrants	2	10%
- Involvement in the ownership of the enterprise of black participants:	1	10%
• In employee ownership schemes		
• Of broad-based schemes		
• Of co-operatives		

1 Voting rights This measure seeks to ensure that black shareholders enjoy the full voting rights that accrue to the percentage shares that they hold. Points are also allocated on the basis of women participation – 10% of the 25% ownership target should be owned by black women.

2 Economic interest This indicator seeks to measure the actual economic interest to which black people are entitled and to ensure that the full economic interest appropriate to the relevant percentage shareholding accrues to the black shareholder. Again, a 10% women shareholding is targeted. In addition, what is termed designated groups (largely broad-based entities involving youth, rural people and black communities, for example) and employee schemes are scored against 2.5% (out of the 25%) shareholding target.

3 Realisation points This measures the net equity value of the BEE shareholders' investment, taking into account the value of the investment less any liabilities (most notably the financing needed to acquire the shareholding in the first place). There is a formula for measuring these points over 10 years, with full marks granted when the shareholding is fully paid off.

4 Bonus points Heavy political pressure to include new BEE entities and to broaden the base of BEE beneficiaries led to the Codes introducing bonus points for new or broad-based BEE entities participating in BEE transactions.

Broadly, BEE ownership is gauged thus:
• A BEE transaction is measured on a continuous basis.
• A BEE investment may unwind, but the formula means that points are lost when a transaction unwinds.
• Economic value and voting rights must ultimately be attributable to a natural person.
• There is provision for certain shareholding to be excluded from the total value of shareholding, thus requiring that the BEE ownership be calculated as a proportion of the total value less such excluded ownership. The exclusion principle covers organs of state or public entities that hold equity in private companies, and mandated investments (the institutionally held shareholdings in listed companies).

Ownership by broad-based ownership schemes: criteria are stipulated for such schemes to qualify as BEE, and there participation in BEE ownership is limited to 10% of the required 25% BEE shareholding, unless certain conditions are fulfilled.

Management control

Management control is aimed at ensuring black representation at the highest levels of company decision-making, covering non-executive and executive board membership and top management. Special provision is made for black women.

Management control indicator	Weighting points	Compliance target
Board participation		
– Exercisable voting rights of black board members using the adjusted recognition for gender	3	50%
– Black executive directors using the adjusted recognition for gender	2	50%
Top management		
– Black senior top management* using the adjusted recognition for gender	3	40%
– Black other top management using the adjusted recognition for gender†	2	40%
Bonus points		
– Black independent non-executive board members	1	

* The Codes envisage senior top management as the chief executive, chief operating and financial officers, while top management may be heads of marketing, sales and public relations.

† The adjusted recognition for gender is a formula that adjusts the score in terms of the representation of black women in board and management positions.

Enterprise Development

The motivation for Enterprise Development lies in the 'high failure rate amongst black-owned start-ups due to lack of access to financing and other business support' and the view that 'job-creation cannot be attained without the growth of the small business sector'.* In brief, measured enterprises (companies above R35 million in turnover) are required to support the development of other enterprises (qualifying criteria are set) – whereas measured enterprises with a turnover of R5 million to R35 million may elect Enterprise Development as one of the four elements of BEE that they are required to implement.

The support provided may be monetary and non-monetary, with the latter given a monetary value. The full monetary value should amount to 3% of net profit after tax (NPAT) over the measurement period – in other words, the contribution is recognised cumulatively. A company may count in its contributions to enterprise development up to five years before the Codes

* BEE Codes Interpretive Guide, June 2007.

were introduced, with measurement continuing until the end of the Codes' measurement period.

Criterion	Weighting points	Compliance target
Average annual value of all Enterprise Development contributions and sector-specific programmes made by the measured enterprise, as a percentage of the target	15	3% of NPAT

There are two categories of enterprises that qualify. The first is micro and small enterprises that are more than 50% black-owned, for which there is a points enhancer in the scorecard – the final score is multiplied by 1.25. The second is any other enterprise that may be 50% black-owned or more than 25% black-owned as long as the enterprise fulfils the BEE Recognition Level conditions. That requirement is not onerous.

There is a long list in the Codes of what a company may do for Enterprise Development – cash contributions, for example, and commitment of effort such as mentoring and employee time, and facilitating access to finance. Some contributions are worth more than others on the scorecard. A benefit factor matrix is provided to determine whether the value of a contribution may be scored at 100% or discounted. A grant provided to an enterprise may thus be counted in full, whereas only 70% of the value of a loan to a micro enterprise at market-related terms may be recognised. There are 16 different categories in this benefit matrix, on the opposite page.

Appendix

Qualifying Contribution type	Contribution Amount	Benefit Factor
Grant and Related Contributions		
Grant Contribution	Full Grant Amount	100%
Direct Cost incurred in supporting enterprise development	Verifiable Cost (including both monetary and non-monetary)	100%
Discounts in addition to normal business practices supporting enterprise development	Discount Amount (in addition to normal business discount)	100%
Overhead Costs incurred in supporting enterprise development (including people appointed in enterprise development)	Verifiable Costs (including both monetary and non-monetary)	80%
Loans and Related Contributions		
Interest-Free Loan with no security requirements supporting enterprise development	Outstanding Loan Amount	100%
Standard Loan to Black Owned EME and QSEs	Outstanding Loan Amount	70%
Standard Loan provided to other Beneficiary Enterprises	Outstanding Loan Amount	60%
Guarantees provided on behalf of a Beneficiary entity	Guarantee Amount	3%
Lower Interest Rate	Outstanding loan amount	Prime Rate – Actual Rate
Equity Investments and Related Contributions		
Minority Investment in Black Owned EME and QSEs	Investment Amount	100%
Minority Investment in Other Beneficiary Enterprises	Investment Amount	80%
Enterprise Development Investment with lower dividend to financier	Investment Amount	Dividend Rate of Ordinary Shareholders – Actual Dividend Rate of Contributor
Contributions made in the form of human resource capacity		
Professional services rendered at no cost and supporting enterprise development	Commercial hourly rate of professional	80%
Professional services rendered at a discount and supporting enterprise development	Value of discount based on commercial hourly rate of professional	80%
Time of employees of Measured Entity productively deployed in assisting beneficiaries	Monthly salary divided by 160	80%
Other Contributions		
Shorter payment periods	Percentage of invoiced amount	Percentage being 15 days less the number of days from invoice to payment

Notes

Introduction

1   *Empowerment 2000: New directions*, BusinessMap SA annual BEE report, p 9. All BusinessMap publications are archived with the Wits Business School, University of the Witwatersrand, Johannesburg.

2   Duma Gqubule, ed, *Making mistakes, righting wrongs: Insights into black economic empowerment*, Jonathan Ball and KMM Review, 2006, p 101.

3   Joel Netshitenzhe, head of the policy co-ordination and advisory services in the Presidency until December 2009, interview, Pretoria, August 2009. Unless otherwise stated, all interviews are with the author.

4   Mark Gevisser, *Thabo Mbeki: The dream deferred*, Jonathan Ball, 2007, pp 538–9.

5   Interview, Pretoria, August 2009.

6   Gevisser, pp 584–5.

7   Jenny Cargill, Behind black empowerment, *Finance Week*, 23–29 April 1992.

8   Vusi Khanyile, Thebe chairman, interview, Johannesburg, June 2009.

9   Jenny Cargill, Politics and profit: Thebe Investment shows need for new rules of the game, *Finance Week*, 10–16 June 1993.

10 Ibid.

11 BusinessMap SA, Face Fax, Ref No: 140/SS, 30 January 1996.

12 *Empowerment 1999: A moving experience*, BusinessMap SA annual BEE report.

13 Khanyile, interview, Johannesburg, June 2009.

14 Ibid.

15 BusinessMap SA, *Empowerment 2000*, p 25.

16 Mamphela Ramphele, *Laying ghosts to rest: Dilemmas of the transformation in South Africa*, Tafelberg, 2008, p 245.

17 Michael Spicer, chief executive officer of Business Leadership South Africa, interview, June 2009.

18 The Nail saga: Vision and vanity, *Financial Mail*, 19 August 2005.

19 PJ O'Rourke, *Eat the rich: A treatise on economics*, Atlantic Monthly Press, 1998, p 228.

20 The BEE ownership measures are all drawn from the annual reviews of BEE by BusinessMap SA, later called the BusinessMap Foundation. The figures here are drawn from *Empowerment 1999*.

21 One can always rely on Evita Bezuidenhout, the alter ego of Pieter-Dirk Uys, for a death-knell one-liner. This one published in the *Sunday Times*, 5 October 2008.

22 Fanaroff, interview, October 2009.

23 Ibid.

24 Gqubule ed.

25 Market capitalisation of MTN Group Ltd on 1 February 2010.

26 Market capitalisation of Vodacom Ltd on 1 February 2010.

27 The Independent Broadcasting Authority Act, No 153 of 1993.

28 *Empowerment guidelines for investors: Mapping state requirements and investor experiences*, a BusinessMap SA report, August 2001.

29 BusinessMap SA Update, Ref No: 8\BEE\SS\96, 14 March 1996.

30 Ibid.

31 Gqubule ed, p 108.

32 Ibid.

33 Ibid.

34 BusinessMap SA, Nail: Drama opens up Pandora's box, Ref No: 1999/020/BEE/TN, 18 June 1999.

35 This week's events at New Africa Investments (Nail) again highlight the uses and abuses of N share, *Business Day*, 23 May 1999.

36 BusinessMap SA, *Empowerment 1999*.

37 Gordon Young, chief executive of Ditikeni, interview, July 2009.

38 Ibid.

39 RSA, Preferential Procurement Policy Framework Act, No 5 of 2000 is available on www.treasury.gov.za.

40 *Business Day*, 2 February 2004.

41 Thabo Mbeki, *ANC Today* 3, 48, 5 December 2003.

42 Peter Haasbrook.

43 Thabo Mbeki, *ANC Today* 4, 36, 10 September 2003.

44 Sven Lünsche and Caroline Southey, Frontier wars, *Financial Mail*, 1 April 2005.

45 Ibid, quoting Adam Habib, then executive director of the Human Sciences Research Council.

46 Lulu Xingwana, minister of Minerals and Energy, as quoted in the *Star*, 15 September 2004.

47 Johann Rupert, chairman of Rembrandt Ltd, University of Pretoria, 15 October 2008, www.antonrupertmemoriallecture.com.

48 RSA, *Black Economic Empowerment Commission Report*, Skotaville, 2001, p 6.

49 Ibid, p 1.

50 Duma Gqubule, No miracle involved, *Financial Mail*, 23 April 2004.

51 Black Business Working Group, A strategy for BEE, Briefing Notes, 2 April 2002.

52 RSA, DTI, *South Africa's economic transformation: A strategy for broad-based black economic empowerment*, March 2003.

53 RSA, Broad-Based Black Economic Empowerment Act, No 53 of 2003.

54 Nicky Oppenheimer and Jonathan Oppenheimer, *South Africa: Our nation delivers*, The Brenthurst Initiative, 5 August 2003.

55 The Financial Sector Charter, November 2003, was drafted by representatives of the financial services sector and the Association of Black Securities and Investment Professionals, www.fscharter.co.za.

Chapter 1 No burst in the BEE bubble … just a pop

1 Paul Krugman, *The return of depression economics and the crisis of 2008*, Penguin, 2008, p 165.

2   There is no longer a consistent set of figures of BEE transactions since the closure of BusinessMap Foundation in 2007. So I have used their figures to 2006, after which I rely on the mergers and acquisitions values released annually by Deloitte & Touche.

3   BusinessMap SA, *Empowerment 2000*.

4   Krugman, p 63.

5   RSA, The codes of good practice on broad-based black economic empowerment, draft for comment, issued by DTI, December 2004, p 9.

6   Mohamad, speech to the Harvard Club of Malaysia, August 2002.

7   Vhonani Mufamadi, founder and chief executive of Ideco Ltd, interview, August 2009.

8   M Jack, Bidvest boss rails against BEE lock-ins, *Business Report*, 18 November 2009.

9   RSA, Financial Sector Charter, 2003, www.fscharter.co.za.

10   Paul Ormerod, *Why most things fail*, Faber and Faber, 2005, p 56.

11   Ibid, p 69.

12   John Kay, Expenses have caught MPs with their pants down, *Financial Times*, 13 May 2009.

13   Stefano Ponte, Simon Roberts and Lance van Sittert, Black economic empowerment, business and the state in South Africa, *Development and Change* 38, 5, 2007, p 950.

Chapter 2 Form over substance

1   Development and underdevelopment: Learning from experience to overcome the two-economy divide, discussion document of the ANC, June 2005, www.anc.co.za

2   Emmanuel (Chief) Lediga, Empowerment needs entrepreneurship too, *Business Day*, 11 November 2006; he is a founder of the black securities firm Legae Securities.

3   Barney Mthombothi, The cheek of it, *Financial Mail*, 1 December 2006.

4   Joel Netshitenzhe, head of Policy Co-ordination and Advisory Services in the Presidency until December 2009, interview, Pretoria, August 2009.

5   RSA, 'Codes of good practice' draft.

6   Philisiwe Buthelezi, chief executive officer of the National Empowerment Fund, interview, Johannesburg, August 2009.

7   Ramphele, p 245.

8   Harvey Leibenstein, Entrepreneurship and development, and William Baumol, Entrepreneurship in economic theory, both articles in *American Economic Review* 58, 2, May 1968.

9   Robert Shiller, Innovations to foster risk-taking and entrepreneurship, paper prepared for the Joint Conference of CESifo and the Centre on Capitalism and Society, 'Perspectives on the performance of the continent's economies', Venice International University, San Servolo, July 2006.

10   Michael Spicer, chief executive of Business Leadership South Africa, interview, June 2009.

11   Clifford Elk, interview, 4 August 2009.

12   JJ Njeke, interview, Johannesburg, June 2009.

13   Ibid.

14   In interview, Johannesburg, June 2009.

15   Cazenove, *Black economic empowerment: Float like a butterfly or sting like a BEE*, South Africa Economic Research report, Cazenove, October 2002.

16   RSA, The Companies Act, No 61 of 1973.

17   Tokyo Sexwale, BEE is very simple: It's about fixing up the mess, Another View, *Sunday Times*, 6 March 2005.

18   Kevin Lester, legal adviser to the DTI drafting team, interview, Johannesburg, August 2009.

19   Dr Michael Yeoh, Asian Institute of Strategy and Leadership, Kuala Lumpur, interview, 21 June 2008.

20   Ibid.

21   Ibid.

22   Scott Shane, Why encouraging more people to become entrepreneurs is bad public policy, Prize Lecture given upon receipt of the Global Award for Entrepreneurship Research, May 2009, Stockholm, www.e-award.org.

Chapter 3 Lessons of the past

1   Roy Cokayne, Truck ban could break the economy, *Business Report*, 20 October 2009.

2   Ramphele, p 246.

3   S'Thembiso Msomi, Afrikaner path to wealth stinks, Rupert warns Nafcoc, *Business Times*, 29 September 2002.

4   No lessons from Afrikaner empowerment, *Business Report*, 23 September 2002.

5   Dr Mahathir Mohamad made the first public criticism of his policies in a speech addressed to the Harvard Club of Malaysia in August 2002. An abridged version appeared in the article 'Ali Baba's crutches', *Financial Mail*, 9 August 2002.

6   Christi van der Westhuizen, *White power and the rise and fall of the National Party*, Zebra, 2007, p 113, citing the work of Hermann Giliomee.

7   Dan O'Meara, *Forty lost years: The apartheid state and the politics of the National Party 1948–1994*, Ravan and Ohio University Press, 1996, p 139.

8   Ibid, p 76.

9   Ibid, p 80.

10   Lim Teck Ghee, Corporate equity distribution: Past trends and future policy, Centre for Public Policy Studies, 2006.

11   Ibid.

12   Professor Fazilah Abdul Samad, Department of Finance and Banking, University of Malaya, interview, Kuala Lumpur, June 2008.

13   Dan O'Meara, 'n Volk red homself: The Afrikaner empowerment movement, *Umrabulo* (ANC publication), 22 February 2005.

14   Lim, p 8.

15   Jayant Menon, Macroeconomic management amid ethnic diversity: Fifty years of Malaysian experience, ADB (Asian Development Bank) Institute Discussion Paper No. 102, ADB, April 2008.

16   O'Meara, Dan, *Volkskapitalisme: Class, capital and ideology in the development of Afrikaner nationalism 1934–1948*, Ravan, 1983, p 219.

17   Mohamad, Ali Baba's crutches, *Financial Mail*, 9 August 2002.

18   Lim, p 16.

19   Syed Husin Ali, *The Malays, their problems and future*, The Other Press, 2008, p 105.

20   Lee Kam Hing, Asian Centre for Media Studies, interview, Kuala Lumpur, June 2008; he is a historian, formerly with the University of Malaya, and at the time of the interview a researcher for the Malaysian newspaper, *The Star*.

21   Donald R Snodgrass, Successful economic development in a multi-ethnic society: The Malaysian case, a paper delivered at a Saltzburg seminar, 17 February 2006. See www.cid.harvard.edu.

22   Studwell, p 130, referring to a comment of the management specialist Michael Porter.

23   KS Jomo, 1990/1, Whither Malaysia's new economic policy?, *Pacific Affairs* 63, 4, p 487.

24   Dr Mohamed Ariff, interview, June 2008.

25   Lim, p 17.

26   Snodgrass.

Chapter 4 If you're black and you're BEE, clap your hands

1   Sibonelo Rabede, Better the BEE you can see? *Financial Mail*, 17–22 February 2006, quoting Mlungisi Hlongwane, president of the South African National Civic Association and mayor of the Sedibeng municipality.

2   Jacob Dlamini, Withering grassroots, *Weekender*, 22–23 August 2009.

3   Julius Malema, *3rd Degree*, SABC programme, 26 November 2009.

4   Dumisani Lubisi and Piet Rampedi, Tax dodger, *City Press*, 7 March 2010.

5   Buddy Naidu and Simpiwe Piliso, How Malema made his millions, *Sunday Times*, 21 February 2010.

6   Jacob Dlamini, While SA laughs, Malema spreads his tentacles, *Business Day*, 11 November 2009.

7   Moipone Malefane, Greed will destroy the ANC, *Sunday Times*, 23 August 2009.

8   Bobby Godsell, chairman of Business Leadership South Africa, in a talk to the Cape Town Press Club, 26 February 2010.

9   Barney Mthombothi, Back to basics, *Financial Mail*, 5 March 2010.

10   Jonathan Hyslop, Political corruption: Before and after apartheid, *Journal of Southern African Studies* 31, 4, December 2005, p 775.

11   Cazenove, p 5 cites foreign multinationals as viewing BEE as 'disguised corruption'.

12   Sue Brown, *Transformation audit: Money and morality*, Institute for Justice and Reconciliation, 2006, p xi.

13   Hyslop, p 775.

14   *The anti-corruption plain language guide*, Transparency International, 2009, p 14.

15   Ibid, p 35.

16   Ibid, p 11.

17   Transparency International, *Corruption perceptions index*, available at www.transparency.org.

18   Stefaans Brümmer, ANC leadership or ANC dealership, *Mail & Guardian*, 23–29 January 2009.

19   Ray Hartley, Nothing to halt public servants' frenzy of corruption, *Business Day*, 9 July 2009.

20   Mondli Makhanya, Bonfires' flames leap ever higher as the people spurn abusive lover, *Sunday Times*, 7 March 2010.

21   Brown, p xi.

22 Ibid.
23 Andile Sokomani, All is not well with government tenders, report for Institute for Security Studies, *ISS Today*, 25 June 2008.
24 Steven Friedman, Politics and money: An exclusive relationship SA can't afford, *Business Day*, 3 June 2009.
25 Hyslop, p 781.
26 Ibid, p 782.
27 Helena Dolny, *Banking on change*, Penguin, 2001.
28 Hyslop, p 784.
29 Ibid., p 783.
30 Ibid.
31 Stefaans Brümmer, Sam Sole and Wisani wa ka Ngobeni, The ANC's Oilgate, *Mail & Guardian*, 3–9 May 2005.
32 Vickie Robinson and Stefaans Brümmer, *Corporate fronts and political funding*, ISS Report No 129, November 2006, p 31.
33 Brown, p xi.
34 Simpiwe Piliso, How ANC bigwigs jostled for Telkom, *Sunday Times*, 15 October 2006.
35 Rob Rose, Cosatu hits at BEE of the worst kind, *Business Day*, 11 November 2004.
36 Gugulakhe Masango, Telkom stock up 7% on BEE move, *Business Report*, 10 November 2004.
37 Buddy Naidu and Simpiwe Piliso, The big cull, *Sunday Times*, 10 May 2009.
38 Robinson and Brümmer.
39 Ibid.
40 Buddy Naidu and Simpiwe Piliso, Saki in ANC payoff scandal, *Sunday Times*, 9 March 2008.
41 Chancellor House Trust.
42 Robinson and Brümmer, p 18.
43 Stefaans Brümmer and Sam Sole, ANC's power grab, *Mail & Guardian*, 1–7 February 2008.
44 Buddy Naidu and Simpiwe Piliso, Saki in ANC payoff scandal, *Sunday Times*, 9 March 2008.
45 RSA, Mineral and Petroleum Resources Development Act, No. 28 of 2002.
46 RSA, Broad-Based Socio-Economic Empowerment Charter for the Mining Industry, 11 October 2002.
47 Manus Booysen, partner with Webber Wentzel Bowen, interview, March 2010.
48 HCI annual report 2009, p 16.
49 Robinson and Brümmer, p 27.
50 Kgomotso Mathe, Mining Charter 'champion' calls it quits, *Business Day*, 5 February 2010.
51 Booysen, interview, March 2010.
52 Robinson and Brümmer, p 24.
53 Kevin Murphy, Andrei Shleifer and Robert Vishny, Why is rent-seeking so costly to growth?, *American Economic Review* 83, 2, May 1993, pp 409–14.
54 Buddy Naidu and Simpiwe Piliso, Saki in ANC payoff scandal, *Sunday Times*, 9 March 2008.
55 Robinson and Brümmer, p 31.

Chapter 5 Sailing amidst a whirlwind

1   Scott, *Seeing like a state: How certain schemes to improve the human condition have failed,* Yale University Press, 1998, pp 77 and 78.

2   Ibid, p 93.

3   Ibid, p 87.

4   Oppenheimer and Oppenheimer.

5   Scott, p 313.

6   Sulaiman Achmad, a Kalk Bay boat owner, interview, Cape Town, March 2009. Other quotation from him comes from this interview.

7   Jacobus Poggenpoel, interview, Cape Town, March 2009. All quotations from him come from this interview.

8   Horst Kleinschmidt, Fishing industry undergoes sea change, *Business Day*, 8 March 2005.

9   Kalk Bay Boat Owners Association, representation made to the MCM on the Draft Traditional Line Fish Application, August 2005

10 Kalk Bay Boat Owners Association, open letter to the Minister of Environment and Tourism, Martinus van Schalkwyk, 27 February 2006.

11 Kalk Bay Boat Owners Association, representation made to the MCM on the Draft Traditional Line Fish Application, August 2005.

12 Scott, p 346.

13 Community-based natural resource management, report to the Department of Environmental Affairs and Tourism and GTZ Transform, by Department of Environmental Sciences, Rhodes University, Grahamstown, 2003.

14 *Traditional line fish policy*, 2005, www.mcm-deat.gov.za.

15 The Masifundise Fishermen's Association is led by Andy Johnson.

16 Kalk Bay Boat Owners Association, representation made to the MCM on the Draft Traditional Line Fish Application, August 2005.

17 Kalk Bay Boat Owners Association, open letter to the Minister of Environmental Affairs and Tourism, Martinus van Schalkwyk, 27 February 2006.

18 Horst Kleinschmidt, former deputy director-general of MCM, interview, Cape Town, April 2009. Unless otherwise stated, all quotations from him come from this interview.

19 Zanele Mbeki, former First Lady of South Africa and founder of the Women's Development Bank, interview, Johannesburg, September 2009.

20 Scott, p 344.

21 Ibid, p 345.

22 Ibid.

23 Stefano Ponte and Lance van Sittert, The chimera of redistribution in post-apartheid South Africa: Black economic empowerment in industrial fisheries, *African Affairs* 106, 424, July 2007, p 437.

24 Scott, p 346.

Part 2

1   Wilson Johwa, New body to expedite empowerment, *Business Day*, 5 February 2010.

Chapter 6 Mass appeal

1   Marcia Klein, Mvela: Everything must go, *Business Day*, 27 September 2009.
2   Phumzile Mlambo-Ngcuka, Broad-based empowerment a must, *Business Day*, 6 August 2003.
3   BusinessMap SA Update, Wiphold: A strategy in the making, Ref No 2000\012\ BEE\JC, 8 June 2000.
4   Michael Spicer, chief executive of Business Leadership SA, interview, June 2009.
5   BusinessMap SA, Satra chooses an unexpected winner, Ref No. 2000/003/BEE/ CU, 3 March 2000.
6   Gordon Young, chief executive of Ditikeni, interview, June 2009.
7   Ibid.
8   Stuart Theobald, Black bankers score big from empowerment deals, *Sunday Times*, 24 January 2010.
9   Gordon Young, interview, June 2009.

Chapter 7 Trade unions toyi-toyi for capital

1   Georgina Jaffee, Co-operative development in South Africa, in *South African review 6*, ed Glen Moss and Ingrid Obery, Ravan, 1992, p 372.
2   Johnny Copelyn, Seizing the moment, *South African Labour Bulletin* 21, 2, April 1997, pp 74–8.
3   Financials reported by MIC for its 2009 financial year.
4   Clifford Elk, interview, August 2009.
5   Ibid.
6   Vicki Robinson, Union companies pose 'grave risk', *Mail & Guardian*, 8–14 July 2005.
7   BusinessMap SA, *Empowerment 1999*.
8   Clifford Elk, former chief executive of MIC, interview, August 2009.
9   Mokgadi Pela, Fund managers accused of pension theft, *Business Report*, 5 March 2004.
10 Cosatu Secretariat report to the Ninth Congress, 21 September 2006.
11 Johnny Copelyn, chief executive of HCI, interview, June 2009.
12 Improvidence funds, *Noseweek*, January 2010.
13 What about the workers? *Financial Mail*, 18 December 2009.
14 Johnny Copelyn, interviewed by *Moneyweb*, 14 April 2009.
15 BusinessMap SA, *Empowerment 1999*.

Chapter 8 BEE's powder keg

1   Rhoda Kadalie, Commission's report gets it wrong on rights, *Business Day*, 4 December 2008.
2   Floors Strauss, co-ordinator of Socio-Economic Projects, Eksteenfontein, interview, September 2008.
3   Susanne Berzborn, Strategies of handling ethnic identity in the Richtersveld land claim, ACACIA Conference: 'Workshop on ethnicity, conflicts over land and political autonomy in contemporary arid Africa', Königswinter, 1–3 October 2003, p.8
4   Ibid, p 7.
5   Geoff Budlender, advocate and former director-general of the Department of Land Affairs, interview, December 2009.

6   Alexkor's mining 'collapsed', Sapa, Cape Town, 16 May 2005.
7   Juan J Buttari, Reassessing privatization in Eastern Europe, 1997, www. amigospais-guaracabuya.org.
8   John Bennett, Saul Estrin and Giovanni Urga, Methods of privatisation and economic growth in transition economies, *Economics of Transition* 15, 4, October 2007, pp 661–83.
9   Ibid, p 662.
10 Phumzile Mlambo-Ngcuka, Broad-based empowerment a must, *Business Day*, 6 August 2003.
11 Mlambo-Ngcuka, *Business Report*, 1 September 2004.
12 Steven A Kennet, *A guide to impact and benefit agreements*, Canadian Institute of Resources Law, May 1999.

Chapter 9 The best of BEE
1   On February 17, the market capitalisation of Implats was R122.8 billion.
2   Vusi Khanyile, executive chairman of Thebe Investment Corporation, interview, June 2009.
3   Tanya Slabbert, chief executive of WBDIH interview, may 2009
4   BusinessMap SA, *Empowerment 2000*, p 70.
5   Ebbe Dommisse in cooperation with Willie Esterhuyse, *Anton Rupert: A biography*, Tafelberg, 2005; the brochure of the early dry-cleaning business of Anton Rupert is cited on p 53.
6   JJ Njeke, chief executive of KTI, interview, June 2009.
7   Jabulani Sikhakhane, Lessons in democracy for ANC from Bafokeng, *Business Day*, 2 November 2009.

Chapter 10 Bridging the fault lines
1   Nick van Rensburg, interview, June 2009.
2   Ibid.
3   RSA, *Annual financial statistics 2008*, Statistics South Africa, pp 63 and 69.
4   RSA, *Guidelines: Equity equivalent programme for multinationals*, DTI, 2007.
5   William Gumede, ANC must spring-clean, nothing less, *Mail & Guardian*, 19–25 March 2010.
6   John Kane-Berman, The ownership revolution, Fast Facts No 09/2008/ September 2008, South African Institute of Race Relations.
7   Ian Fife, Blacks cross ownership bar, *Financial Mail*, 30 May 2008.
8   Yolandi Groenewald, Who owns what land in South Africa? *Mail & Guardian*, 23–29 January 2009.
9   Alan Hirsch, *Season of hope: Economic reform under Mandela and Mbeki*, University of KwaZulu-Natal Press, 2005, pp 227–8.
10 Joseph Stiglitz, *Freefall: Free markets and the sinking of the global economy*, Allen Lane, 2010, p 198.

Chapter 11 Beyond BEE
1   Tenth five year plan 2008–2013, Gross National Happiness Commission, Royal Government of Bhutan.

2   The Commission on the Measurement of Economic Performance and Social Progress reported in 2009, www.stiglitz-sen-fitoussi.fr.

3   A Craig Copetas, Bhutan puts happiness and karma into investment, *Business Report*, 26 March 2008.

4   Carol Graham, Happy talk: The economics of happiness, *Washington Post*, 3 January 2010.

5   Ibid.

6   Andrew Oswald, *A non-technical introduction to the economics of happiness*, 1999, www.warwick.ac.uk

7   Peter Sanfey and Utku Teksoz, Does transition make you happy? *Economics of Transition* 15, 4, 2007, pp 707–31.

8   Report by the Commission on the Measurement of Economic Performance and Social Progress, 2009, p 7.

9   Stephan Hofstatter, Government drive to set up white SA farmers in Africa, *Business Day*, 12 October 2009

10   Brendan Boyle, Massive farm failure, *The Times*, 3 March 2010.

11   John Kay, There is no universal economic theory, *Business Day*, 15 April 2010.

12   Jonny Steinberg, Whole stratum of whites in SA still 'postponing the inevitable', *Business Day*, July 16, 2007.

13   Development indicators 2009, the Office of the Presidency, www.thepresidency. gov.za, pp 54–6.

14   Trevor Manuel, interview, February 2010.

15   Neva Makgetla, Shunning stakeholders is no way to make policy, *Business Day*, 14 April 2010.

16   Trevor Manuel, interview, 2010.

17   Paul Hoffman, Cadre deployment hurt in battle to build a better SA, *Business Day*, 16 April 2010.

18   Ramphele, p 27.

19   Sampie Terreblanche, *A history of inequality in South Africa 1652–2002*, University of Natal Press and KMM Review, 2002, p 4.

20   William Gumede, Building a democratic political culture, in *The poverty of ideas* ed William Gumede and Leslie Dikeni, Jacana, 2010, p 25.

21   Ramphele, p 144.

22   Moeletsi Mbeki, *Architects of poverty: Why African capitalism needs changing*, Picador Africa, 2009, p 70.

23   Ibid, p 83.

24   Ibid, p 74.

25   Neville Alexander, Racial identity, citizenship and nation building in post-apartheid South Africa, edited version of a lecture delivered at the East London campus, University of Fort Hare, 2006, www.ecsecc.org.

26   Kgalema Motlanthe, Deputy President of South Africa, interview, January 2010.

27   Jeffrey Sachs, *Common wealth: Economics for a crowded planet*, Penguin, 2008, p 81.

28   Ibid, p 315.

29   Nicky Newton-King, Call to courage, *Financial Mail*, December 2009.

30   Neva Makgetla, Tough rural decisions need more open debate, *Business Day*, 17 March 2010.

31   Sachs, p 292.

32   Malcolm Gladwell, *Outliers: The story of success*, Allen Lane, 2008, p 236.

33   Ibid, p 233.

34   Vietnam's IT sector growing fast: UN agency, *China Post*, 27 August 2009.

35   IT prosperity stifled by labour shortage, opportunity abounds, *Vietnam Economic Portal*, 2008, www.vnep.org.vn.

36   Gladwell, p 144.

37   Thomas Sowell, *Race and culture: A world view*, Basic, 1994, p 2.

38   Ibid, p 16.

39   RSA, Ninth Commission of Employment equity report 2008/9, Department of Labour, www.labour.gov.za.

40   *Aiming high: Vietnam development report 2007*, joint donor report to the Vietnam Consultative Group Meeting, Hanoi, 14–15 December 2006 (for 2007), available from the Vietnam Development Information Centre, www.vdic.org.vn.

41   Gevisser, p 56.

42   Ibid, p 77.

43   Scott Shane, *Why encouraging more people to become entrepreneurs is bad public policy*, Research Institute of Industrial Economics, 2009, www.e-award.org.

References

Republic of South Africa (RSA)

The Companies Act, No 61 of 1973

Independent Broadcasting Authority Act, No 153 of 1993

Preferential Procurement Policy Framework Act, No 5 of 2000.
www.treasury.gov.za

Mineral and Petroleum Resources Development Act, No 28 of 2002

Broad-Based Black Economic Empowerment Act, No 53 of 2003

Black Economic Empowerment Commission Report. 2001. Johannesburg:
Skotaville

Broad-Based Socio-Economic Empowerment Charter for the South African
Mining Industry, October 2002. www.dme.gov.za/minerals/mining_charter.stm

*South Africa's economic transformation: A strategy for broad-based black economic
empowerment*, Department of Trade and Industry, 2003

Financial Sector Charter, November 2003. www.fscharter.co.za

The codes of good practice on broad-based black economic empowerment.
Draft for comment, issued in December 2004 by the Department of Trade
and Industry

Traditional line fish policy, 2005. www.mcm-deat.gov.za

Guidelines: Equity equivalent programme for multinationals, Department of
Trade and Industry, 2007

Annual financial statistics 2008, Statistics South Africa. www.statssa.gov.za

Ninth commission of employment equity report 2008/9, Department of
Labour. www.labour.gov.za

Development indicators 2009, Office of the Presidency. www.thepresidency.gov.za

BusinessMap SA and BusinessMap Foundation

All BusinessMap SA and BusinessMap Foundation publications are archived at the Wits Business School, University of the Witwatersrand, Johannesburg.

BusinessMap SA. 1996a. Face Fax, Ref No: 140/SS, 30 January

Businessmap SA. 1996b. Update, Ref No: 8\BEE\SS\96, 14 March

BusinessMap SA. 1999a. *Empowerment 1999: A moving experience.* Annual BEE report

BusinessMap SA 1999b. Nail: Drama opens up Pandora's box, Ref No: 1999/020/BEE/TN, 18 June

BusinessMap SA, 2000a. Satra chooses an unexpected winner, Ref No. 2000/003/BEE/CU, 3 March

BusinessMap SA. 2000b. *Empowerment 2000: New directions.* Annual BEE report

BusinessMap SA. 2000c. Wiphold: A strategy in the making. Update Ref No 2000\012\BEE\JC, 8 June

BusinessMap SA. 2001a. *Empowerment 2001: Better outcomes.* Annual BEE report

BusinessMap SA. 2001b. *Empowerment guidelines for investors: Mapping state requirements and investor experiences.* Report, August

BusinessMap Foundation. 2003. *Black ownership of the South African banking sector.* Study commissioned by the South African Banking Council

General

African National Congress (ANC). 2005. Development and underdevelopment: Learning from experience to overcome the two-economy divide. ANC Discussion Document, June. www.anc.co.za

Alexander, Neville. 2006. Racial identity, citizenship and nation building in post-apartheid South Africa. Edited version of a lecture delivered at the East London campus, University of Fort Hare. www.ecsecc.org

Baumol, William. 1968. Entrepreneurship in economic theory, *American Economic Review* 58, 2, May, pp 64–71

Bennett, John, Saul Estrin and Giovanni Urga. 2007. Methods of privatisation and economic growth in transition economies, *Economics of Transition* 15, 4, October, pp 661–83

Berzborn, Susanne. 2003. Strategies of handling ethnic identity in the

Richtersveld land claim, ACACIA Conference: 'Workshop on ethnicity, conflicts over land and political autonomy in contemporary arid Africa', Königswinter, 1–3 October, p 7

Brown, Sue, ed. 2006. *Transformation audit: Money and morality*. Cape Town: Institute for Justice and Reconciliation

Buttari, Juan J. 1997. Reassessing privatization in Eastern Europe. www. amigospais-guaracabuya.org

Cazenove. 2002. *Black economic empowerment: Float like a butterfly or sting like a BEE*. South Africa report, October. Johannesburg: Cazenove South Africa

Congress of South African Trade Unions (Cosatu). 2006. Secretariat Report to the Ninth Congress, 21 September

Copelyn, Johnny. 1997. Seizing the moment, *South African Labour Bulletin* 21, 2, April, pp 74–8

Dolny, Helena. 2001. *Banking on change*. Johannesburg: Penguin

Dommisse, Ebbe, in cooperation with Willie Esterhuyse. 2005. *Anton Rupert: A biography*. Cape Town: Tafelberg

Ernst & Young. 2007. Mergers & acquisitions report. Johannesburg: Ernst & Young

Ernst & Young. 2008. Mergers & acquisitions report. Johannesburg: Ernst & Young

Gevisser, Mark. 2007. *Thabo Mbeki: The dream deferred*. Johannesburg: Jonathan Ball

Gqubule, Duma, ed. 2006. *Making mistakes, righting wrongs: Insights into black economic empowerment*. Johannesburg: Jonathan Ball and KMM Review

Gladwell, Malcolm. 2008. *Outliers: The story of success*. London: Allen Lane

Gumede, William. 2009. Building a democratic political culture, in *The poverty of ideas: South African democracy and the retreat of intellectuals*, ed William Gumede and Leslie Dikeni, pp 11–34. Johannesburg: Jacana

Hirsch, Alan. 2005. *Season of hope: Economic reform under Mandela and Mbeki*. Scottsville, Pietermaritzburg: University of KwaZulu-Natal Press

Husin Ali, Syed. 2008. *The Malays, their problems and future*. Kuala Lumpur: The Other Press

Hyslop, Jonathan. 2005. Political corruption: Before and after apartheid, *Journal of Southern African Studies* 31, 4, December, pp 773–89

Jaffee, Georgina. 1992. Co-operative development in South Africa, in *South*

African Review 6, ed Glen Moss and Ingrid Obery, pp 364–77. Johannesburg: Ravan

Jomo, KS. 1990/1. Whither Malaysia's new economic policy? *Pacific Affairs* 63, 4, p 487

Kaufmann, D and P Vicente. 2005. Legal corruption. Mimeo. World Bank

Kennet, Steven. A 1999. *A guide to impact and benefit agreements.* Calgary: Canadian Institute of Resources Law

Krugman, Paul. 2008. *The return of depression economics and the crisis of 2008.* London: Penguin

Landsburg, Steven. 1993. *The armchair economist: Economics and everyday life.* New York: Free Press (Simon & Schuster)

Leibenstein, Harvey. 1968. Entrepreneurship and development, *American Economic Review* 58, 2, May, pp 72–83

Lim, Teck Ghee. 2006. Corporate equity distribution: Past trends and future policy. Centre for Public Policy Studies (CPPS) Paper. Kuala Lumpur: CPPS

Mbeki, Moeletsi. 2009. *Architects of poverty: Why Africa's capitalism needs changing.* Johannesburg: Picador Africa

Menon, Jayant. 2008. Macroeconomic management amid ethnic diversity: Fifty years of Malaysian experience. ADB (Asian Development Bank) Institute Discussion Paper 102. Tokyo: ADB

Murphy, Kevin; Andrei Shleifer and Robert Vishny. 1993. Why is rent-seeking so costly to growth? *American Economic Review* 83, 2, Papers and proceedings of the hundred and fifth annual meeting of the American Economic Association, pp 409–14

O'Meara, Dan. 1983. *Volkskapitalisme: Class, capital and ideology in the development of Afrikaner nationalism 1934–1948.* Johannesburg: Ravan

O'Meara, Dan. 1996. *Forty lost years: The apartheid state and the politics of the National Party 1948–1994.* Johannesburg: Ravan; Athens, Ohio: Ohio University Press

O'Meara, Dan. 2005. 'n Volk red himself: The Afrikaner empowerment movement. *Umrabulo* (ANC publication) 22, February

Oppenheimer, Nicky and Jonathan Oppenheimer. 20003. *South Africa: Our nation delivers.* Report. The Brenthurst Initiative. www.thebrenthurstfoundation.org

Ormerod, Paul. 2005. *Why most things fail*. London: Faber and Faber

O'Rourke, PJ. 1998. *Eat the rich: A treatise on economics*. New York: Atlantic Monthly Press

Oswald, Andrew. 1999. *A non-technical introduction to the economics of happiness*. www.warwick.ac.uk

Ponte, Stefano, Simon Roberts and Lance van Sittert. 2007. Black economic empowerment, business and the state in South Africa, *Development and Change* 38, 5, pp 933–55

Ponte, Stefano and Lance van Sittert. 2007. The chimera of redistribution in post-apartheid South Africa: Black economic empowerment in industrial fisheries, *African Affairs* 106, 424, July, pp 437–63

Ramphele, Mamphela. 2008. *Laying ghosts to rest: Dilemmas of the transformation in South Africa*. Cape Town: Tafelberg

Rhodes University (Grahamstown), Department of Environmental Sciences. 2003. Community-based natural resource management. Report to the Department of Environmental Affairs and Tourism and GTZ Transform

Robinson, Vickie and Stefaans Brümmer. 2006. *Corporate fronts and political funding*. ISS (Institute for Security Studies) Report No 129, November. Cape Town: ISS

Sachs, Jeffrey. 2008. *Common wealth: Economics for a crowded planet*. London: Penguin

Sanfey, Peter and Utku Teksoz. 2007. Does transition make you happy? *Economics of Transition* 15, 4, pp 707–31

Scott, James C. 1998. *Seeing like a state: How certain schemes to improve the human condition have failed*. New Haven, Conn and London: Yale University Press

Shane, Scott. 2009. Why encouraging more people to become entrepreneurs is bad public policy. Research Institute of Industrial Economics. www.e-award.org

Shiller, Robert. 2006. Innovations to foster risk-taking and entrepreneurship. Paper presented at the Joint Conference of CESifo and the Centre on Capitalism and Society, 'Perspectives on the performance of the continent's economies', July, at the Venice International University, San Servolo

Snodgrass, Donald R. 2006. Successful economic development in a multi-ethnic society: The Malaysian case. Paper presented at a Saltzburg Seminar, 17 February. www.cid.harvard.edu

Sokomani, Andile. 2008. All is not well with government tenders. Report for Institute for Security Studies (ISS) in *ISS Today*, 25 June

Sowell, Thomas. 1994. *Race and culture: A world view*. New York: Basic

Stiglitz, Joseph. 2010. *Freefall: Free markets and the sinking of the global economy*. London: Allen Lane

Stiglitz, Joseph, Amartya Sen and Jean-Paul Fitoussi. 2009. Report by the Commission on the Measurement of Economic Performance and Social Progress. www.stiglitz-sen-fitoussi.fr

Studwell, Joe. 2008. *Asian godfathers*. London: Profile

Terreblanche, Sampie. 2005. *A history of inequality in South Africa 1652–2002*. Pietermaritzburg: University of Natal Press; Sandton, Johannesburg: KMM Review

Transparency International. 2009. *The anti-corruption plain language guide*. Berlin: Transparency International

Van der Berg, Servaas and Ronelle Burger. 2002. *The stories behind the numbers: An investigation of efforts to deliver services to the South African poor*. Report prepared for the World Bank. www.worldbank.org

Van der Westhuizen, Christi. 2007. *White power and the rise and fall of the National Party*. Cape Town: Zebra

Vietnam joint donors. 2006 (for 2007). *Aiming high: Vietnam development report 2007*. Joint Donor Report to the Vietnam Consultative Group Meeting, Hanoi, 14–15 December 2006, available from the Vietnam Development Information Centre, www.vdic.org.vn

AccountAbility and World Economic Forum. 2005. *Mainstreaming responsible investment*. Geneva: World Economic Forum

Yunus, Muhammad. 2007. *Banker to the poor: Micro-lending and the battle against world poverty*. New York: Public Affairs

About the author

Jenny Cargill been involved in black economic empowerment since its inception in the early Nineties. She started her career as a journalist but soon got caught up in the political turmoil of the Eighties and joined the ANC, working underground inside South Africa and then from exile in Zimbabwe. Her experiences are documented in the award-winning film *Memories of Rain*. With democracy, she founded a think-tank on economic transformation, later becoming an adviser in the investments designed to increase black ownership in the major corporations. Cargill is a mother to one son and focuses her voluntary efforts on education and youth organisations, believing that the future of South Africa will be defined by how it treats its children.